Outside
MAGAZINE'S

Urban Adventure

Seattle

Outside MAGAZINE'S

Urban Adventure

Seattle

Maria Dolan

Outside BOOKS W. W. Norton & Company New York · London

Copyright © 2004 by Mariah Media Inc.

All rights reserved
Printed in the United States of America
First Edition

For information about permission to reproduce selections from this book,
write to Permissions, W. W. Norton & Company, Inc., 500 Fifth Avenue,
New York, NY 10110

Manufacturing by The Haddon Craftsmen, Inc.
Book design by Chris Welch
Production manager: Diane O'Connor

ISBN 0-393-32397-8 (pbk.)

W. W. Norton & Company, Inc.
500 Fifth Avenue, New York, N.Y. 10110
www.wwnorton.com

W. W. Norton & Company Ltd.
Castle House, 75/76 Wells Street, London W1T 3QT

1 2 3 4 5 6 7 8 9 0

Contents

9

Acknowledgments

PAUL EDMONDSON, my partner in love and adventure, supported this project in countless ways. He shared his vast sea kayaking and backpacking experience, was unflaggingly enthusiastic about heading out on any adventure I proposed, and cooked me many a meal while I typed away at my desk. Brangien Davis, a talented writer and unwavering friend, provided excellent research and word tweaking on the horseback and surfing chapters. Julie Walker, one of my oldest and dearest pals, provided brilliant snow sports research. Dear friend and baker extraordinaire Lyanda Haupt was, as always, the final word on anything to do with birds (though any errors in the matter are mine). Her sidekick, sea kayaker Tom Furtwangler, rescued me from a computer-induced breakdown. The inimitable Kathryn True, naturalist, writer, and font of Vashon knowledge, was wise counsel. My brother Patrick Dolan let me download a few hours worth of his fly-fishing knowledge, helped out with descriptions of some of the fly-fishing rivers in the fishing chapter, and passed along a pile of books. My wild-minded parents, in their different ways, gave to me a love of being outside. A special thanks to Maria Lee and her pack of rock-climbing women and men who offered thorough beta and refused to let me buy them a pitcher of beer in return. Mel Furrer gave cheerful and generous whitewater advice and inspired me with her enthusiasm. Diver Karlista Rickerson of Washington Scuba Alliance passed on 20-plus years of knowledge about local scuba diving. Thanks to Wayne Pallson, fisheries biologist at the Washington Department of Fish and Wildlife; bikers Heather Johnston, Peter Wobber, and Ben Spencer; surfers Therese Littleton, Paul Fleming, and Ernest Martin; sailor Roger Coulter; birder Kevin Li; bike mechanic Andrew McColm; and Cici Carson of West Side Stables on Vashon. The people at Seattle Audubon and Washington Audubon were very helpful with bird knowledge—thanks in particular to Hilary Hilscher and Christi Norman. Tom Deschner explained local kayaking history to me and was a gracious host. The paddle fanatics at Pacific Water Sports are an amazing source of information about local kayaking—thanks in particular to Lee Moyer, Judy Moyer, and Chris Hivick. Conservationist and fly-fisherman Bill McMillan was an inspiration and a great interview, in spite of the fact that he thought I should write about someone more worthy. Thanks to the fishing folks at Spot Tail Salmon Guide and Emerald Water Anglers, Charles Eldridge of Turns-All-Year for backcountry chat, and Robin Ogaard at Urban Surf for windsurfing and kiteboarding lowdown.

I'm also grateful to David Takami, Chuck Ayers, Bob

Schafer, Fred Zeitler, Patti Wold, and Barb Maynes for their assistance.

Thanks to my generous and thoughtful editor, John Barstow, to keen-eyed copyeditor Kristin Camp, mapmaker Susanna Fillingham, production manager Diane O'Connor, managing editor Nancy Palmquist, and the rest of the adventurers at W. W. Norton.

An apology to anyone who shared their urban adventure with me and didn't make it onto these pages—there were so many helpful people along the way, I was sure to forget a few.

Finally, to Josephine, my newest and best reason for going outside.

Introduction

WHEN I WAS GROWING UP in the dead center of this city in the 1970s, "outdoorsy" was not a term, and flannel was not a fashion statement. The outdoors was where Seattleites lived, and fine, Northwest-made, buffalo-plaid Pendelton was what you threw on to deal with it. Maybe a yellow slicker, brand name unknown, if things got too soggy by December. REI had been selling its serviceable, style-free outdoor gear since 1956. The Mountaineers, that venerable Northwest institution, had been around since 1906 and had just begun adding singles hikes to its busy schedule of activities. We were fishing and camping in layers of cotton and a hefty wool sweater, plunking in worms and yanking out trout in our flush streams with the regularity of automatons. No one in the rest of the country thought about joining us. In fact, I don't think anyone even thought of Seattle at all, unless they were considering relocating for a job at Boeing.

Clearly, things have changed.

Ever since the 1980s, when some clever soul from a magazine proclaimed Seattle the Most Livable City in America, people from all over the world have wanted to see the superlatives for themselves.

This influx has brought some much-needed change. Great coffee roasters moved up from California, lyric poets flew in from London, jazz musicians road-tripped out from New York and opened the windows of this once-provincial city, giving us a wider and more sophisticated view. The drawbacks of this deluge are notable, too. More traffic (our city now has one of the worst traffic problems in the country), fewer trout, fewer days when one can see the white cap of Mount Rainier through the charcoal smog. Not to mention the shift from plaid gear to pricey polyester fleece.

What I've noticed is that the people who really manage to love Seattle, and sometimes even make a home here, are the ones who can appreciate the city's extraordinary natural setting. Despite our world-class opera house, our flourishing theater community, and our rockin', Microsoft-funded, Frank Gehry–designed blob of a music museum, we will never be Paris or New York. Our populace, though chic-er than ever before, still shelters a fair number who ride their bikes to dinner and sit down to eat in quick-dry Gramiccis.

So, to the visitors who wish we could be a bit more cultured, I say, there are other cities waiting, with fewer rain clouds and a much bigger Barneys. To those for whom the sharp spikes of the Olympics seem more elegant than any high-heeled shoe, who can be satisfied with the music of a

Snoqualmie waterfall when opera season ends, this guide is for you.

What to Do

If anything stops the intrepid Seattleite from getting outside, it's the confusion of choices. I've got some gentle advice for those of us living in a place where traffic congestion starts the moment you leave the driveway: Begin with something human-powered and local. There's nothing more satisfying than whizzing your skinny tires down a major arterial while pitying the fools stuck in traffic, and in-city paddling is even more fun when you slip under a drawbridge that's stopped the SUVs in their tracks. Take your road bike on a bird-watching trip to Discovery Park, visited by nearly 300 species of birds a year, or to a paddle (there are plenty of boat rentals around) along the West Seattle shoreline, where my friend Lyanda Haupt, author of an award-winning book of essays on Northwest birds, likes to do her research. Summer weekends, on the days when they close Lake Washington Boulevard to traffic, get out early on your bike (or team up with the Cascade Bicycle Club) and ride from one shoreline park to the next; they are strung out like jewels along the lake's western shore. Or get over to Green Lake for fly-casting practice, like I do sometimes with my brother. (If you can't find Pat that day, talk to the contacts in the fishing chapter about hiring a guide.) Prepare for the Cascades on the climbing rocks at the University of Washington. In-line skate on Alki Beach, where the first white settlers hunkered down, and which now, with its wide flat sidewalks, sandy beach, and fruit-smoothie cabanas, looks like a piece of California that broke free and floated north.

Who Else Does It

There are experts here for every kind of sport, lured by the mild year-round climate and the fact that you can be on the water in ten minutes, in the mountains in forty-five. Seattle also supports a healthy if unruly pack of conservationists who don't want to see it all spoiled. In this book I've profiled a few of these groups and individuals, people like Bill McMillan, renowned steelhead fisherman and president of Washington Trout.

Only when you've exhausted this city's wealth of self-propelled pleasures (and that might include taking your touring kayak out through the Chittenden Locks, heading North up the Cascadia Marine Trail to Alaska and back, all without getting into a car or plane) should you even *start* looking farther. When you do, you could be forced to leave your day job.

Farther Afield

There's whitewater kayaking on the Snoqualmie River, where you might cross water with Mel Furrer of the Werner Paddle family, playing with her boat in Rodeo Hole. There are the hikes along the I-90 corridor, many not more than 45 minutes from your door—steep, rocky, blanketed in wildflowers every spring and in a variable Northwest snow in winter. When that winter weather isn't producing the kind of powder you'd like, there are climbing gyms for training, crazy waves for the advanced surfer, a migratory bird festival on the coast, and winter steelhead fishing. There are streams and alpine lakes and Mount Rainier, where the serious international mountaineering contingent cuts its teeth. And I haven't even started in on sea kayaking, from day trips to Blake Island and the South Sound, to the famous (and therefore summer-glutted) San Juans, to British Columbia and its scatter of islands, sprinkled like the crumbs of a carbo-loading feast on the floor of the car.

Hiking season here, despite first impressions, can be almost year-round. Just ask the folks at the Issaquah Alps Trails Club, who have made it their job to learn about those below-snow-level but still wild hills just outside Seattle. For serious backpacking you'll have to wait until summer, but that's just enough time to pick from all the choices. The Olympic Peninsula is famous for its rain forest. Few visitors realize that the leeward side of the Olympic Mountain range is in what's called a rain shadow, sheltered from southwest winds and weather. Here is where I'd go in May, before hiking season officially opens, before the rain stops, when you are completely alone with the black bears, deer, and all the morels the locals have overlooked. At the cusp of spring last year my partner, Paul, and I hiked out in that shadow on the Dungeness Spit when Seattle was socked in a cold mist. We came home (it takes about two hours to get back from there, including the ferry ride) with a sunburn. If you actually *want* to get wet, you can take another hour to get to the rain forest. Or how about a two-hour drive from Seattle to Washington's real coast (visitors occasionally forget we don't live right on the ocean here, but on Puget Sound, our own inland sea) and Westport, where burly Al Perlee holds court at The Surf Shop. He *is* a piece of California that broke off and floated north, come to tell where to surf, when to go, and exactly how many millimeters thick your wet suit should be. Go in August to check out the Longboard Classic competition, the biggest surf gathering in the state. Speaking of events, you'll be busy with them. There's the Chilly Hilly ride around Bainbridge

Island in February, the "Duck Dodge" for sailboats on Lake Union all summer, and a riot of half-pipe and snowboard demos all winter.

You won't be able to do all of it, of course—I can't either. But give it your best shot. From kayaking past great blue herons in a restored wetland to taking a world-class week-long backpack by the close of which you're hallucinating fried chicken and chocolate pie, I promise you'll never be bored.

How to Use This Book

As I've said, there's a lot to do. I've tried to make things easier by cross-referencing within chapters. I also recommend that you spend some browsing time between these pages and come up with your own creative ways to expand the options even farther. For instance, bird-watching destinations are almost always great places for a hike or walk. They also tend to be near water, so consider bringing a boat. Many rock-climbing meccas are located in great hiking terrain. Road-biking routes recommend themselves to joggers and in-line skaters, and vice versa. Whitewater rapids might be on great fishing rivers; the opposite is, of course, also true. Keeping these things in mind, you'll find new options.

Multisport getaways: Another way to get mileage out of this book is to plan a multiday adventure in one area of the state, collecting a variety of activities from different chapters and linking them up for a series of busy days outside. Try making a list and narrowing it down. Certain areas lend themselves to certain sports. For example, Seattle and its suburbs offer bird-watching, sailing, saltwater fly-fishing, windsurfing, road biking, and short hikes. Central and east-

Introduction

20

ern Washington are great for whitewater outings, trout fishing, rock climbing, and backpacking.

A few words on how the chapters are organized: Most are
divided into City Limits, Backyard, Short Hops, and Meccas. Unlike some cities, Seattle is lucky enough to have a
lot of things to do within a fairly close range. *City Limits*
means you could get there on the bus. *Backyard* could be
anywhere from 15 to 45 minutes away, depending on traffic. The suburbs, and the islands that are a short ferry ride
from downtown, are all Backyard adventures, though they
may feel a lot wilder. *Short Hops* are within about an hour
and a half of the city. Sometimes closer. Occasionally I
have included *Longer Hops*, which are farther than that,
but they are rare. Generally, if something is farther away, it
has been chosen because it is a *Mecca*, a don't-miss destination for that particular sport. A Mecca can be anywhere
from two to eight hours away, though it's usually in the
two- to five-hour range.

Speaking of meccas, understand that there are more meccas in this area than can fit between one book's covers. For
instance, much of Oregon, which starts only three hours
away, could be a mecca. The entire Cascade Range *is* a
mecca, and every time I thought I had things covered I cast
my thoughts up north to British Columbia, also a three-
hour drive and teeming with great adventures. Though this
book visits a few choice spots in each of these areas, you'll
want to gather more resources to do these destinations jus-
tice. See *Where to Connect* sections in each chapter for
additional ideas.

Sidebars can contain important pieces of information
about a particular sport (etiquette or safety tips) or they can
be profiles of local adventures or places. I wrote this book
intending to offer more than great routes. I wanted to cap-
ture some of Seattle's lively and diverse outdoor culture.

It's a place that has drawn adventurers from all over the world. One sidebar, titled *Pitching Tent*, appears throughout the book and describes camping opportunities near your destination. These aren't just convenient camping spots, they're standouts.

A few words on terminology: Each entry starts with a list of information. Certain information essential for, say, hiking (elevation gain) is not necessary for sea kayaking, where you'll need details on water, so the information provided may vary a bit. Here are the terms and how to interpret them:

Location: Tells where the spot is located in relation to downtown Seattle—direction and name of neighborhood, if appropriate. Miles from downtown Seattle are given for *Backyard*, *Short Hops*, *Longer Hops*, and *Meccas*.

Two terms used here and elsewhere in the book are "Eastside" and "east of the mountains." They mean two different things.

"Eastside" refers to the east side of Lake Washington, the location of such suburbs as Bellevue, Kirkland, and Redmond, also the location of Microsoft. When I talk about the "east side of the mountains," well, you've probably guessed that refers to somewhere a lot farther away—the other side of the Cascades. People occasionally think of these two sides as two different states, and both parties sometimes threaten to secede, with eastern Washington teaming up with the more compatible eastern Oregon, and western Washington webfoots planning nuptials with Portland and the Oregon coast. People who love the outdoors wouldn't enjoy that very much. The east side of the mountains often holds the sunny weather hostage. It's more arid, colder and drier in winter and hotter in summer.

Length: Depending on sport, this could be trail miles or nautical miles. Many sports don't need this section—rock

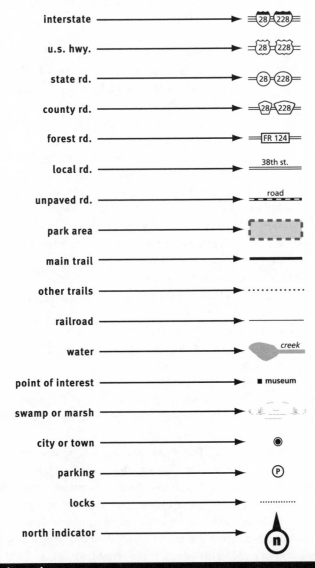

interstate	⊨28⊨228⊨
u.s. hwy.	⊨28⊨228⊨
state rd.	⊨28⊨228⊨
county rd.	⊨28⊨228⊨
forest rd.	⊨FR 124⊨
local rd.	38th st.
unpaved rd.	road
park area	
main trail	
other trails	....
railroad	
water	creek
point of interest	■ museum
swamp or marsh	
city or town	◉
parking	Ⓟ
locks	....
north indicator	n

Legend

climbing, surfing, and windsurfing come to mind. Some entries, for instance in the mountain biking chapter, give you the total amount of trail in a given area, rather than the distance of one designated route.

Difficulty: Take this assessment with a grain of salt, and use your own judgment. When I say a bike ride is "easy," it probably means there isn't much elevation gain, and nothing technical to worry about, though it may be long. By looking under elevation gain, the route description, and the length, you'll get a better sense of whether it's an easy outing by your standards. If an outing is described as difficult, you can assume that if you've never done the sport it's not a good place to start.

Water: This refers to what kind of water you're getting yourself into: freshwater lake, saltwater, estuarine, or riverine.

Tides and weather: This is included for some water sports to give a sense of local conditions and how much of a concern they might be.

Dogs: In a few chapters, such as hiking, I'll let you know if you can bring your dog or not. Double-check with the authorities, as these rules can change.

Outfitters: People and places to contact for gear, instruction, or guiding. The name of the outfitter will appear here; detailed contact information is listed at the end of the chapter in *Where to Connect*.

Books and maps: The more you get into an activity, the more you'll need extra books to sate your appetite for adventure. Many of those listed were essential, during the writing of this book, when trying out a new sport long ago, or in helping me find new places to explore. The maps included here are not meant to offer detailed guidance; you will often need to move to a more technical source. NOAA charts, Green Trails maps—they're listed here if they're available.

Heads up: Highlights, hazards, permits you'll need, nearby restaurants, or other activities to consider.

Description: An overall description of what you'll find at your destination. Sometimes it's just the facts, sometimes I wax rhapsodic.

Route: Trail, road, or river directions, more detailed than the description.

Directions: How to get there by car.

Conservation

If there hadn't been good people fighting to preserve and restore the many destinations in this book, there would be nothing to write about. Everywhere I could find the space I tried to list or highlight such people and organizations. If you love these places, make it your project to preserve and restore them as well. This means donating time to build a trail, or money to help lobby the government. You can also help by writing a letter to the people in charge of a natural area, telling them how important it was to you as a visitor and encouraging them to keep the place protected.

When you're out there, be sure to follow the Leave No Trace ethics embraced by countless outdoorspeople. Some simple rules include:

1. Don't travel in large packs, particularly in wilderness areas. Big groups are great for a whitewater outing, but they can wreak real havoc on a delicate Mount Rainier meadow.

2. Use established trails; camp in established campsites. I've tried to highlight areas where this is particularly important. You may encounter delicate alpine areas, endangered wildlife, and rare birds. Follow the etiquette described where necessary.

3. In most cases, use a camp stove, rather than building a fire.
4. Camp at least 200 feet from water sources, and don't use soap in them.
5. Bury human waste in a cat hole, or, in such instances as rock climbing in arid places, pack it out. Pack out all other trash.

I discuss Leave No Trace ethics further in "Hiking."

Other chapters have etiquette sidebars, or information on such specific subjects as avalanche preparation and water safety. The farther afield you go, the more prepared you should be. Plenty of classes and books out there are loaded with information.

Most of all, have fun.

WHAT SKIING IS to Colorado, what surfing is to Hawaii, sea kayaking is to the Pacific Northwest. Kayaking's North American revival pretty much started here in Washington in the 1950s and has been gaining popularity ever since. It almost seems impossible to properly experience this area *without* trying the sport. Your goal in western Washington should be to get as close to water as possible, and this is about the best you can do short of swimming. Our area offers every kind of paddling, from easy and flat in-city day trips to extremely challenging, outer coast excursions that will test your navigation and bracing skills to the limit.

Of course, people were canoeing and rowboat-ing here long before the first kayak put in, and there are still places to use these as well as other small boats. Just don't be surprised if you don't find them for rent as readily as kayaks. Rowboats, which can often hold an entire family with dog, are easy to use, and usually cheap to rent. Rowboats rentals are available on lakes and occasionally on some of Puget Sound's sheltered coves; they're not a great choice for rainy days or challenging saltwater conditions. Likewise for open canoes; however, these boats, particularly the shorter, more nimble versions, can be better than a long, ruddered sea kayak for paddles on rivers that are shallow or hard to navigate. Shops and outfitters that offer canoes and rowboats almost always rent kayaks—see *Where to Connect* to learn more. Outings that are equally good for open boats will be flagged under *Heads up.*

This chapter describes a range of local lake and Puget Sound paddling. River paddles are generally focused on the estuaries and sloughs at the mouth of a waterway. These areas are more easily navigated by kayak, don't require serious river knowledge, and are rich in wildlife.

The sidebar *Keeping Afloat* offers some boating safety tips; consider them carefully before strapping on that life-jacket and paddling blithely into the Sound. There's not usually much to worry about on the small inland lakes, particularly in summer, but kayaking in salt water requires skill. With Seattle's changeable weather, a calm day can quickly turn into the windstorm of the decade. Fortunately, there are many great shops and classes that offer instruction; these are also good opportunities to find paddling companions, troll for additional outing ideas, or upgrade your gear. Sea kayakers are just about the happiest outdoorspeople you'll meet—attuned to the rhythm of the water, their boats floating cargo holds for gourmet picnics and favorite books, how could they be otherwise? If this sounds appealing, it's time you joined them.

Flatwater Paddling

ASIDE FROM THE Skagit River delta, the Snohomish River slough, and the much-altered Duwamish, this chapter spends little time on rivers. The sea kayaks many people buy or rent in this area, the ones that are great for lakes and saltwater, are long and ruddered, and usually tough to navigate in even Class II rapids. Canoes are also divided into lake and river styles. That said, when you've exhausted your trips to lakes, bays, estuaries, and islands, you might want to throw some flatwater trips into the mix. Look no further than Verne Huser's *Paddle Routes of Western Washington* for advice and lots of great outings. His book also offers advice on the right equipment, describes techniques, and discusses safety and etiquette.

City Limits

NORTH LAKE UNION TO ARBORETUM

Location: Seattle
Length: Variable, depending on where you go. See map for details.
Difficulty: Beginner, but intermediate in the cut
Water: Urban lake
Tides and weather: No tidal concerns. If the winds are strong it can be challenging for weak or beginning paddlers.
Outfitters: Northwest Outdoor Center; Agua Verde Paddle Club
Maps: Maptech Chart for Seattle and Lake Washington; Lakes-to-Locks Water Trail map, West Section
Heads up: If you rent at Agua Verde you can get margar-

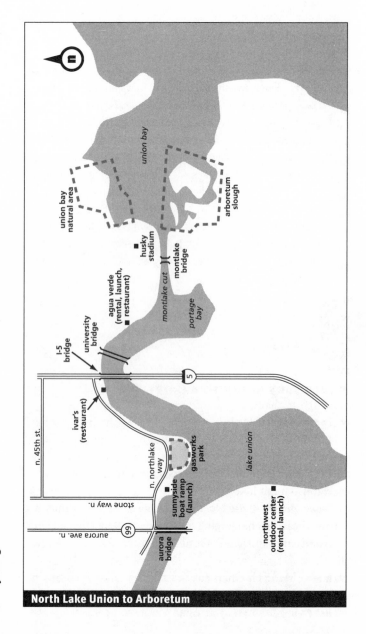

North Lake Union to Arboretum

itas and fish tacos upon return. Dock at Ivar's, on the north side of Lake Union, for fish and chips and chowder.

Description: This working urban lake is a rarity: at the south end, downtown shimmers in the near-distance; along the eastern edge, dry docks share a shoreline with quirky houseboats. Overhead are honking geese, cormorants, and low-flying float planes. On this route you'll paddle northeast on Lake Union and pass under the I-5 and University Bridges into Portage Bay. Along the way is Ivar's Seafood restaurant and one of glass artist Dale Chihuly's workshops (watch for a row of colorful birdfeeders). In Portage Bay you can pull up to the Agua Verde Paddle Club on the north side of the bay for delicious Baja fare (they'll tell you where to dock—if you haven't rented one of their boats you'll need to pull up to one side).

The Montlake Cut provides access to Lake Washington, if you want to go farther. At one time these two bodies of water were separate, but the Army Corps of Engineers created this passage as part of an early 20th-century project to connect the Sound to Lake Washington. The passage is fairly narrow, and on a sunny weekend you'll be sharing it with yachts and motorboats. Use caution. Don't get too close to the banks or you'll be dealing with treacherous wave reverberation; don't get too close to the boats either. Might want to go fast while you're at it. Or come on a calmer day, or in the off-season. On the other side of the cut are some great areas for exploration. To the right after the cut is the Arboretum slough, a swampy bayou with turtles, beavers, muskrats, nesting birds, and overhanging cottonwoods. To the left is University of Washington property along the shoreline, including Husky Stadium and the Union Bay Natural Area, a sanctuary for all kinds of birds. Watch for great blue herons and a huge variety of ducks in winter. (For more about this area see "Bird-Watching," page 229.)

Directions: If you're renting, the outfitters listed offer access to the lake. Agua Verde is closest to the Arboretum, but is technically past Lake Union on the route outlined. NWOC is probably the best bet. Self-launchers have several access points, including the Sunnyside Boat Ramp at 2301 N. Northlake Way in lower Wallingford. To get there take I-5 north from downtown Seattle to exit 169, North 45th St. Stay in the left lane as you exit and turn left over the freeway. Continue on North 45th St. to Stone Way N. Turn left. Continue about 12 blocks to the end of the street, crossing N. 34th St. and curving left as Stone Way becomes N. Northlake Way. The boat launch is about 0.7 mile from 34th, next to the Puget Sound Yacht Club.

Canoeing the Arboretum

F YOU WONDER why your kayak is far outnumbered by canoes and rowboats on your paddle in the Arboretum, look no further than the University of Washington, where renting boats is a long-standing sunny day tradition. You can join the fray by going to the Waterfront Activities Center (WAC) located just north of the Montlake Cut, next to Husky Stadium, and renting your own vessel. It is fairly inexpensive, and there are lots of boats available, except on the warmest summer days. For more information: (206) 543-9433 or http://depts.washington.edu /ima/IMA.wac.html

SOUTH LAKE UNION TO CHITTENDEN LOCKS

Location: Seattle
Length: Variable, depending on where you go. See map for details.

Difficulty: Beginner–intermediate

Water: Urban lake

Tides and weather: No tidal concerns. If the winds are strong it can be challenging for beginning paddlers.

Outfitters: Moss Bay Rowing and Kayak; Northwest Outdoor Center

Maps: Maptech Waterproof Chart for Seattle and Lake Washington; Lakes-to-Locks Water Trail map, West Section

Heads up: Seaplanes dock near here. Wear bold colors and be alert for their takeoffs and landings.

Description: The Fremont Cut is an Army Corps of Engineers project built around the turn of the 20th century. This canal widened tiny Ross Creek, a former Native American fishing grounds, into a channel for boat passage. Above the canal walls on each side are poplars, where cormorants often perch. The shoreline is a mix of marine industry and other businesses, and if you make it to the end of the canal you'll see Fisherman's Terminal on the left. This is one of the few urban wharves in the country still devoted primarily to commercial fishing, not tourism or some other purpose, and has been since 1913. This trip stops at the Hiram M. Chittenden Locks, which operate much like those in the Panama Canal, allowing boats to go between the fresh water of Lakes Union and Washington and the salt water of Puget Sound. You can choose to "lock through" in your kayak here, but it can be a fairly long and stressful process, particularly in the summertime. Check with the Army Corps of Engineers for details.

Route: From Lake Union's south end, head north along the west shoreline. Turn west down the Fremont Cut.

Directions: South Lake Union Park is a decent launch site, if you're willing to keep your eyes peeled for taxiing float planes from nearby Kenmore Air. To get there, take Westlake Ave. around the south side of Lake Union to where it heads north toward the Fremont Bridge. The park

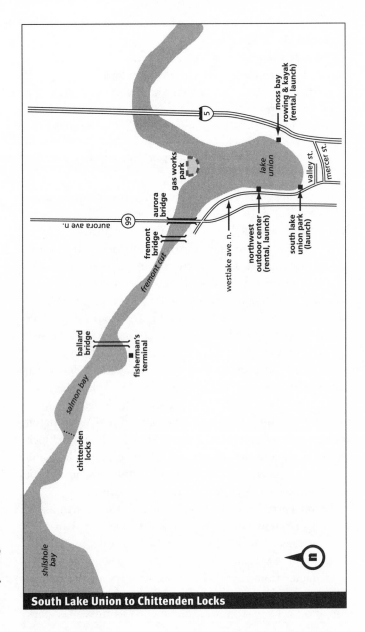

South Lake Union to Chittenden Locks

is just south of Kenmore Air, across from Jillian's and the Marriott Courtyard on Westlake Ave. The Seattle Park floating dock is nice, though it can be green with goose poop if you're unlucky. Good parking.

DUWAMISH WATERWAY

Location: Seattle

Length: About 3 hours, depending on skill level

Difficulty: Strong beginner–intermediate; boat traffic can be intimidating

Water: Tidal river

Tides and weather: If it's low tide, bring rubber boots for the put-in, which will be muddy. Going upstream on a strong ebb current can be difficult and cause problems for novice boaters, so try for a slack or flood tide.

Outfitter: Pacific Water Sports rents canoes and kayaks for carportage to the launch, teaches classes, offers tours, and has tips for other launch sites along the Duwamish.

Maps and books: Maptech Waterproof Chart for Seattle and Lake Washington; Lakes-to-Locks Water Trail map, West Section; Seattle tide table; *Kayaking Puget Sound, the San Juans, and Gulf Islands*; *Nature in the City: Seattle*

Heads up: This is an industrial area and its waters are heavily used by barges, tankers, and the like. If you see any headed your direction, give them a wide berth.

Description: If David Lynch were going paddling, he'd come here. Last time I went I foolishly wore sandals, and wondered if my feet would glow for a day or two after sinking into the arsenic muck. The lower Duwamish is a Superfund site. But hidden among the rust and clang of industry is a string of salmon habitat restoration projects (People for Puget Sound, www.pugetsound.org, has a current list) where you can glimpse this former estuary's glorious past.

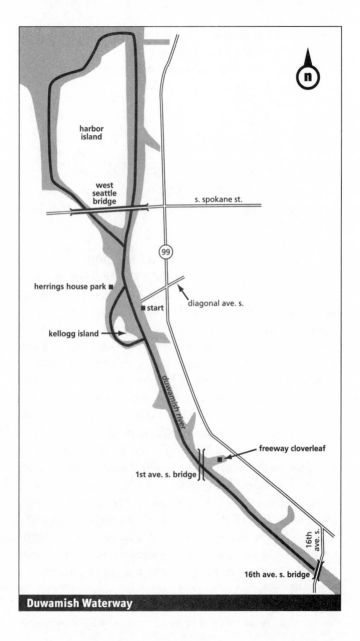

harbor
island

west
seattle
bridge

s. spokane st.

(99)

herrings house park ■

■ start

diagonal ave. s.

kellogg island

duwamish river

freeway cloverleaf

1st ave. s. bridge

16th ave. s.

16th ave. s. bridge

Duwamish Waterway

This is also a great place to get a water-level view of Seattle's port; your boat will put you right in the middle of things. Its possible to circumnavigate Harbor Island, getting up close and personal with the huge cranes that lift trainloads of goods to and from the shore, or to dip beneath the docks for a dark excursion into the industrial underbelly. Those who do like it here will probably love it: A guy I met who comes for weekly paddles (he's usually the only one in the parking lot) says he returns for the thrill of seeing something new—sunken boats, migrating birds, salmon jumping, huge ships from distant ports being nosed into dock by tugboats.

There are several entry points to the Dumawish, and you can arrange a car shuttle and kayak its length if you choose. It's possible to paddle south all the way to Auburn, but, depending on the current, this can be a serious athletic event.

Route: The Diagonal Ave. S. put-in described below is just across from Kellogg Island, a wild remnant of the Duwamish past. The bend in the river on the west side of Kellogg is the only original crinkle in the 4.5 miles of dredged and straightened lower Duwamish. Osprey, eagles, herons, and kingfishers fish here. Rare purple martins (our largest swallows) snuggle in nest boxes constructed on pilings to the south of the island and monitored by martin enthusiasts. With luck, you may see a river otter, beaver, harbor seal, or sea lion here, especially if the salmon are running.

After visiting Kellogg you can head off either north or south.

If you head north: Just north of the island along the west bank of the river is Herring's House Park, a restored wetland where you can dabble your paddles at high tide. For a 3-hour tour, continue on toward Elliott Bay under the West Seattle Bridge and head counterclockwise around Harbor Island.

If you head south: Upriver from Kellogg Island you will pass under two bridges, the first being 1st Ave. S. From the west bank you can pass through a culvert into a small wetland in the middle of a highway cloverleaf, a surprisingly good place to stop and eat lunch. Continuing upriver, explore any patches of beach or greenery you see, which may be restoration projects in the making. A good turn-around point is the next car bridge, 16th Ave. S.

Directions: From downtown Seattle drive south on WA 99. At 0.25 mile south of the Spokane St. overpass (West Seattle exit) turn right (west) onto Diagonal Ave. S. Drive straight back between industrial buildings to the Duwamish. Park here and launch just below the lot.

WEST SEATTLE

Location: West of downtown

Length: 2 to 6 miles

Difficulty: Intermediate

Water: Puget Sound

Tides and weather: From glass to whitecaps, depending on the weather. Minimal tidal concerns.

Outfitters: Bring your own boat. For rentals see *Where to Connect.* Tahoma Outdoor Pursuits offers some trips here.

Map: Maptech Waterproof Chart for Seattle and Lake Washington

Heads up: Sunset splendor. Bring binoculars for marine mammal and bird viewing. Stop at the Alki Bakery for snacks or go to Spuds for fish and chips.

Description: West Seattle has some of the best parks and wildlife viewing in the city. This route starts at the south end of Lincoln Park, right beside the Fauntleroy Ferry dock, and hugs the shoreline for as long as you're interested, up to 12 miles out and back. You might be watched by curious

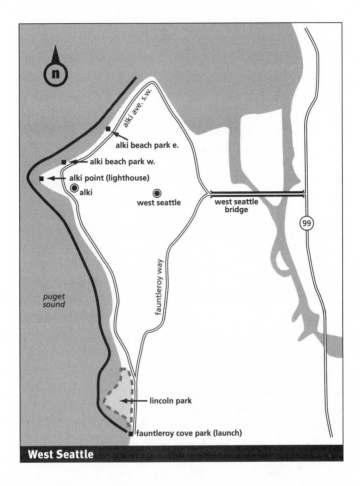

alki ave. s.w.

alki beach park e.

alki beach park w.

alki point (lighthouse)

alki

west seattle

west seattle bridge

99

fauntleroy way

puget sound

lincoln park

fauntleroy cove park (launch)

West Seattle

seals or the occasional mammoth sea lion, and you'll certainly get your fill of seabird sightings, especially in winter.
Bald eagles and ospreys also hunt here—watch for them
soaring or diving over the water. The alert may even spy
orcas in the distance, down for a visit from the San Juans.
If you paddle the 3.5 miles to Alki Point you can spot a historic lighthouse. Rounding this point, you'll soon find
yourself at Alki Beach. Alki is where pioneers established

residence in Seattle, imagining it would one day become a mini-Manhattan. If you need a break, pop out here (you'll have to be comfortable leaving your kayak on the beach), and cross the street to get fish and chips or an espresso. Alki, along with Golden Gardens Park in the north end of the city, is about as close as Seattle gets to California dreaming, with beachfront condos and in-line skaters in short-shorts come summer. This strip is congenial even in the evening in winter. From Alki Point to the end of the route on the map is over 2 miles. See the bird-watching, scuba diving and in-line skating chapters for more on Alki Beach.

Directions: From WA 99 take the West Seattle Bridge exit (don't go to Harbor Island) and cross the bridge. The road becomes Fauntleroy Way. Stay in the left two lanes. Follow Fauntleroy as it turns left (south) at Alaska St. Continue about 2.8 miles to the second Lincoln Park parking lot on your right.

Cove Park, a tiny strip of sandy beach about 50 feet wide, is just north of the Fauntleroy ferry dock, south of Lincoln Park. Unload here and find street parking in nearby neighborhoods. Or put in at the south end of Lincoln Park itself. Here you can drive almost to the water, unload your kayak, then return to the park's lot. Easier parking access, but the trade-off is a less forgiving gravel beach.

EASTSIDE: MERCER SLOUGH AND OPTIONS

Location: Bellevue, a few miles east of Seattle
Length: 2 miles, plus options for more
Difficulty: Beginner
Water: Freshwater lake and freshwater slough
Tides and weather: Not a concern
Outfitters: The slough's Winters House Visitor Center

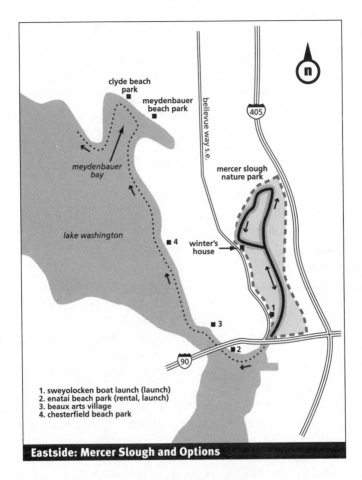

clyde beach
park
meydenbauer
beach park
bellevue way s.e.
405
mercer slough
nature park
meydenbauer
bay
lake washington
■ 4   winter's
house
■ 3
90
■ 2

1. sweyolocken boat launch (launch)
2. enatai beach park (rental, launch)
3. beaux arts village
4. chesterfield beach park

Eastside: Mercer Slough and Options

(425-452-2752) offers naturalist-guided canoe trips on Saturdays May through October. Cascade Canoe and Kayak Center at Enatai Beach Park has boat rentals.

Map and book: Maptech Waterproof Chart for Seattle and Lake Washington; *Nature in the City: Seattle*

Heads up: An easy, rewarding paddle. The slough is open only to nonmotorized boat use.

Description: Paddling along past the cattails and willows, past great blue herons fishing intently from logs or shoreline, you'll find this waterway a humid, soothing escape from city life—even with the hum of I-90 in the background. The slough is a short paddle, but what it lacks in distance it makes up for in accessibility and richness of habitat. The park, nearly in downtown Bellevue, is one of the last large stretches of shoreline wetland in the Seattle area and shelters an enormous number of animal species, from coyotes, foxes, beaver, and muskrats to over one hundred bird species. Trails on land are great for wandering through woods and over marshes and meadows, and the Winters House Visitor Center offers plenty of information. From the water you'll probably spot those great blue herons, and perhaps green herons and American bitterns. In the waterside brush watch for red-winged blackbirds and a variety of songbirds, including chickadees, bushtits, and kinglets. You may also spot bald eagles fishing—there's plenty for them to hunt for in the slough's green depths. Salmon species spawn or pass through here headed up Kelsey Creek; in the fall they can be seen making the passage into the creek from a modified concrete culvert at the Slough.

Route: From the Sweyolocken boat launch you can't get lost—just head up the slough (if you're standing at the boat launch facing the water, it's on your left), loop around the Bellefields Office Park (you'll know it when you see it), and return to the launch. Enatai Park is slightly farther away but nearly as simple. Slough waters are calm and protected from other boat traffic. To extend the journey, you can continue past the launch and under I-90, turning right (roughly north) to head past Enatai Beach Park. You'll next cruise past Beaux Arts Village; first established in 1908 as an art colony, it's now an upscale Eastside community. Glide just under a mile to reach the next shoreline access, Chesterfield Beach Park, where there's swimming and a grassy slope for a picnic. If you're still feeling ambitious, continue north along Lake Washington's east shore as far as you're able. A couple more miles brings you to Meydenbauer Bay, with several more landing sites, and a couple of miles after that you'll get close to Bill Gates's waterfront estate in Medina. It's a slightly different escape fantasy than the one offered by the Mercer slough.

Directions: *To self-launch at Sweyolocken boat launch,* take I-90 east from Seattle to the Bellevue Way exit north. Watch for signs for the boat launch on the right along Bellevue Way before 112th Ave. S.E. *To get to Enatai Beach Park for boat rentals,* take I-90 east from Seattle to the Bellevue Way exit. Travel north for 1 mile. Veer left at the "Y" and turn south, left, onto 108th Ave. S.E. and go to the lake. The Cascade Center is at 3519 108th Ave. S.E.

Short Hops

Keeping Afloat

GENERALLY SPEAKING, the inland lakes—Union, Washington, and Sammamish—are easy places to learn paddling, with little risk provided you wear your lifejacket. Paddling on Puget Sound is an entirely different prospect, particularly when you leave the Sound's sheltered bays and inlets and head out on an open crossing. Weather can turn suddenly, and nothing is more intimidating than finding yourself in the path of a Russian trawler in one of the busiest ports in the United States. As a breakable rule, the Sound becomes more unwieldy as you move south to north. Though there are sheltered coves for wetting a novice paddle in the San Juan Islands, this seemingly carefree place has some of the strongest and most unpredictable currents around. Begin on salt water with a guide, or hone your skills before you go. Also, find a more experienced open-water kayaker to join you. Solo kayaking on the Sound is unwise. *Where to Connect* offers plenty of outfitters willing to take or teach you; there are hour-long sessions and week-long trips to suit every interest. The cheapest, most painless way to get started is to take a class on an inland lake in the summer. You'll have to learn how to "wet exit" your boat and self-rescue, and you'll be grateful to do it in warm water.

BLAKE ISLAND

Location: 475-acre Blake Island is located in Puget Sound, about 4 nautical miles west of Seattle.

Length: 2.75 to 5 miles one way, depending on route

Difficulty: Intermediate–advanced, weather and tide dependent

Water: Puget Sound

Tides and weather: Both are concerns. See individual routes below for details

Maps and book: Maptech Chart for Puget Sound; Seattle tide table; *Kayaking Puget Sound, the San Juans, and Gulf Islands*

Heads up: Call ahead to have dinner at Tillicum Village on Blake Island

Outfitters: Puget Sound Kayak Company on Vashon offers overnight trips and rentals from Vashon; Pacific Water Sports and Tahoma Outdoor Pursuits lead occasional trips.

Description: Spend a day or overnight on this local gem, sharing the area with deer, bald eagles, seals, and maybe even orcas. The northwest end has a beautiful sand beach

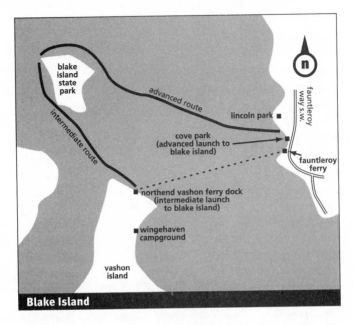

Blake Island

with driftwood, and you'll listen to waves lap against the shore as you eat your lunch. The center of the island is wooded, with cedar, fir, alder, and mosses. Several miles of trails and unused dirt roads cross the island, so there's walking available, too. If you go on a summer weekend you're likely to share space with yachters, motorboaters, and perhaps other kayakers, but there's room to spread out. Go during the week to avoid crowds. There are gorgeous views of the Olympic Mountains, and you can also see the city lights at night. Touristy Tillicum Village (800-426-1205), on the northeast side of the island, is a developed area for groups to camp or to spend the evening at an Indian-style longhouse, eating a salmon feast and watching a dance performance. A tour boat brings most guests from Seattle, but if you want to investigate (or feast on salmon) you can call in advance for a reservation.

Route: For this you have two options.

If you are an intermediate paddler, and if the water is anything but glass calm (and perhaps even in the best conditions), take the Fauntleroy Ferry, just south of Cove Park, to Vashon Island and start your journey from here. If you're going alone and leaving your car behind you'll need a wheeled portage cart to get your kayak on and off the ferry efficiently. The ferry staff will direct you—you will generally load and unload after cars. Just south of the Vashon ferry terminal, next to the Mexican restaurant, is a small boat launch where you can put in. The trip from Vashon Island to the Blake Island campsite is about 2¾ miles. The exposed part of the crossing is about 1¼ miles. Be aware of the rips that can occur between these two points. However, this crossing is still shorter and less exposed than a crossing directly from Seattle.

If you are an advanced or very strong intermediate paddler, launch from West Seattle and paddle to Blake Island. The crossing is exposed and about 4 miles long. If there is any wind it can be challenging, and definitely intimidating to anyone without experience. Cove Park, a tiny strip of sandy beach about 50 feet wide, is just north of the Fauntleroy Ferry dock, south of Lincoln Park. Unload here and find street parking in nearby neighborhoods. Or put in at the south end of Lincoln Park itself. Here you can drive almost to the water, unload your kayak, then return to the park's lot. However, you can't leave your car here overnight, so this is a day-trip option only. The latter has easier parking access, but the trade-off is a less forgiving gravel beach.

The trip from Cove Park to the Blake Island campsite is about 5 miles. To get to the sand beach, aim for the northwest side of Blake Island.

Directions: To get to Lincoln Park, take WA 99 to the West Seattle Bridge exit (don't go to Harbor Island) and cross the bridge. The road becomes Fauntleroy Way. Stay in the left two lanes. Follow Fauntleroy as it turns left (south) at Alaska St. Continue about 2.8 miles to the second Lincoln Park parking lot. The Vashon Ferry is just past Cove Park.

PITCHING TENT
blake and vashon islands

IT'S NOT IMPOSSIBLE to do a day-trip to Blake Island and get home in time for dinner. However, many paddlers will want to extend their trip once they get there. It's hard to resist the option of a beautiful boat-up campsite within a couple of paddle hours from home. For a great weekend outing, consider tacking on a second night on Vashon Island, where a charming, small Cascadia Marine Trails campsite, Wingehaven, is tucked into the first bay south of the Vashon ferry dock, about one mile from the dock. The site is easy to miss; look for the Cascadia Marine Trails sign on beach. Access is by foot or boat only, and only kayakers (and others in human-powered craft) may camp here. The quiet, undeveloped 12-acre campsite features great views east and southeast to Mount Rainier, with a picnic table and a grassy clearing for camping. A mixed woodland surrounds the area. Remnants of a former estate, including an ornate wall and part of a birdbath and sculpture, have survived. Be sure to bring extra water if you're going to spend the night.

Blake Island camping details: Consult Washington State Parks for up-to-date information. The sites are first-come, first-served, with fresh water and restrooms available. Washington State Parks Information Center is at (360) 902-8844, www.parks .wa.gov.

Wingehaven camping details: Camping is free, with three first-come, first-served sites. No fresh water, primitive toilet. Owned by the Vashon Park District (206-463-9602, www .vashonparkdistrict.org) but part of the Washington Water Trails.

NISQUALLY DELTA

Location: 8 miles northeast of Olympia

Length: Variable

Difficulty: Beginner–intermediate. The paddle is sheltered but you'll need to pay attention to tides so as not to get stuck in mudflats.

Water: Estuary

Tides and weather: Higher tides mean more access to the fingers of marshland you'll want to explore here. A 10-foot tide or more is ideal, though anything past 14 feet will cover much habitat. You'll get stuck in mudflats if you get too far up one of these fingers when the tide is going out.

Outfitters: NWOC and Tahoma Outdoor Pursuits offer some tours.

Maps and Books: Maptech Chart for Puget Sound or Maptech Chart Book, Puget Sound; *A Sea Kayaker's Guide to South Puget Sound; Nisqually Watershed: Glacier to Delta*

Heads up: Luhr Beach access is from a state boat launch. To park here you will need a Vehicle Use Permit. Buy one at most sporting goods stores, on-line at www.fishhunt.dfw.wa.gov, or by calling (866) 246-9453. Cost is about $10. Also, be aware of the hunting season. Exact dates (and other information) available at the wildlife refuge (360-753-9467).

Description: The Nisqually delta contains the Nisqually National Wildlife Refuge, 3,000 acres of protected habitat, from salt- and freshwater marshes to mixed forest. The nearly untouched state of the area is extraordinary compared with nearly every other estuary in the area, and for this it ranks near the top of most kayakers' favorite local destinations. Expect to see a rich diversity of birds (see "Bird-Watching," page 239). The waters are frequented by loons, grebes, cormorants, herons, swans, geese, ducks,

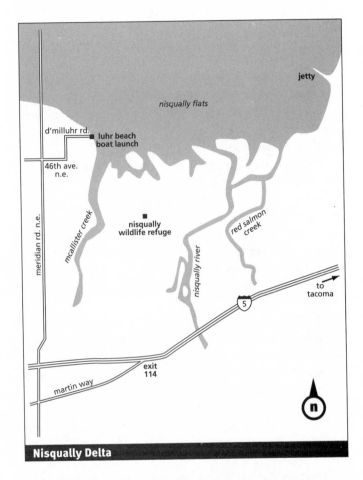

Nisqually Delta

gulls, and such raptors as bald eagles, golden eagles, red-tailed hawks and ospreys. The estuary also provides passage for salmon and steelhead in season, and habitat for seals that may look you over from a safe distance (do not disturb these creatures if you happen upon them on shore). You can roam the area freely if you've caught the right tide.

Route: One popular choice is to paddle up McAllister Creek, accessed by heading right (south) from the launch.

An incoming tide makes this route easy. A great blue heron colony on the shoreline about a mile up on the right provides a view of these huge birds in their breeding and nesting habitat. Depending on how long your trip lasts (and how late into the incoming tide you started out), you may be able to return on an outgoing tide, gliding all the way. McAllister is a particularly good foul-weather destination, because there is some shelter from wind.

If you want to cut across the delta you should be able to head easterly if the tide is high. Otherwise, you'll need to go north toward the flats to cut across and then head back down either the Nisqually River or, with enough water, Red Salmon Creek. On the east side, a sand jetty is a good spot to pull over for a break and lunch. For information on a good walk here, see "Bird-Watching," page 239.

Directions: Take I-5 south to exit 114, Martin Way, about 60 miles from Seattle. You will go up and over the freeway, to the left. At the light go straight uphill, east on Martin Way. In about a mile turn right onto Meridian Rd. and go about 2.5 miles. Turn right on 46th Ave. Take the first left onto D'Milluhr Rd. and continue to the parking lot for the Luhr Beach boat launch.

SNOHOMISH RIVER ESTUARY

Location: Everett, about 33 miles north of Seattle
Length: 5 to 30 miles
Difficulty: Intermediate
Water: Tidal estuary
Tides and weather: Parts of this estuary are too shallow for passage at low tide. For best access, aim for high or slack tide. Currents are generally not too strong, but keep in mind that you will be paddling against the tide in one direction or the other unless you time your outing properly.

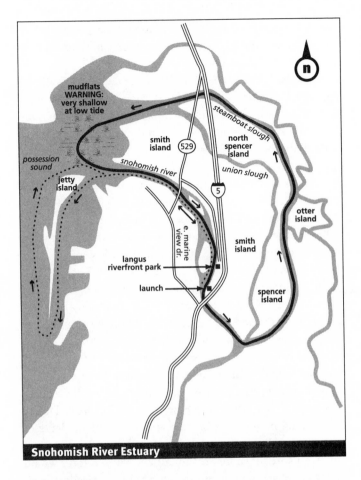

Snohomish River Estuary

Do not paddle here during flood conditions unless you have ample experience.

Outfitters: Popeye's Marine in Everett (425-339-9479) rents boats; Pacific Water Sports, and Tahoma Outdoor Pursuits offer occasional trips here.

Maps and book: *Snohomish River Estuary Recreation Guide*, available from Snohomish County Parks and Recreation (425-339-1208, www.co.snohomish.wa.us/parks), includes history, some flora and fauna descriptions, and a map. Maptech Puget Sound Waterproof Chart or NOAA Chart 18443 are also options.

Heads up: When the Snohomish River near Langus Riverfront Park is open for fishing, it may be crowded with motorboats. Avoid these times or prepare to share the river and breathe exhaust fumes between the launch site and the protected sloughs. (Consult Washington Department of Fish and Wildlife for fishing season details.)

Spencer and Jetty Islands are currently the only ones that are open to the public for walking. Spencer is accessible from a trail at Langus; you can land your boat on Jetty.

Description: Everett is an industrial city, and its port was once lined with sawmills. The Snohomish River Estuary is created where the river meets Possession Sound's salt water. As in other estuaries around Puget Sound, this enticing mix of salt and fresh water draws a remarkably rich mix of wildlife. For those in small boats, the many sloughs and channels seem tailor-made; you can spend hours, if you time the tides right, wandering from one area to the next. Spencer Island, which has an accessible nature trail, is known as one of western Washington's best bird-watching destinations (see "Bird-Watching," page 237). Jetty Island, a 2-mile long manmade island created from the dredging of Port Gardner Bay, has a sandy beach and other landings and draws all sorts of shorebirds in fall and winter. Jetty would be a good place to wait out an ebb tide before heading back upriver. Huge stick nests at the estuary's entrance belong to ospreys. Keep your eyes out for the black heads of harbor seals, popping up to take a look at you.

Route: From the put-in at Langus Riverfront Park you have a couple of alternatives, heading either southeast to explore Union and Steamboat Sloughs or northwest and out to Everett Port to pay a visit to Jetty Island. The map shows possible routes for each of these options, or you may choose your own.

Directions: Head north on I-5 and take exit 195, Marine View Dr. Turn left off the exit ramp onto E. Marine View Dr., which becomes WA 529 N. Take the first exit, signed for Langus Riverfront Park. Follow signs to the park—at one point the road will fork; stay to the right. Access for nonmotorized craft is beyond the main, fee boat ramp.

SOUTH PUGET SOUND: OLYMPIA TO HARTSTENE ISLAND

Location: Boston Harbor in Olympia, about 60 miles south of Seattle

Length: 21 miles out and back; 6-mile option

Difficulty: Intermediate–advanced

Water: Puget Sound

Tides and weather: Plan with the tides for the easiest paddling experience. As on all Puget Sound excursions, foul weather or high winds will make the outing for advanced paddlers only. Weather and winds tend to be gentler in summer.

Outfitters: Tahoma Outdoor Pursuits and Pacific Water Sports have occasional trips to South Puget Sound.

Maps and book: Cascadia Marine Trail Map from Washington Water Trail Association (WWTA); Maptech Chart for Puget Sound; *A Sea Kayaker's Guide to South Puget Sound*

Heads up: The South Sound is the newest leg of the Washington Water Trails Association's marine trail, and it's not yet well known. This is a worthwhile alternative to the crush (and hazards) of the San Juan Islands. For information on Boston Harbor Marina go to www.bostonharbormarina .com/home.htm or call (360) 357-5670.

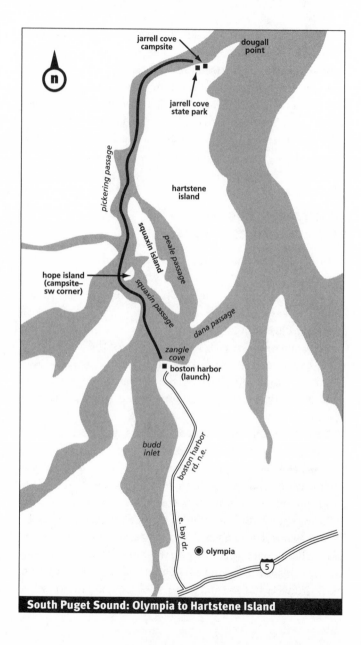

jarrell cove campsite

dougall point

jarrell cove state park

hartstene island

pickering passage

squaxin island

peale passage

hope island (campsite– sw corner)

squaxin passage

dana passage

zangle cove

boston harbor (launch)

budd inlet

boston harbor rd. n.e.

e. bay dr.

olympia

5

South Puget Sound: Olympia to Hartstene Island

Description: The quaint Boston Harbor, north of Olympia, is a nice launch point for this outing. From the moment you put in you'll feel miles away from the bustle of the I-5 corridor. Using WWTA information you can chart your own course between idyllic islands and inlets, or follow the route described here for a fairly easy (depending on weather and tides) one- or two-night trip. For a short outing cut across northeast to Squaxin Passage, named for the Indian tribe living on nearby Squaxin Island. The paddling will be easiest at end of flood or at slack tide. From here, visit 106-acre Hope Island for the day—a round-trip of about 6 miles. All of Hope is a state park, accessible only by boat. The island offers 2 miles of hiking trails, and you might share them with deer and other wildlife. In fall you can pick up to 5 pounds of apples from the island's trees for free. Views of Mount Rainier, apples in an old orchard—what more could you want? There's camping available (see *Pitching Tent*, page 56, for details), or continue on up Pickering Passage to Jarrell Cove on Hartstene Island, about 8 more miles, which is shorter than it sounds if you're going with the tide. This larger island is sparsely inhabited and equally picturesque. The WWTA site is tucked into woods, with views of the Sound (see *A Trail Through Water*, page 64). Watch at both locations for bald eagles, great blue herons, river otters, seals, and a variety of other wildlife. Return to Boston Harbor the way you came.

Directions: Take I-5 about 60 miles south to Olympia and exit 105B toward State Capitol/City Center/Port of Olympia. Take the ramp toward the port, and merge onto E. Bay Drive. Make a slight right onto Plum St. SE, which becomes E. Bay Dr. N.E., and then Boston Harbor Rd. Continue 6 miles to 73rd Ave. N.E. and turn left. The ramp and parking lot are about 0.25 mile farther, next to the Boston Harbor Marina, which has a general store. Public parking lot and restrooms are across the street.

south puget sound—
hope island and hartstene island

MANY KAYAKERS HAVE NEVER tried the Cascadia Marine Trail's (CMT's) southernmost campsites in South Puget Sound. That might change once paddlers realize the area is nearly as scenic as the San Juan Islands, without the crowds or long ferry lines.

Both the Hope Island and Jarrell Cove campsites are water-side heaven. The Hope Island campground is on the southwest side, 200 feet west of the main stairs, and has six tent sites. It has no fresh water and a vault toilet. Jarrell Cove is at the north end of Hartstene Island, 2 miles south of Dougall Point. Time your arrival to avoid low tide, when the landing area becomes a mudflat. The site is above the small dock on the east shore of the cove. *Restrooms.* The island's main, non-CMT campground uphill has restrooms with hot showers and fresh water. Limited supplies may be available at the marina across the shoreline from the site. Both Hope and Jarrell work on a first-come, first-served basis. Camp fees are $8 to $10 a night. Check out www.parks.wa.gov for more information and current prices, or call Jarrell Cove directly at (360) 426-9226. For information on other state parks sites call (360) 902-8608. For a complete listing and descriptions of South Sound campsites on the trail contact the Washington Water Trails Association.

Meccas

OLYMPIC PENINSULA

Location: West of Seattle, across Puget Sound and the Kitsap Peninsula

Sea Kayaking

Difficulty: Beginner–advanced, depending on the outing

Outfitters: Olympic Raft and Kayak; Kayak Port Townsend

Maps and book: NOAA Charts 18465 for Port Townsend to beyond Port Angeles; NOAA chart 18460 for Port Angeles to beyond Neah Bay; *Kayaking Puget Sound*

Heads up: A wide variety of paddles is available, from wild coastal waters to the sheltered bays of the Port Townsend area. Incredible abundance of wildlife. When you travel through Port Angeles, eat at Michael's Divine Dining.

Description: Kayaking Seattleites are so flush with options that it can be years before they dip their paddles in peninsula waters. Once they get there, a whole new watery world opens up. There are many great destinations, though choices will be narrowed by experience and time available. Those with less experience should start at Indian and Marrowstone Islands, near Port Townsend, or even at Port Townsend itself, taking a class or guided tour in the bay and then settling in at a campground or historic Victorian B&B. This area of the peninsula is in what's called a rain shadow, and can often be drier and sunnier than Seattle, another draw. It's also a reasonable day-trip, if you start early, from Seattle. Sheltered coves on central Hood Canal are another place to head for some protected paddling. Farther north and west, along the Strait of Juan de Fuca, the Dungeness Spit National Wildlife Refuge offers slightly more exposed conditions at a renowned bird-watching destination. West of here the strait becomes more and more challenging. Finally, the shoreline on the northwest and west coasts, in places such as Neah Bay near the peninsula's northwest tip, offer excitement for the most advanced paddler.

Directions: There are several driving routes for getting to the Olympic Peninsula. The best way to get to the northern end, where much of the kayaking is found, is to go north on I-5 to Edmonds-Kingston ferry (exit 177). Follow signs to the ferry, another 6 to 7 miles. Take the ferry to Kingston and follow signs to WA 104. Take this west to the Hood Canal Bridge. Cross, and continue west to US 101. Indian and Marrowstone Islands, Port Townsend, Dungeness Spit, and other kayaking destinations are accessed from this highway.

West Coast Sea Kayak Symposium

'M SITTING ON THE FRONT STEPS of the registration building for the annual West Coast Sea Kayak Symposium on the Olympic Peninsula, poring over the program of events. Up to 10 classes, including one or two on the water, take place simultaneously, and I'd like to attend them all. Impossible, of course, so I huddle over every page.

It's an exercise in self-definition: What kind of paddler am I or should I be? Do I go with "Cold Water Immersion/Hypothermia," to prepare myself for the worst? Or the crafty "Feasting on Flotsam," a class on gathering wild foods in which I will learn to make Sea Cheetos and Chocolate Ocean Pudding? Am I awake enough after one espresso to go for "Celestial Mechanics," or would "Wacky Strokes Demo" be easier on my morning brain? Who among the many kayaking luminaries here would be the most inspiring?

I turn to a guy on the other side of the steps. He's hunched over his program, too, finger scrolling down the page. A straw-blond ponytail sticks out from under his cap.

"Which classes are you going to?" I ask him.

"I don't know," he moans. "It's all good."

The symposium is one of North America's most popular sea kayaking events. It takes place over three days each September at Fort Warden State Park in Port Townsend, in the rain-shadow region of the famously wet Olympic Peninsula, an area protected by mountains from too much damp weather. This weekend is no exception, and blissed-out paddlers stroll from one event to the other in golden autumn sun.

The atmosphere here is jovial, communal, and all about boats. The park is crawling with paddle freaks: They're carbo-loading in the dining area; gathered around a kayak for a repair class, awash in wood glue; or tromping down to the beach to try out a folding kayak or an ultralightweight paddle. Evening gatherings, including ice cream socials, barbecues, and slide shows, offer plenty of time to socialize. If you come alone, as I did, you're sure to find plenty of camaraderie in this group.

But first you have to experience the pleasurable pain of picking between all the great offerings. Having recently heard of a friend's near-death experience while kayaking in the surf, I opt for self-preservation and head to "The Ins and Outs of the Surf Zone." But like the man said: It's all good.

SAN JUAN ISLANDS

Location: The Anacortes ferry terminal, gateway to the San Juans, is 85 miles north of Seattle.

Difficulty: Beginner–expert

Outfitters: Too many to list here; see *Where to Connect.*

Maps and book: Sea Trails Marine Maps, San Juan Series; Maptech Waterproof Chart Book, Puget Sound and San Juans; *Kayaking Puget Sound, the San Juans, and Gulf Islands*

Heads up: Gorgeous but overrun in summer and early fall. In the high summer season, you will have to wrestle strangers for a campsite. The waters here can be dangerous for beginners.

Description: Justifiably known for their beauty, the San Juan Islands draw visitors from all over. Four main islands—Lopez, Shaw, Orcas, and San Juan—are served by Washington State Ferries; and the rest, all 743 of them stretching up to Canada, are sparsely occupied. There are tiny beaches, sheltered coves, and rocky bluffs to which auburn madrona trees cling tenaciously. Expect to encounter resident orcas, seals, porpoises, tufted puffins, and bald eagles, just to mention a few of the more flamboyant members of the community.

There are kayak rental companies on most of the main islands. Many waterfront B&Bs and hotels make boats available for short paddles. It's likely that even if you're visiting for some other reason you'll end up paddling around a quiet bay at some point, if only to fit in. If the Northwest is a kayak destination, this may well be its epicenter.

That said, the San Juans are also a place where people overconfident in their paddling abilities are sometimes taught a serious lesson. More than one boat outfitter in Seattle has mentioned getting calls from people looking to gear up for a trip that was far out of their league. There's a world of difference between a shoreline paddle and a jaunt out between islands on open water. For a day-long journey across any exposed water, or a multiday camping trip, you should come prepared with solid self-rescue and paddling skills and a good understanding of local weather and currents. This isn't meant to discourage, however. If you're still working on your skills, contact an outfitter for guided trips—he or she will show you places that are nearly risk-free and will knock your binoculars off.

For more sheltered paddling nearby, try out some areas on the mainland east of the San Juans. Padilla Bay, east of Anacortes and accessible from I-5, is a destination for waterfowl and very scenic. Chuckanut Bay in Bellingham, farther north, offers a similar experience off the shores of

an engaging college town. *Kayaking Puget Sound* has good
descriptions of these and other routes.

Kayak Fever

VISITORS TO SEATTLE often think of sea kayaking as a
traditional local sport. But fifty years ago, only a few
wild-minded locals had even dipped a kayak paddle in
western Washington waters.

Native Americans had been using canoes to travel and earn
a living from the rivers, lakes, and Puget Sound long before
that, but kayaks, an Inuit invention, weren't commonly used
here, and in the 20th century they were more likely to be found
in Europe than anywhere in the United States.

It wasn't until I talked to 83-year-old Washington Water
Trails Association cofounder Tom Deschner, who still heads out
whitewater and sea kayaking regularly, that I learned Seattle
was home port for the birth of 20th-century kayaking in the
mainland United States. According to Deschner, legendary
local skiing and climbing pioneer Wolf Bauer offered a YMCA
whitewater kayaking course in 1954. When Deschner took the
class they used Fold-A-Boats, canvas boats with wooden ribs
brought over from Europe. There was no such thing as a hard-
shell whitewater kayak, and kayakers had to backpaddle to
maneuver.

By the time Deschner, a Boeing engineer, returned with his
family from several overseas jobs in the late 1960s, a kayak
club had formed, today's Washington Kayak Club. "I thought
I'd get my kids involved in something to keep them out of
drugs," he says explaining why he enrolled them in kayak
classes. As a result, his son, Whit Deschner, has crisscrossed
the world with a kayak, writing *Travels with a Kayak* and *Does
the Wet Suit You?* in the process.

Deschner recalls the early years of Seattle-area sea kayaking as obsessive ones. "In 1969 there were probably 80 to 100 people with kayaks," says Deschner. "You knew when you saw a kayak on the car who they were, where they were going, and what they were doing." The intrepid group cobbled together equipment from the contents of their garages. "Back then you made your own car rack out of pipes and things," says Deschner; his was installed on the top of a Volkswagen Bug. Club members worked up designs for making fiberglass kayaks, and bought their paddles from "one guy in Kirkland who was in charge of making them." In the late 1960s and early '70s Bauer and Lee Moyer, now the co-owner of Pacific Water Sports, began to make their own sea kayaks with a skeg, or fixed rudder.

Deschner and his wife, Laura, took their first sea-kayaking trip to the Gulf Islands in British Columbia after encountering difficulties with shoreline access around Puget Sound. "All the land seemed to be privately owned," he says. "People were yelling at us." As they, and the club, found themselves forced to head north for paddle outings, the idea of the Washington Water Trails Association gestated.

The popularity of the sport within the club hit a high point with *Kayak Fever,* a 1971 musical written by Char Baker, a musician and club member. The group rented the Carco Theater in Renton and performed with piano, drummer, and club members playing the parts. "The people who were sea kayaking here in the 1960s and '70s glued themselves together as a family," says Deschner. "We're welded." A couple of years ago Tom and Laura were the oldest members on a paddle trip in south Puget Sound, traveling from Olympia's Boston Harbor north to Blake Island by way of Anderson and Vashon Islands. The pair struggled with a pair of 1970 paddles weighing 4½ pounds apiece. When they decided to take a more direct, but separate, route home in their kayaks, they were prevented by concerned trip members. The two were forced to sneak away from Blake Island before dawn. Deschner believes the key to gaining more access to local shoreline, and keeping it, is encouraging more people to get into boats. As he puts it: "We need more people on the water."

BRITISH COLUMBIA

Location: About 120 miles north of Seattle. However, it can take 3 to 12 hours to get to a paddle, depending on border crossing time, ferry schedules, destination, and other variables. Getting to Vancouver takes between 3 and 4 hours.

Difficulty: Beginner–advanced

Outfitters: The industry is booming here, and new outfitters start up (and fold) all the time. A great resource is the Web site www.wavelengthmagazine.com. This B.C.-based paddling magazine has entertaining and informative articles and is a terrific source of information on area outfitters.

Maps and books: Various Canadian chart books and individual charts are available. Call or visit the Armchair Sailor (2110 Westlake Ave. in Seattle, 206-283-0858, www .armchairsailorseattle.com) for help. *Kayak Routes of the Pacific Northwest Coast; Kayaking Puget Sound, the San Juans, and Gulf Islands* are all useful.

Heads up: It can seem like a long haul, but British Columbia has great shoreline access, beautiful camping, and, in Desolation Sound, some of the warmest salt water north of the Gulf of Mexico. Ferry information is available at www.bcferries.bc.ca.

Description: From the warmer, more protected waters on the mainland coast to the wild outer coast of Vancouver Island to the cities of Vancouver and Victoria, British Columbia is at least as blessed with paddle opportunities as western Washington, and all at favorable exchange rates.

The area is outrageously scenic, a diverse mix including the sandstone walls of the Gulf Islands, the snowy backdrop of the Coast Range, and the rain forests of Clayoquot Sound. There are islands just big enough for one campsite and others with enough wilderness to support a few bears. Some beaches are inches thick with oysters, and blue mussels hang in giant clumps wherever they can gain purchase, like oversized bunches of grapes.

Kayaking has become more popular in British Columbia in recent years, which means there are more outfitters if you don't want to schlep your own gear, but also, of course, means a boom in fellow boaters. In certain areas, like the Gulf Islands, you'll want to watch out for popular yacht cruising spots, which can get busy in summer. The shoulder seasons, late spring and mid-fall, can be an ideal time to visit—fewer people but, if you're lucky, nice weather. The farther north you go, generally, the more solitude you'll find—you can get to the edge of serious wilderness within a few hours of some of the busier destinations.

A Trail Through Water

WITH A SHELTERED INNER COASTLINE, placid lakes, and tumbling rivers, western Washington is about as close as you get to small-boat heaven. Or is it? Our setting may be glorious, but Washington State has a history of selling off public shoreline access. While British Columbia, Oregon, and California have retained public rights to shores up to the high tide line, Washington beaches can and have been sold to developers and individuals. About 60 percent of Washington tidelands were sold by Washington State into private ownership before the 1970s, when that practice ended. Boaters, anglers, scuba divers, and even strolling beachgoers often travel long distances between one public access point and the next.

Puget Sound shoreline is also threatened by "hardening," the modification of shores with riprap and bulkheads for development, piers, docks, boat ramps, and marinas.

Fighting a pitched battle against this sorry state of affairs, the nonprofit Washington Water Trails Association (WWTA), works to preserve and expand shoreline access for small watercraft. Inspired in part by the Maine Island Trail Association, the WWTA creates "blue trails" by linking a string of access points along lake or Puget Sound shorelines.

The WWTA's first and ongoing project is to create the Cascadia Marine Trail (CMT), a blue trail stretching over 140 miles from the shorelines of Olympia to the Canadian border. It's the first National Recreation Trail on water, inspiring the kind of love among paddlers that the Pacific Crest and Appalachian Trails inspire among hikers. There are not only launch and landing points but also over 40 campsites, from charming, privately owned beaches campers are likely to have to themselves to big state park sites packed with boating camaraderie. The WWTA would like to have 250 or more camping spots on the trail—enough so that boaters wouldn't have to travel more than 5 to 8 miles between each site—but finding enough open space continues to be a challenge. To learn more about the WWTA, see *Where to Connect*.

Where to Connect

The Basics

There are lots of outfitters willing to take you on a tour or multiday trip. For going out on a city lake in a kayak, canoe, or rowboat you'll only need a few tips before taking off in a borrowed or rented boat. Out on Puget Sound in a kayak, however, you'll want at least a couple of lessons and possibly many more. Check out the clubs and outfitters in this section to get started.

Clubs and Organizations

- Associated Students of the University of Washington (ASUW) Experimental College (206-543-4375, www .experimental.asuw.org) offers cheap boating classes (and lots of other stuff) to the entire community through their quarterly catalog.

- Duwamish River Cleanup Coalition (5410 1st Ave. N.E., 206-954-0218, www.duwamishcleanup.org) is an alliance of groups working to ensure cleanup of the city's Duwamish River.

- Green Lake Small Craft Center (5900 W. Green Lake Way N., 206-684-4074) is one of the city's best boating deals. Run by Seattle Parks and Recreation and the Seattle Canoe and Kayak Club, the center offers classes in canoeing, rowing, sailing, and kayaking, and boat access to members. This club is one of the training centers for the U.S. Canoe and Kayak Team.

- Lesbian and Gay Sea Kayakers (1202 E. Pike #896, Seattle, 98122)

- The Mountaineers (300 3d Ave. W., 206-284-6310, www .mountaineers.org) offers all kinds of paddle classes and trips for those who have completed course requirements.

- North Sound Sea Kayaking Association, at www .nsseakayaker.homestead.com, has information on the Everett and Snohomish River Delta area.

- Paddle Trails Canoe Club (206-444-4313, www .paddletrails.org)

- People for Puget Sound (206-382-7007, www.pugetsound
  .org) works to protect Puget Sound.

- Puget Soundkeeper Alliance (206-297-7002, www
  .pugetsoundkeeper.org) is a local conservation group working to protect and preserve Puget Sound.

- Seattle Sea Kayak Club (www.Seattlekayak.org) meets at
  the REI flagship store on the last Tuesday evening of each
  month.

- Washington Kayak Club (206-433-1983, www.Wakayakclub
  .com) is a big, established whitewater and sea kayaking
  club with hundreds of trips a year.

- Washington Water Trails Association (4649 Sunnyside Ave.
  N., Rm. 305, 206-545-9161, www.wwta.org) is a nonprofit
  championing public access to water. See p. 65.

Shops and Outfitters

- Agua Verde Paddle Club (1303 N.E. Boat St., 206-545-8570
  or 800-308-7991, www.aguaverde.com) offers kayak rental
  on Portage Bay. Seasonal passes or hourly rates available.
  Great, reasonably priced Baja Mexican food upstairs at the
  Agua Verde Café, and a laid-back staff. Good for paddles
  into Union Bay or Lake Union.

- Center for Wooden Boats (1010 Valley Street, 206-382-2628,
  www.cwb.org). A boat-lover's dream museum of classic
  wooden watercraft. Classes in sailing and rowing and
  rentals of various watercraft, such as rowing shells, sailing
  dinghies, and rowboats. No kayaks.

- George Gronseth's Kayak Academy and Expeditions
  (2512 N.E. 95th St., 206-527-1825, www.kayakacademy
  .com) provides beginner to advanced sea kayaking classes
  and tours after lessons. Rentals available for classes.

- Moss Bay Rowing and Kayaking Center (1001 Fairview Ave.
  North #1900, 206-682-2031, www.mossbay.net). Very nice

people offering daily beginner to advanced paddle classes and rentals. Located on South Lake Union. They also teach rowing and sailing and rent rowboats, canoes, rowing shells, and small sailboats.

- Northwest Outdoor Center (NWOC), (2100 Westlake Ave. N. Suite 1, 206-281-9694, www.nwoc.com) is the city's busiest outfitter, opened in 1980, teaching at least 1,500 people to kayak each year. Rent a kayak (prepare for crowds on a sunny afternoon), buy a life vest, or sign up for classes or a tour. Class and trip catalog available on Web site. Also rents whitewater kayaks and sells sea kayaks and some whitewater. Web site has good weather and river-level links.

- Pacific Water Sports (11011 Tukwila International Blvd. in Tukwila, 206-246-9385, www.pwskayaks.com) is the grandaddy of local kayak stores, around since 1973. Rental on- and off-site, classes, tours, repairs, and modifications. Year-round. Also rents canoes and whitewater kayaks. The experienced staff has a wealth of information.

- Puget Sound Kayak Company (Jensen Point Boathouse, Burton Acres Park, Vashon Island, 206-463-9257, www .pugetsoundkayak.com) offers kayaks to rent or buy, classes, and tours. Great place for renting and launching to Blake Island, around Vashon, or to points farther south on Puget Sound.

Eastside
- AquaSports Paddle Center (Kayak Pursuits) in Redmond (7907 159th Place N.E., 425-869-7067, www.aqua-sports .com) rents kayaks near Lake Washington. Also offers classes and retail.

- Cascade Canoe and Kayak Centers, Inc. (www.canoe-kayak .com), has two Eastside locations: in Bellevue (Enatai Beach Park, 3519 108th Ave. S.E., 425-430-0111) and in Renton (Cedar River Boat House, 1060 Nishiwaki Ln., 425-822-6111). Classes, trips, conditioning programs for canoes and kayaks. Also boat rental. Gets very crowded on sunny weekends. Reservations recommended.

- Klub Kayak in Issaquah (18869 S.E. 42d St., 425-957-7673, www.klubkayak.com) or Lake Sammamish has kayak rentals, classes, and tours operating May to September. Also does custom multiday trips, women's trips, and San Juan Islands tours.

South Puget Sound

- Tahoma Outdoor Pursuits (5206 South Tacoma Way in Tacoma, 253-474-8155, www.tahomaoutdoorpursuits.com) is a well-established outfitter offering rentals, classes, and trips, particularly in the South Sound.

Olympic Peninsula

- Olympic Raft and Kayak (123 Lake Aldwell Road in Port Angeles, 888-452-1443, www.raftandkayak.com) offers tours on the Olympic Peninsula, rentals, and retail. Kayak, surf kayak, and whitewater classes, local river rafting.

San Juan Islands

- Crystal Seas, in Friday Harbor (877-SEAS-877, www .crystalseas.com) offers San Juan Islands guided tours: sunset, 3-hour, multiday, and custom.

- Elakah Sea Kayak Expeditions in Bellingham (800-434-7270, www.elakah.com) does San Juan Island multiday trips. Guides are eco-sensitive and know natural history.

- Island Outfitters (formerly Eddyline Watersports Center, at 2403 Commercial Ave. in Anacortes, 360-299-2300, www .seakayakshop.com) offers rentals on- and off-site, classes, tours, a shuttle and delivery service, and a retail store.

- Leisure Kayak (in Friday Harbor, 360-378-5992 or 800-836-1402, www.leisurekayak.com) offers San Juan Island tours and boat rentals. Catered seafood lunches available.

- Lopez Kayak (Fisherman Bay Rd. on Lopez Island in the San Juans, 360-468-2847 www.lopezkayaks.com) is a longstanding kayak shop with rentals, tours, and equipment, and offers guided trips in the San Juans. Also rents camping equipment. Open May to October.

- Orcas Outdoors, at the ferry landing on Orcas Island (360-376-4611 or 360-376-2971, www.orcasoutdoors.com) provides kayak rentals and tours.

- Osprey Tours (in Eastsound on Orcas Island in the San Juans, 360-376-3677, www.fidalgo.net/~kayak /osprey.html) sells hand-crafted Aleut-style wood-frame kayaks. Classes, tours, and rentals to experienced paddlers. Guided trips around Orcas.

- Outdoor Odysseys Sea Kayaking Tours (206-361-0717 or 800-647-4621, www.outdoorodysseys.com) leads San Juan kayak tours, mostly out of Friday Harbor. B&B tours and trips with naturalist guides.

- REI Adventures (800-622-2236, www.reiadventures.com). REI's tour company offers multiday trips to the San Juan Islands and Vancouver Island.

- San Juan Kayak Expeditions in Friday Harbor (360-378-4436, www.sanjuankayak.com) offers guided tours and rentals.

- San Juan Safaris (360-378-1323, 800-450-6858, www .sanjuansafaris.com) offers 3-hour sea kayak tours from Friday and Roche Harbors and sit-on-tops for rental.

- Sea Quest Expeditions (360-378-5767, http://sea-quest-kayak .com) offers San Juan Island tours led by biologists and scientists.

- Shearwater Adventures (in Eastsound on Orcas Island in the San Juans, 360-376-4699, www.shearwaterkayaks.com) offers half- and multiday guided tours, instruction for all levels, plus kayak and gear sales and rentals. Skills clinics and private instruction.

- West Beach Resort (190 Waterfront Way in Eastsound on Orcas Island, 360-376-2240 or 877-WEST-BCH, www .westbeachresort.com) provides guided kayak tours and rentals. Guided trips May through September, rentals year-round.

Books

- Burch, David. *Fundamentals of Sea Kayak Navigation.* Guilford, CT: Globe Pequot Press, 1999.

- Campbell, Ken. *A Sea Kayaker's Guide to South Puget Sound.* Tacoma, WA: Little Bay Press, 1999.

    ———. *Shades of Gray: Sea Kayaking in Western Washington.* Tacoma, WA: Little Bay Press, 1999.

- Dolan, Maria, and Kathryn True. *Nature in the City: Seattle.* Seattle, WA: Mountaineers Books, 2003.

- Dowd, John. *Sea Kayaking: A Manual for Long-Distance Touring.* Vancouver, B.C.: Greystone Books, 2003.

- Hahn, Jennifer. *Spirited Waters: Soloing South Through the Inside Passage.* Seattle, WA: Mountaineers Books, 2001.

- Huser, Verne. *Paddle Routes of Western Washington: Fifty Flatwater Trips for Canoe and Kayak.* Seattle, WA: Mountaineers Books, 2000.

- Lembersky, Mark, photographer and David George Gordon, writer. *Nisqually Watershed: Glacier to Delta, A River's Legacy.* Seattle, WA: Mountaineers Books, 1995.

- McGee, Peter. *Kayak Routes of the Pacific Northwest Coast.* Vancouver, B.C.: Greystone Books, 1998.

- Moyer, Lee. *Sea Kayak Navigation Simplified.* Mukilteo, WA: Alpenbooks Press, 2001. One of the owners of Pacific Water Sports lays it all out for you.

- Mueller, Marge and Ted. *Seattle's Lakes, Bays and Waterways Including the Eastside.* Seattle, WA:

Mountaineers Books, 1998. *See also other books in the Afoot and Afloat series.*

- Renner, Jeff. *Northwest Marine Weather.* Seattle, WA: Mountaineers Books, 1993.

- Washburne, Randel. *Kayaking Puget Sound, the San Juans, and Gulf Islands: Fifty Trips on the Northwest's Inland Waters.* Seattle WA: Mountaineers Books, 1999.

  ———. *The Coastal Kayaker's Manual.* Guilford, CT: Globe Pequot Press, 1998.

Links

www.atmos.washington.edu/data for almost too much information on water, weather, mountain forecasts, and the like. Data-lovers will go crazy.

www.wsdot.wa.gov/ferries/index.cfm for Washington State ferries

www.bcferries.bc.ca for British Columbia ferries

www.wcsks.org/wcsks.htm for information on the West Coast Sea Kayak Symposium

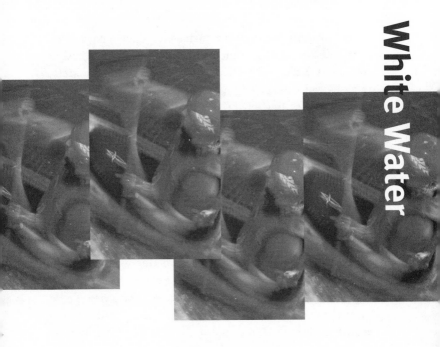

THE ONLY RIVERS actually within Seattle city limits have been narrowed and tamed until they're more accurately called waterways. But outside the city, even within an hour of the sprawling metropolis, lie several gorgeous, rollicking rivers that have been spawning more whitewater enthusiasts every year. "There's been a boom," says long-time kayaker Mel Furrer, "sort of like with extreme skiing. A lot of people are getting out there and going crazy. They're on the water almost every day, trying the serious stuff." Mel is more a river runner than a "destination" paddler—she likes to take the time to scout rapids and run an entire stretch of territory, rather than heading out to just one play spot. But there's room for both camps. Some rivers, such as the Green, have dams with releases—you'll want to call ahead so your Class II run doesn't turn into a Class IV+ swim. Unfortunately, releases can be decided on as late as a day in advance, so don't bother calling until the day before your outing. Other rivers are greatly affected by spring runoff and should be closely monitored during the late spring and early summer months. Still others get dried out and rocky in late summer. The United States Geological Survey (USGS) measures the quantity and variability of river waters via stream gages, and you can check their Web site for flow updates.

It's important to make sure you've got the best river information and the right training for the job. Just about anyone interested in trying white water would be well served by taking a class or refresher course from a local, reputable shop; check *Where to Connect* for a list. These same shops can provide up-to-date information, advice, and gear. For water flow information, the NOAA River hotline at (206) 526-8530 is another good source.

This chapter offers a taste of the best nearby outings for the beginning and intermediate paddler, and a roundup of some of the paddling hot spots farther afield. If you're looking for more trips, details, or places for advanced paddling, a great sourcebook is *A Guide to the Whitewater Rivers of Washington* by Jeff and Tonya Bennett.

If you're not ready to jump into the paddling scene just yet but are still raring for river spray, look to the rafting outfitters listed in *Where to Connect*. Rafting is a great way to get initiated into river boating without being in charge. For more on most of these rivers look to the fly-fishing section of "Fly-Fishing & Sportfishing."

Waterchick

WATERCHICK'S A POWERHOUSE of a woman, 39 going on 29, whose athletic boldness and enthusiastic spirit never fail to impress. Her favorite river is the Wenatchee. Her favorite sea kayaking destination is the northwest side of Vancouver Island. Her favorite drink is a martini. Waterchick (the beginning of her e-mail address, as well as a pretty good summation of her existence) is Seattlelite Melinda Furrer, a whitewater, sea, and flatwater racing kayak fanatic who was in a boat "before I could walk" and is the younger sister of the guy who brought you Werner paddles. "I grew up hanging out with local kayak icons," she says, "Dave Halpern, John Day [after whom the John Day River is named], and local Olympian Scott Shipley." I first met Mel outside her family's cabin on the banks of the Wenatchee River in eastern Washington, where she was slipping herself into a chili-red rodeo kayak for a photo shoot. As the photographer shouted above the roiling water, "Look this way! Smile!" Mel tossed back her unruly thatch of strawberry red hair, grinned, and kept on playing in that standing wave so casually you'd have thought she was treading water.

"Kayaking has been my life," she says. "I like that it can be peaceful, wild, everything." She makes her athletic accomplishments seem casual, though she undertakes challenges, such as cross-Sound races, that have her speed-paddling from Seattle to Bainbridge in boats with men twice her size, or kayaking major rivers running at 20,000 cfs. "I've probably swum every rapid in the state of Washington," she says. "I like to call those my fish surveys." Fortunately, she is also studying for her advanced nursing degree. This comes in handy on the river, where she's attended to scrapes, bruises, and a broken nose.

But kayaking's not about danger or big water for Mel any more. Or so she tells it. She likes the thrill of scouting a run, going the length of a river, and taking the time to play. Her best kayak memories involve paddling near wildlife, whether alongside orcas on the San Juans or black bears on Oregon's Rogue River.

And then there are her family vacations.

The Furrer family are firm proponents of "sea kayak deluxe," constantly trying to outdo each other with the most decadent camp amenity. "Oh yeah," she says. "We make hot tubs with sheets of Visqueen film and heated rocks; my brother's got hot saltwater showers rigged up with copper coils and things; meanwhile I'm working on the fresh-caught crab appetizers." And martinis, of course. Making it all look easy.

Short Hops

Only 40 or so miles southeast of Seattle, the Green River has everything, from Class I to Class IV rapids, and is long on scenery to boot. The two runs described are beginner-intermediate. Nearby on the same river, more advanced paddlers should look into the classic Green River Gorge run, which takes you through a dripping, mossy canyon rimmed with old growth.

East of Seattle is the Snoqualmie, perhaps the most accessible river in the area, only 30 miles away and right off I-90. The various forks of the river offer a variety of white-water, particularly for beginner-intermediate paddlers. Powerhouse to Plum's Landing and The Club Stretch are classics for practice and training close to town; Middle-Middle offers more challenge with some difficult rapids.

Up north the Skykomish, also a favorite fly-fishing desti-nation, runs past the town of Index, where rock climbers scale world-class granite walls. The river offers every level of paddling but is best known for some intense rapids known as Boulder Drop, where three sections of big boulders provide a proving ground for advanced paddlers. The entire area offers intermittent views of forests and mountain ranges. The Train Bridge Run doesn't offer quite the adrenaline rush of Boulder Drop, but is a beauty in its own right.

GREEN RIVER: FLAMING GEYSER STATE PARK TO WHITNEY BRIDGE (THE YO-YO STRETCH)

Location: Near Black Diamond, about 40 miles south of Seattle

Difficulty: Class II

Season: Year-round possible

Gage: Green River near Auburn (USGS). For information on water releases at the Howard Hanson Dam, call the Army Corps of Engineers at (206) 764-6702

Heads up: Great beginner-intermediate run in a gorgeous setting; the Black Diamond Bakery is famous for its goodies; Black Diamond Pizza and Deli is a kayaker/biker gathering spot.

Description: Pacific Water Sports takes their beginner classes here for their first river day. The 2¾-mile run starts with Class I water through Flaming Geyser State Park, giving you plenty of time to catch your stride before hitting the Class II rapids. Just past the high cliff on the left bank before those rapids is a gravel bar on the right bank where you can do some scouting. The ending is plenty of fun with a little bang as the river narrows for a few hundred yards of rapids. Watch out for woody debris and log jams. "Flaming geyser" refers to methane seeps in the park that indicate coal seams—this was once a major coal mining area. The geysers were apparently much more impressive 40 or 50 years ago and were included in the *Guinness Book of World Records.* All along the river watch for eagle, ospreys, and

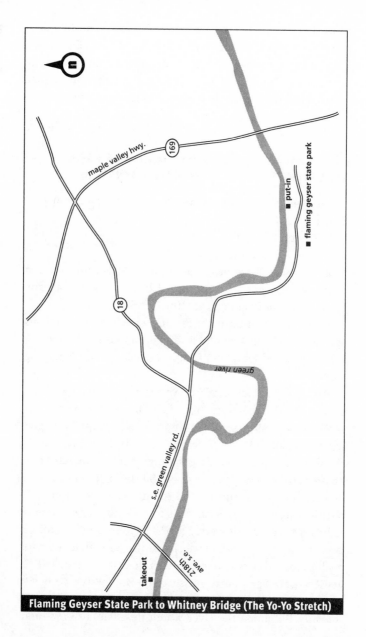

Flaming Geyser State Park to Whitney Bridge (The Yo-Yo Stretch)

hawks. The park also has hiking and mountain bike trails, should you wish to biathlon.

Directions: From Seattle take I-5 south to I-405 north toward Renton, a left-hand exit number 154A. Merge onto S.E. Maple Valley Highway/WA 169 South via exit 4 toward Maple Valley and Enumclaw. Stay straight onto the highway through Black Diamond. Turn right onto Green Valley Rd. In about 2 miles turn left into Flaming Geyser State Park. Turn right at the T intersection and go the marked kayak launch.

To get to the takeout, return to Green Valley Road and turn left. Drive about a mile, then turn left onto 218th Avenue S.E. Park on right in the parking lot.

GREEN RIVER: HEADWORKS TO KANASKAT-PALMER STATE PARK (THE HEADWORKS)

Location: About 40 miles south of Seattle

Difficulty: Class II+ or III

Season: November to early May

Gage: Green River near Palmer (USGS), or the Army Corps of Engineers (206-764-6702)

Heads up: Once you've mastered the Yo-Yo Stretch, try this one. Don't miss the takeout—things quickly get dangerous if you end up in the gorge. Good eats at Black Diamond Pizza and Deli and the Black Diamond Bakery. The town is south of the WA-516 turnoff on the Maple Valley Hwy.

Description: At the base of the dam, the well-known Headworks Stretch is still favored by those in the know. "It has a little bit of everything," says Pacific Water Sports instructor Chris Hivick, "and it's beautiful and feels remote." He takes beginner classes here after a couple sessions on the Yo-Yo Stretch. The beginning can be easily

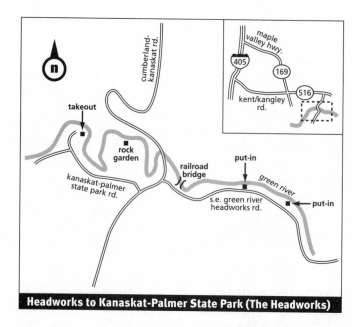

Headworks to Kanaskat-Palmer State Park (The Headworks)

scouted from your boat, but at about 1½ miles the river takes a sharp right. A railroad bridge is just downstream—play in the eddies here before passing under the bridge to the Railroad Bridge Drop. This ledge *must* be scouted. Past this 4-foot ledge things will slowly ease up. Watch for houses on the right and a sign warning of dangerous rapids; it's time to take out.

Directions: From Seattle take I-5 south to I-405 north toward Renton, a left-hand exit number 154A. Merge onto S.E. Maple Valley Highway/WA 169 south via exit 4 toward Maple Valley and Enumclaw. Stay straight onto the highway. At the intersection with WA 516 turn east. This becomes Kent-Kangley Rd. Turn right in 3.3 miles onto Retreat-Kanaskat Rd. Turn right and go 3 more miles, then right onto Cumberland-Kanaskat Rd. In 1.5 miles turn left onto Green River Headworks Rd. SE. Go to the end of the road to the signed put-in.

To get to the takeout, Kanaskat-Palmer State Park, from the put-in, return to Cumberland-Kanaskat Rd. and turn left. The park is in 0.4 mile on your right. Drive into the park, staying right, to upper takeout parking area.

SNOQUALMIE RIVER: POWERHOUSE TO PLUM'S LANDING

Location: About 30 miles east of Seattle

Difficulty: Class II+

Season: Year-round possible

Gage: Snoqualmie below Falls (USGS) or King County Public Works (206-296-8100)

Heads up: Logs and debris following rain

Description: "Every beginning kayaker cuts their teeth on this run at one time or another" says Chris Hivick.

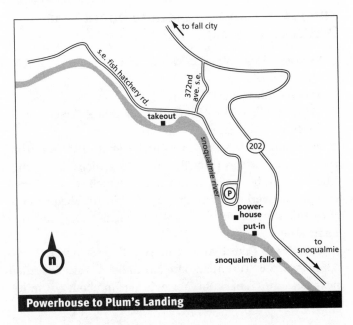

Powerhouse to Plum's Landing

Kayaker Melinda Furrer calls it her favorite post-work outing. It's a short run, a destination spot where you can play around in currents, eddies, and rock gardens and practice maneuvering. The river can be scouted from the parking lot. And you've got Snoqualmie Falls as your backdrop.

Directions: Drive east on I-90, take exit 22 (Preston/Fall City Rd.), and go left. Turn right at the T intersection. Drive down Preston/Fall City Rd. for about 5 miles. Cross the bridge and turn right onto WA 202. Drive 2.5 miles and turn right onto 372nd Ave. Turn left onto Fish Hatchery Rd. and park in the parking lot at the end. Walk down the access road to the river and follow the trail that leads behind the powerhouse.

To get to the takeout, drive back down Fish Hatchery Rd. for 1.5 miles to the large parking lot on the left.

SNOQUALMIE RIVER: TANNER TO NORTH BEND (THE CLUB STRETCH)

Location: About 30 miles east of Seattle
Difficulty: Class II
Season: Fall through late spring
Gage: Middle Fork Snoqualmie near Tanner (USGS)
Heads up: Rock gardens
Description: This beginner–intermediate run is fairly easy most of the way through, with rock gardens to play in. The ease can be deceptive at the end, which requires lots more maneuvering during the last 300 yards. When you're tired this can get difficult, so save a bit of energy for the home stretch.

Directions: Take I-90 east to exit 32 and turn left on 436th Ave. S.E. Turn right onto North Bend Way. Take the next left onto Tanner Rd. You will put in about 0.5 mile

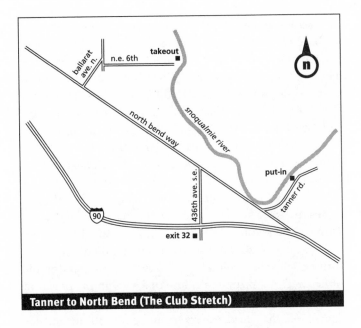

Tanner to North Bend (The Club Stretch)

down this road—watch for gate on left. Park on the right side of the street.

To get to the takeout, go south on North Bend Way and turn right on Ballarat Ave. N. Turn right on N.E. 6th. Drive to the end and take the trail to water.

MIDDLE FORK OF THE SNOQUALMIE (THE MIDDLE-MIDDLE)

Location: East of Fall City, about 30 miles east of Seattle
Difficulty: Class III+
Season: Late April through June
Gage: Middle Fork Snoqualmie (USGS)
Heads up: House Rocks

Description: This is more advanced than the other Snoqualmie runs, and more conveniently accessed than comparable runs on other rivers. The whole thing can generally be done top to bottom in about 4 hours. It's best when water levels are up around 1,500 to 4,000 cfs. Lower and you'll hit shallow boulder fields early on that can be difficult. Much higher and the run is rollicking, rough, and full of holes and big waves. Of particular note are House Rocks, granite boulders that create a maneuvering challenge about 5½ miles into the run. This area is not easy to scout. Save some energy for playing at the end, right near the takeout.

Directions: Take I-90 to exit 32 and head north 0.6 mile. Turn right on North Bend Way. Continue to S.E. 140th St. and turn left. Take this just over a mile to Middle Fork Rd., turning left. Continue 3.5 miles to Island Drop (the old Mine Creek Campground), close to a bend in the river. Put in here or, at higher water levels, continue up to where a concrete bridge crosses the river and put in to the left side of the bridge.

To get to the takeout, return to North Bend Way and go back to S.E. Tanner Rd. Turn right. Follow this 0.5 mile to a gravel pullout on the right. Public access to the river is beneath the powerlines that cross the road. Be sure to respect private property boundaries in this location.

SKYKOMISH RIVER: TRAIN BRIDGE RUN TO BIG EDDY

Location: East of Goldbar, about 45 miles northeast of Seattle

Difficulty: Class II+

Season: Year-round, water dependent

Gage: USGS at Goldbar, or NOAA hotline (206-526-8530)

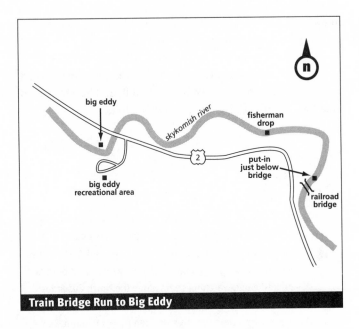

Train Bridge Run to Big Eddy

Heads up: Fisherman Drop. The nearby Sky Run from Index to Goldbar is a great Class III/IV for those up to it.

Description: This run takes about the same skills as the Skykomish Powerhouse run, but it's shorter. A Class II+, it is a fairly long and flat 3 miles, with one rapid, Fisherman Drop, worth a mention. The rapid can be a boulder garden approaching Class III at times—in general, the run gets harder above 4,000 cfs. During fishing season you will have to dodge the lines of eager casters on the shoreline near the drop. Other than this it's an excellent beginner run.

Directions: Take I-5 to WA 520E (exit 168B) toward Belle-vue/Kirkland. In about 9 miles, merge onto I-405 north to exit 23 and drive northeast on WA 522E to Monroe. Turn left onto US 2. Drive through Sultan, Start-Up, and Gold-bar, crossing the Skykomish River in Goldbar. Pass mile marker 32 and park on the side of the highway, preferably at the gravel parking area on the left (north). Be careful crossing the highway here as this is a blind corner.

To get to the takeout, Big Eddy Recreation Area, return on US 2 to the bridge just before Goldbar. The recreation area has a public fishing access on the left.

Floating with the Big Birds

EVERY WINTER THE SKAGIT RIVER serves as a banquet hall for one of the United States's largest congregations of bald eagles, which migrate down from Canada and Alaska for a feast of spawned-out salmon. People gather, too, both at designated eagle-watching spots along the North Cascades Scenic Highway and on rafts that float right into the action. Quite a few outfitters run trips through here, including Eco Orca Raft Trips and Tours and Downstream River Runners. For advance scouting you can visit the area by road, where various interpretive stations are set up in season. The viewing is generally between Rockport and Marblemount. The Skagit River Bald Eagle Interpretive Center in Rockport (360-853-7283, www.skagiteagle.org) offers exhibits and information about the birds and runs the Upper Skagit Bald Eagle Festival in early February. An Eagle Watchers Program is set up along the highway from December into February to direct people to safe places to pull out and see the eagles. The naturalist interpreters field questions and provide spotting scopes.

The area is about 100 miles northeast of Seattle. Drive north on I-5 to WA 20 (North Cascades Highway) and continue about 40 miles to Rockport. Viewing areas include Howard Miller Steelhead Park in Rockport, Sutter Creek Rest Area at Milepost 100 on WA 20, and Marblemount Fish Hatchery.

Meccas

WENATCHEE RIVER

Location: About 120 miles northeast of Seattle

Difficulty: Class I to III+

Season: Spring–Summer

Gage: USGS at Peshastin

Outfitters: Tons of outfitters here, including Osprey, ZigZag, River Runners, and Go Big

Heads up: Those in the know recommend "going left" through the river if you want to make it a little easier on yourself.

Description: This is perhaps the most popular white water in Washington, a place boaters flock to from the west side of the Cascades in late spring to get the jump on good weather. The sun, dry air, and sweet smell of ponderosa pine on the arid east side of the mountains are all balm to mossy Puget Sound types, and kayakers are no exception. For this reason, you won't find solitary communion with nature here, and the scenery varies. Some spots offer gorgeous views of the Stuart Range, while other river sections are flanked by houses, trailers, or the fruit orchards that dominate local industry. The headwaters of the river are at Wenatchee Lake, and flow all the way through Leavenworth and Cashmere before joining the Columbia River in Wenatchee. It's best to run the river at 5,000 to 10,000 cfs, which will give you places to play but nothing more drastic. Too high and you'll get a flush, whacking debris with every stroke. Too little and the river is littered with rock gardens that are a hazard to equipment and body parts. There are several popular play holes, and you are likely to find a line of people waiting to frolic if you're there at a good time. One of the recent favorites is Rodeo Hole, just west of Cashmere.

There are a few good put-ins for the Wenatchee. One of the most popular is in Peshastin, off US 2. For more information see the *Guide to the Whitewater Rivers of Washington* or get in touch with the people at Pacific Water Sports. River rafting is quite popular on the Wenatchee as well, and is served by many outfitters. The town of Leavenworth is also a rock climbing hot spot (see "Rock Climbing," page 208).

OLYMPIC PENINSULA RIVERS

Location: West of Seattle

Outfitter: Olympic Raft and Kayak

Heads up: Wilderness, solitude, and incomparable beauty. Also, risky business.

Description: The Olympic Peninsula, with its renowned national park and sharp-toothed mountain range, naturally harbors some of the most beautiful and pristine rivers in Washington, and perhaps the country. There are many, many things to do here, from low-water runs in winter on the Elwha, the Soleduck, or other rivers to big-water rivers to surf kayaking in the Pacific. But before you go, it's good to keep in mind the dangers involved in venturing west into a landscape where continued logging has created landslides, and tree falls may mean multiple portages and unseen hazards. As the banks of each river change, the conditions change and, in many cases, require extensive scouting. The beauty and solitude of peninsula rivers bring with them increased responsibility, both for preserving the environment and for avoiding errors that will get you into trouble.

There's no room to go into detail here, and no need. The

guide book has already been written that will tell you everything you could possibly want to know about over 35 rivers and creeks in the area. If you are even *thinking* about going to the peninsula, be sure to pick up Gary Korb's *A Paddler's Guide to the Olympic Peninsula,* the result of 20-plus years and lunatic numbers of hours spent playing in the area. He even gives his phone number if you want further assistance. The guide is available at Pacific Water Sports and elsewhere.

Surf Pummel

EVERY YEAR, SURF KAYAK FANATICS spend the first weekend in January at the Surf Frolic in La Push, on the upper left corner of the Olympic Peninsula. The informal event is more familiarly (and accurately) known as the "surf pummel." Here at the Indian reservation on the Quillayute River people venture out in their kayaks to surf behind the breakwater and occasionally expose themselves to the big waves just beyond, particularly during storms. Every year, says Pacific Water Sports instructor Chris Hivick, a few daredevils get a little beat up. "Last year was especially bad: someone got a helmet ripped off, and I think another had a dislocated shoulder. But it's fun." And Chris says you don't have to be an expert to join—sometimes brave intermediate paddlers come out and either stay well behind the jetty, which is there to protect fishing boats at the mouth of the river, or, during foul weather, hang out and watch the mayhem from the beach. The nearby Ocean Park Resort is ground zero, and fills with paddlers and their families. If you're looking to meet people to learn from, or for inspiration to try this risky business yourself, you could do worse than to plant yourself here for the weekend, watching techniques and joining in the annual crab and salmon feed.

Where to Connect

Clubs and Organizations

- Associated Students of the University of Washington (ASUW) Experimental College (206-543-4375, www .experimental.asuw.org) offers cheap boating classes and lots of other stuff to the entire community through their quarterly catalog.

- League of Northwest Whitewater Racers (206-933-1178, nwwhitewater.org) promotes and organizes area slalom racing.

- The Mountaineers (300 3d Ave. W., 206-284-6310, www .mountaineers.org) offers all kinds of paddle classes and trips for those who have completed course requirements.

- Pacific Rivers Council (P.O. Box 10798, Eugene, OR 97440; 541-345-0119; www.pacrivers.org) is a West Coast river conservation organization.

- Paddle Trails Canoe Club (206-444-4313, www.paddletrails .org) organizes canoe trips, from flatwater to Class IV river. Also workshops and training.

- Washington Kayak Club (206-433-1983, www .washingtonkayakclub.org) is a big, established whitewater and sea kayaking club with hundreds of trips a year.

- Washington Recreational River Runners (www.nwwf.com /wrrr) is a nonprofit club for inflatable-boat river-running enthusiasts.

Shops and Outfitters

- Northwest Outdoor Center (2100 Westlake Ave. N, Suite 1, 206-281-9694, www.nwoc.com) has been in business since 1980, teaching at least 1,500 people to kayak each year. Class and trip catalog available on their Web site. Rents

whitewater kayaks and sells sea kayaks and some whitewater. Site has good weather and river level links.

- Olympic Raft and Kayak (123 Lake Aldwell Rd., Port
  Angeles, 888-452-1443, www.raftandkayak.com) offers
  tours on the Olympic Peninsula, rentals, retail, and classes.

- Pacific Water Sports (11011 Tukwila International Blvd. in
  Tukwila, 206-246-9385 www.pwskayaks.com) is the
  grandaddy of local kayak stores, open since 1973. Off-site
  rentals, classes, tours. Year-round. Also rents canoes and sea
  kayaks. The experienced staff has a wealth of information.

Eastside and Beyond

- Cascade Canoe and Kayak Centers (www.canoe-kayak
  .com) has two Eastside locations: in Bellevue (Enatai Beach
  Park, 3519 108th Ave. S.E., 425-430-0111) and in Renton
  (Cedar River Boat House, 1060 Nishiwaki Ln., 425-822-
  6111). Classes, trips, conditioning programs for canoes and
  kayaks. Also boat rental. Gets very crowded on sunny
  weekends.

- Kayak Pursuits (7907 159th Place NE, Redmond, 425-869-
  7067, www.aqua-sports.com) offers classes, rentals for off-
  site, and retail.

- Olympic Raft and Kayak (123 Lake Aldwell Rd., Port
  Angeles, 888-452-1443, www.raftandkayak.com) offers
  tours on Olympic Peninsula, rentals, and retail. Kayak,
  surf kayak and whitewater classes, local river rafting.

- Tahoma Outdoor Pursuits (5206 South Tacoma Way,
  Tacoma, 253-474-8155, www.tahomaoutdoorpursuits.com)
  is a well-established outfitter offering rentals, classes, and
  trips, particularly in the South Sound.

Rafting Outfitters

Following are just a few of the many river rafting outfitters in
the area.

- Downstream River Runners (www.riverpeople.com/rafting
  .htm) offers rafting trips on a number of Washington rivers,
  including the Skagit (featuring a bald eagle winter float)
  Sauk, Skykomish, Suiattle, Tieton, Klickitat, and Green.

- Eco Orca Raft Trips and Tours (866-298-6287,
  alaskafloattrips.com) leads bald eagle float trips on the
  Skagit.

- Go Big (888-979-9600, www.gobigwhitewater.com) offers
  rafting on the Wenatchee.

- Osprey (800-743-6269, www.shoottherapids.com) has 12
  years experience and offers rafting and dory floats on the
  Wenatchee, Tieton, and Methow Rivers.

Books
- Bennett, Jeff. *The Complete Whitewater Rafter.* Portland,
  OR: McGraw Hill Professional, 1996.

- Bennett, Jeff, and Tonya Bennett. *A Guide to the
  Whitewater Rivers of Washington: 300 Trips for Raft,
  Kayak and Canoe Throughout the Pacific Northwest.*
  Swiftwater Publishing Company, 1998.

- Korb, Gary. *A Paddler's Guide to the Olympic Peninsula:
  A Comprehensive Guide to 75 River Runs on Washington's
  Beautiful Olympic Peninsula.* 3d ed. Gary Korb, 1997.

Links
www.americanwhitewater.org lists many local rivers with
  details.

www.wa.waterdata.usgs.gov/nwis/current?type=flow provides
  Washington water resources data from USGS.

www.nwd-wc.usace.army.mil/nws/hh/basins/rivers.htm provides Seattle District Army Corps of Engineers water flows
  for river basins.

White Water

WHAT IS IT about perching on a slim little bike frame in a Mickey Mouse jersey that makes the world seem so serious? That's what road rider and bike designer Ben Spencer wants to know. He waves and smiles broadly at fellow cyclists on trails and roads, an effort that's rarely reciprocated. For a while he even took up singing the Barney song while ascending hills during road races to dispel the air of grim intensity. The tune's sing-song insidiousness was nothing compared to the realization that this big lug of a guy in a cheap, 1960s thrift-store golf shirt was going to pass your narrow, Lycra-clad behind, leaving you with only that damn melody.

I have to admit I've crossed spokes with these same riders, and I'm afraid they'll scare away those who are new to cycling. You'll see them on the Burke-Gilman Trail, a quiet riot of polyester, zipping pickle-faced and depilated past dreadlocked in-line skaters and joggers with bouncy pony-tails. They are hunched and intent along Lake Washington Boulevard on a sunny day, somehow unfazed by spectacular water views and damp slivers of beach that to me always seem worth at least a quick side trip.

If you're new to this sport, don't let the stony faces fool you. Seattle is a great place for biking—surrounded by pretty countryside and hunkered beside salt water dotted with bike friendly islands. It's home to the biggest bike club in the country, amazing bike advocacy groups, lots of stores, and events for nearly every week of the year. More casual riders might want to start with some of the nearby routes, where the inclines are gentler and there are plenty of amenities. For those who are beginning to get serious rider syndrome, or just want a challenge, I've included some hilly rides. A couple of this chapter's outings are on islands. Though I offer routes for these, keep in mind the opportunities for exploration such discrete patches of land offer and consider charting your own way—it's a lot tougher to get lost on Lopez Island than on the backroads of Snohomish, and whatever you do you won't end up dead-ended at a freeway on-ramp.

North, south, east, and west of Seattle are many, many more rides than I can list here. Since this book has an urban focus, I included a lot of rides that start right in the city. When you're ready to explore from there, check out the books listed in *Where to Connect* and take a look at the rides offered on the Cascade Bicycle Club Web site. You won't run out of good routes.

City Limits

MAGNOLIA LOOP

Location: Downtown Seattle
Length: 10-mile cherry-stem loop
Difficulty: Easy to moderate with a couple of hills
Map: Seattle Cycling Map
Heads up: A cruiser ride with splendid views of Puget Sound and islands at the top. Links up nicely with the Discovery Park Loop section of the Gas Works to Discovery Park Ride (see next route).

Description: This is a nice way to ride out from downtown, a reasonable late-afternoon trip on a trail and some mostly wide, quiet streets. There's one slightly arduous climb at the start, but when you get to the top the rest is smooth. Houses in this part of the Magnolia neighborhood have fancy views, high price tags, and, sometimes, really weird landscaping—count how many ways there are to sculpt a shrub. Planning for a sunset stop at Magnolia Bluffs, about halfway through the ride, is highly recommended. Expect views toward the Olympics and islands, and a pink glow on the madrone trees clinging to bluff's edge.

Route: Begin at Myrtle Edwards Park. Ride the Elliott Bay Trail northwest along the water, past the Pier 86 grain elevator, to the Pier 91 Bike Path (signed). Stay on this for about a mile until you can either continue left or go right up to 20th Ave. W. Go right. There is a hairpin turn left at intersection onto Thorndyke Ave. W., heading uphill. At the top continue on Thorndyke as it jogs left. This ride follows the Magnolia Scenic Loop; watch for the signs. Pass

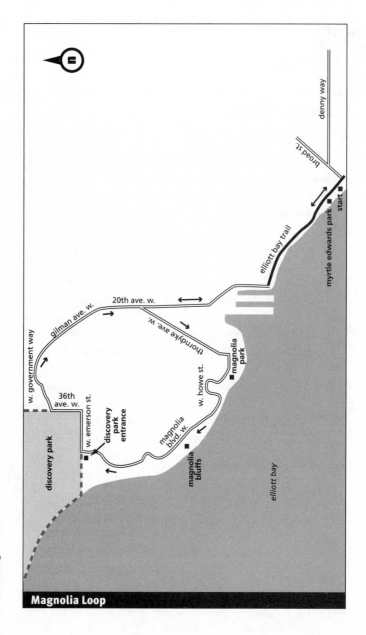

Road Biking

96

Magnolia Loop

(map labels:)

denny way

broad st.

elliott bay trail

myrtle edwards park

start

20th ave. w.

gilman ave. w.

w. government way

thorndyke ave. w.

36th ave. w.

w. emerson st.

discovery park entrance

magnolia park

w. howe st.

magnolia blvd. w.

discovery park

magnolia bluffs

elliott bay

N

Magnolia Park on your left. Turn left onto W. Howe Street and cross a small bridge. Curve left onto Magnolia Blvd. W. Soon you'll have sweeping views of the Sound. Stay on Magnolia Blvd. to the T intersection at W. Emerson St. Discovery Park (see the next ride) is in front of you. If you want to explore the city's largest park, turn left and then immediately right into the park entrance. To complete the Magnolia Loop ride, turn right on Emerson, then left on 36th Ave. W. Go right at W. Government Way (another park entrance is on your left). Stay on W. Government, following Scenic Loop signs. It becomes Gilman Ave. W. and 20th Ave. When road forks (you'll see the Thorndyke Ave. hill climb again) veer left down the dead end road that meets up with bike path. Return to start.

Directions: Take I-5 to Olive Way (exit 166). Turn left onto Denny Way. Go about 1 mile and turn left onto Broad St. At the end of Broad, turn right into the parking area.

GAS WORKS–DISCOVERY PARK LOOP

Location: 5 miles north of downtown

Length: 12-mile cherry-stem loop

Difficulty: Hilly in Discovery Park; nerves will be jangled on a short jaunt from the bike trail to the locks.

Map: Seattle Cycling Map

Heads up: Watch for in-line skaters, Yorkshire terriers, and other impediments along the trail. Picnic facilities at all three parks. For food in Fremont, eat in at Jai Thai or Still Life in Fremont Café, or get takeout from the deli at the Puget Consumer's Co-op. In Ballard try the Other Coast Café for sandwiches and salads to go.

Description: This ride is an old, time-tested standby for me, visited over years of random "Hey, let's go to Discovery Park" summer afternoons, and I was curious to see how

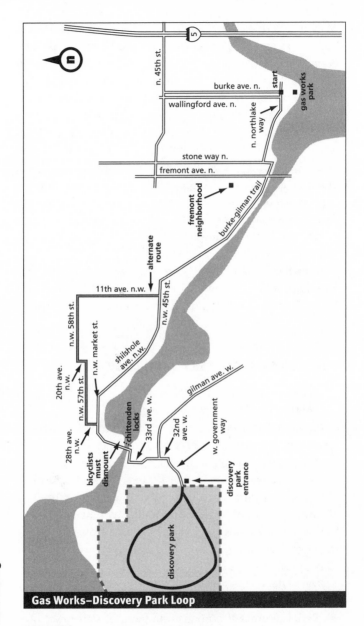

Gas Works–Discovery Park Loop

it would hold up to closer inspection. I'm happy to report it's as cool as ever, a real slice of Seattle. It's a mix of parks, waterside industrial areas, and quiet neighborhoods—very urban, but at a manageable level. (If you're looking to ride without stopping, this one won't work—there's even a little stretch where you have to walk your bike.) Start at Gas Works, a park built around the retired bones of a gasification plant, and a radical statement in the 1970s when landscape architect Richard Haag unveiled the plans. There's an artsy mosaic sundial from the free-love period at the top of the kite-flying hill. From here the ride takes off on the Burke-Gilman Trail, heading west through Fremont. (Stop for coffee on or near Fremont Ave. or for on-site brewed beer at Hale's Brewpub on your way back.) Upon entering Ballard the trail ends, and you'll negotiate one irritating patch of city streets for a mile or so before reaching the Ballard Locks (I've included a more peaceful detour if you're riding with kids or if old railroad tracks and a lack of bike lanes make you nervous). At the locks, watch the city's pleasure cruisers being lowered to sea level courtesy of the Army Corps of Engineers—boats have been "locking through" since 1917. There's a fish ladder here where you can watch salmon migrate. A short jaunt through the lower Magnolia neighborhood leads you to Discovery Park, the city's largest, visited by hundreds of birds and featuring a nature center, beach, and beautiful trail walks. Ride the loop and be done with it, or park your bike and explore.

Route: Exit the Gas Works Park lot and cross the street to pick up the Burke-Gilman Trail (in front of Fisheries Supply). Head west, staying in the bike lane. At the intersection with Stone Way, as you cross the street, the trail continues to the left of the building in front of you. Continue on the trail past office buildings, along the Fremont Canal, and finally past a Fred Meyer store on your left, at which point the trail ends (a sign makes this clear) at the intersection of Northwest

45th St. and 11th Ave. N.W. Merge onto 45th here and head west until you reach the light at N.W. Market St. Turn left onto Market, and in ¼ mile turn left into the locks, just past the Lockspot Restaurant.

Alternate Route: To take the longer but more peaceful route to the locks, head north on 11th to N.W. 58th St., turn left onto 58th, left onto 20th, right onto N.W. 57th, and left onto 28th Ave. N.W. In two blocks, turn right at N.W. Market St. and left into the locks, just past the Lockspot Restaurant.

Walk your bike straight through the grounds and on the pathway across the locks. A ramp ascends right (west) at the end of the locks. Take it to the top and exit right onto W. Commodore Way, then immediately (10 feet) left at 33rd Ave. W. (A sign here says DEAD END but a green sign shows that bike and foot traffic are allowed.) Immediately bear right (instead of topping the hill) and cross a footbridge. Continue up to 32nd Ave. W., taking you into W. Government Way, where you merge into a marked bike lane going right (west) straight into Discovery Park. From here, follow the park's bike route signs on a loop that will return you to this entrance. Return back across the locks and to Gas Works the way you came.

Directions: Take I-5 to the 45th St. exit. Turn left (west) across I-5 and left onto Wallingford Ave. Turn left onto N. 34th St. and then right onto Burke Ave. N. The parking lot for Gas Works is directly in front of you at the end of the street.

ARBORETUM TO SEWARD PARK

Location: About 4 miles northeast of downtown

Length: 15 miles out and back (17 miles with the Seward Park Loop option)

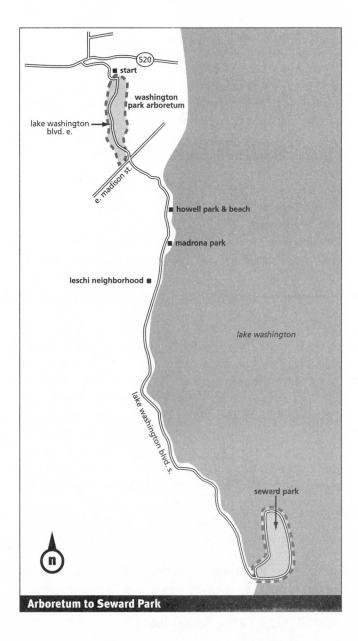

520

■ start

washington
park arboretum

lake washington
blvd. e.

e. madison st.

■ howell park & beach

■ madrona park

leschi neighborhood ■

lake washington

lake washington blvd. s.

seward park

n

Arboretum to Seward Park

Difficulty: Moderate

Map: Seattle Cycling Map

Heads up: Leafy green goodness. Be aware of traffic on the rather narrow Arboretum Rd. The old cyclist hangout Perk's Coffee and recent interloper Starbucks in Leschi compete across the street from one another for your business. Also, Lake Washington Blvd. is closed to auto traffic about ten times a summer for Bicycle Saturdays and Sundays, which are especially good times to ride. Bring a swimsuit if you want to brave the lake (and if it's August or September).

Description: When riding through the arboretum, the enormous plant collection managed by the University of Washington, hog the narrow road and let the cars pass when they can. Then ride past some of the city's swankiest real estate down a winding road to Lake Washington. Take a dip at Howell Beach, the thin crescent moon of public access just after you descend on Lake Washington Boulevard, but be aware that a certain gazillionaire may be watching you from the next property over—it's said he's been fighting the nude swimmers and sunbathers here since at least the advent of the bikini. The long, curvaceous road along Lake Washington passes several small parks, most of which were designed by the sons of Frederick Law Olmsted. (Yes, the designer of New York's Central Park left his mark on our little burg.) About a third of the way through the ride is Leschi, where the city's serious cyclists gather for weekend rides and courage-instilling espresso. Finally, arrive at Seward Park, the emerald on the big thumb of the Bailey Peninsula. Its only-in-Seattle features include a nesting pair of bald eagles, a small stand of old growth Douglas firs and cedars, and the city's only flock of parakeets, which escaped from captivity. There's a nature center planned to open here soon, where you can get further details on all of the above. Or ride around and see for yourself; there's a loop around the park.

One other note: The Seward Park Criterion rides take place on summer evenings. Plan your evening ride around catching it and find yourself inspired to zip home at twice the pace. Go to www.bikeride.com for dates and times.

Route: From the arboretum, take Lake Washington Blvd. E. going southeast. Cross E. Madison St. Continue on the Boulevard as it winds through a neighborhood and down a cool, shaded series of switchbacks to the lake. At the bottom tiny Howell Beach will quickly come up on the left. Stay on the boulevard another mile or so to Leschi, with its cafés and shops. From here it's a little over 4 miles to Seward Park. The loop trail in Seward Park is 2 miles. Return the way you came.

Directions: From downtown take I-5 north to exit 168B (WA 520). Merge onto WA 520 east. Immediately, take the Montlake Blvd. exit. Cross Montlake Blvd. onto E. Lake Washington Blvd. Follow this into the arboretum. The Graham Visitors Center, with parking, is located near the north end of Arboretum Dr. E. and is accessible by turning left as you enter the arboretum and following signs. Other parking is evident if you turn right as you enter.

Bike on Board

ALL METRO BUSES have bike racks on the front. This is convenient for people who don't have the energy to bike their entire round-trip commute or whose brakes give out unexpectedly halfway to their destination. But if you're a bike rack novice, or have issues about holding up traffic, the whole thing might make you damp in the armpits. To prepare yourself, review the following.

First, remember that, as someone who is going *at some point* to actually ride this awkward piece of luggage, you are doing the lungs of your fellow passengers a favor. They can afford to wait while you fumble a bit. Then, realize that you probably won't have to fumble, because the rack is designed even for those who have experienced one too many endos. Follow these three steps: 1. While waiting for the bus, remove anything that might fall off your bike—bottles, pumps, bulging panniers. 2. (This is very important.) Signal to the driver that you are going to be loading your bike. Make sure he or she has seen you before placing yourself in front of the bus. 3. Approach the front rack and follow the posted instructions. The basics, which will make sense when you stand there, are these: Squeeze the handle and pull it down. Lift your bike onto the rack, which is marked for front and rear wheels. It goes in the outside slot unless that's full. Then raise the support arm over the top of the front tire, and make sure it's resting on the tire, not the frame of your bike. When you go to remove your bike, lift the support arm off the tire and out of your way, get your bike, and put the arm back up. If you dash off to an appointment and forget your bike, leaving it on the bus until the end of the day, there's actually something you can do about it. Call the Bike Alliance hotline (206-903-8075). The Alliance takes in forgotten bikes (around 500 a year, they say, so you're not alone) and stores them for 30 days. Those left longer (almost 60 percent) are donated to nonprofits.

GAS WORKS PARK TO BREWPUB AND WINERIES

Location: 5 miles north of downtown

Length: 42 miles round-trip, Gas Works to Woodinville. An option to ride to Marymoor Park adds another 10 miles round-trip.

Difficulty: Easy—long and flat

Maps: Seattle Cycling Map; *Washington Atlas and Gazetteer*

Heads up: On sunny weekends, watch out in the congested early section for in-line skaters, Yorkshire terriers, and other impediments along the trail. Either end of this ride is a great picnic spot. In Woodinville (20 miles into the ride) are the Chateau St. Michelle and Columbia Wineries, and the sunny patio of the Red Hook Brewery's pub. **Tip:** If riding back at sunset (and I'm guessing you will), wear goggles and keep your mouth shut to avoid swallowing a cloud of gnats.

Description: This ride starts in the university area, which can get clogged on weekends. But soon the hand-holding couples and skateboard punks get lost, and you can fall into whatever traffic-free cadence you like. The trail is mostly flat and hugs the north end of Lake Washington, offering the usual Seattle spectacles of water, greenery, and big lakeside houses. The first part is in the woods; the latter parts are mostly open, with views. Your ride out can come to a stop, as mine usually have, when you sprawl out with your picnic on the lawns of a winery, or at the Red Hook Brewery's big outdoor tables. (Best not to indulge in libations now, though you could tuck a bottle into the panniers to celebrate when you get home.) Or continue on 5 more miles to enormous Marymoor Park, where you can look for birds by the shoreline, and, if you're here on a Friday evening in summer, watch the velodrome racers and their gravity-defying antics (see *Welcome to the Velodrome*, page 106).

Route: Cross over from the Gas Works parking lot to the Burke-Gilman Trail (in front of Fisheries Supply) and go right (northeast). The trail (later becoming the Sammamish River Trail) is well signed and has occasional street crossings. At about 20 miles you'll come to Woodinville. Detour just off road to the Columbia Winery (in a Victorian mansion), the Chateau Ste. Michelle Winery (in a French château), or the Red Hook Ale Brewery, (a relaxed brewpub with a deck). All 642 acres of Marymoor Park is another 5 miles along the trail. Park maps are available at the recreation office. Return the way you came.

Directions: Take I-5 to the 45th St. exit. After exiting, turn left (west) over the freeway. Turn left onto Wallingford Ave. Turn left on North 34th St. and then right onto Burke Ave. N. The parking lot for Gas Works Park is directly in front of you at the end of the street.

Welcome to the Velodrome

WHEN LISA MERRELL MOVED to Seattle at age 25, she figured this was her last shot at dedicating herself to a competitive sport—possibly road cycling. She never imagined she'd find herself on the intensely competitive track of a velodrome. "I'd gotten on this cycling team, and one night my coach told me they were going someplace called the velodrome to practice skills. I'd never heard of the sport before, but it turned out I had just the body type for it—strong and stocky, for power, instead of those lanky, floaty, distance types."

Ginger Rogers did everything Fred Astaire did, but backward. Velodrome racers do what cyclists do, only on a steeply banked oval or circular track, sometimes at over 40 miles per hour. The variety of velo-specific races include the Scratch, the Tempo, and the Chariot. It's an amazing spectator sport, and very intense for the riders, who are on ultralight bikes with no gears or brakes, packed close together. "It's like being in a tunnel when you're up there," says Merrell. "You can feel the energy of the group sucking you in. It's a rush." The Marymoor Velodrome, on the east side of Lake Washington, is a rarity in the Northwest and dates from the 1970s. To see a race for yourself, bike out to the 'drome on the Burke-Gilman Trail (or drive if you must) on rain-free Friday nights in late spring and summer for the serious adult racing. If you want to try it yourself, sign up for a track class. Road cyclists swear by the track as a way of improving their bike-handling skills. The velodrome is located in Marymoor Park in Redmond, at 6046 W. Sammamish Pkwy. N.E. For more information check www.marymoor.velodrome.org.

Backyard

VASHON ISLAND

Location: The West Seattle ferry terminal is about 7 miles west of downtown.

Length: 30-mile loop

Difficulty: Moderate to difficult—hilly

Maps: Vashon–Maury Island Map (available free on the island at local realtors); King County Bike Map; *Washington Atlas and Gazetteer*

Heads up: Plenty of good food, including tasty baked goods at Bob's Bakery in town. Saturdays in summer there's a farmer's market from 9 to 1 on the village green. For a biathlon, combine your ride with a paddle (see "Sea Kayaking," page 46).

Description: This is the island to which Seattleites dream about moving when the world becomes too much for them, or when their start-up folds. It's a groovy sort of place, one where you can sit all day behind a potter's wheel in your yurt and no one bats an eye. Unless you restrict your mileage, or at least stick to the center of the island, you're going to need more than a soy shake to get around, however—it's a hilly, strenuous ride, starting with the road to town from the Northend ferry dock, a steep uphill grind.

Don't be daunted. Wait until the cars unload and then follow them, maintaining distance from the exhaust pipes.

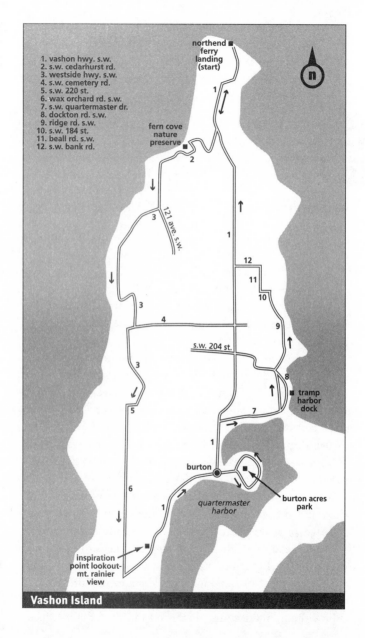

1. vashon hwy. s.w.
2. s.w. cedarhurst rd.
3. westside hwy. s.w.
4. s.w. cemetery rd.
5. s.w. 220 st.
6. wax orchard rd. s.w.
7. s.w. quartermaster dr.
8. dockton rd. s.w.
9. ridge rd. s.w.
10. s.w. 184 st.
11. beall rd. s.w.
12. s.w. bank rd.

northend ferry landing (start)

fern cove nature preserve

121 ave. s.w.

s.w. 204 st.

tramp harbor dock

burton

burton acres park

quartermaster harbor

inspiration point lookout- mt. rainier view

Vashon Island

You will be rewarded with good food, views of Mount Rainier and the Olympics, beach stops, and pretty country roads. There are plenty of good places to put on the brakes, including several mentioned in the route description. For a description of bird-watching on Vashon, see that chapter, page 235.

Route: From the Northend ferry dock, head uphill on Vashon Hwy. S.W. Do not not turn off until you reach S.W. Cedarhurst Rd., about 1.8 miles (look for the John L. Scott office). Head downhill and right, away from the highway. Wind down the hill as it curves through woods. In a little over a mile you'll see the Fern Cove Nature Preserve on the right. Stop for a short walk to the beach and estuary, where salmon counters watch for coho spawning in the fall. Cedarhurst Rd. takes a sharp left and becomes Westside Hwy. S.W. Stay right with the highway, enjoying views of the Olympics and Colvos Passage. Turn right with Westside Hwy., as 121 Ave. S.W. continues uphill. In 3 miles, as Cemetery Rd. goes left, continue to follow the highway to its end at S.W. 220th St. Soon turn left onto Wax Orchard Rd. S.W. Take a hard left on Vashon Hwy. S.W., following the signs for Vashon. Look for the Roadside Attraction sign and pull off for a drop-dead view of Rainier. Continue on the highway downhill and around the edge of Quartermaster Harbor. In Burton, refresh yourself at the coffee stand at the four-way stop, or continue on, taking a right on S.W. Burton Dr. to the Burton Peninsula. Turn right onto 97th Ave. S.W., which becomes S.W. Bayview Dr. and S.W. Harbor Dr. and makes a loop around the peninsula. In about a mile is King County Burton Acres Park. Turn off, or continue on, turning right on Burton Dr. S.W. Return to Vashon Hwy. and turn right. Turn right again onto S.W. Quartermaster Dr., following the sign for Dockton. You will pass the northern reaches of Quartermaster. Called "Portage," this used to be a waterway separating Vashon from Maury Island to the east. Turn left onto Dockton Rd. S.W. Keep right along Tramp Harbor on Chautauqua Beach Dr. S.W. and head uphill as Ellisport Rd. veers left. Turn left onto S.W. 204th St., uphill, veering right onto Ridge Rd. S.W., and left again onto S.W. 184th St. Turn right onto Beall Rd. S.W. and turn left onto S.W. Bank Rd. Turn right onto Vashon Hwy. SW. Bob's Bakery, the Farmer's Market, and other shops and restaurants are here. From here to the ferry it's a 5-mile ride on flats, with a final downhill coast.

Directions: From Seattle, take I-5 or I-99 to signs for the West Seattle Bridge (exit 163 on I-5). Cross to West Seattle, staying in the center or left lane to head uphill. Continue through West Seattle on Fauntleroy Ave., following ferry signs. Park in the north parking lot of Lincoln Park, then ride the three blocks south to the ferry terminal on the right. Ferries depart at least every hour, and the crossing is 15 minutes. For ferry schedules phone 800-84-FERRY or download a schedule at www.wsdot.wa.gov/ferries.

Club Bike

NOT MANY ROAD CYCLISTS will admit to the desire to join a club. Cycling is, as my roadie friend Peter Wobber described it, kind of an "interior" sport. And most riders I know, when not seeking solitude under that plastic helmet, stick with a reliable stable of companions, friends who will maintain the pace and know instinctively when it's time to pull over for an espresso.

And yet there are several thriving bike clubs around town, and one in particular that beats all odds. Seattle's Cascade Bicycle Club has managed to attract over 4,000 members since its debut in 1970 and is now the largest bike club in the United States. Their near-daily group rides are particularly useful to those new to town, introducing great local routes and fellow fanatics to explore them with. Cascade also sponsors just about every major local bike event, from the Chilly Hilly that kicks off the cycling season to the STP, a 200-mile weekend ride from Seattle to Portland. They've developed bike safety training for children, and they push for better access for cyclists in Seattle and central Puget Sound. "We're one of the only bike clubs in the country that combines advocacy and riding," says executive director Chuck Ayers. Break out of your roadie reticence and check out what they do at www.cascade .org or call (206) 522-3222.

FLYING WHEELS

Location: 15 miles northeast of Seattle

Length: 47.5 miles

Difficulty: Challenging

Maps: King County Cycling Map; *Washington Atlas and Gazetteer*

Heads up: There's one grocery stop a little over halfway through. There are also a lot of turns, so trace your finger over a road map before you set out, and keep two steps ahead of the directions so as not to miss any streets.

Description: Dave Douglas is a well-known local bike race organizer with a reputation for designing spectacular rides. He also works for the Cascade Bicycle Club. The Flying Wheels ride in June is considered a warm-up for the Seattle-to-Portland ride later in the summer and is popular because it's gorgeous. Ride past open fields, through farmland, cross rivers, and enjoy views of the Cascades. Go on your own and you won't have to contend with the bike mob. Man-of-few-words Dave says "What makes this a great ride is that it's not very far from civilization and you go through some very beautiful farmland and rolling terrain."

Route: Start at Marymoor Velodrome. Turn left, heading

east, out of the park. In a mile, turn right at E. Lake Sammamish Pkwy. In 3.4 miles turn left onto Inglewood Hill Rd. Stay straight through roundabouts and lights all the way to 244th Ave. N.E. and turn left. Turn right at the stop sign onto busy N.E. Redmond Fall City Rd. Turn left onto N.E. Ames Lake Rd. Keep straight on Ames at its junction with Union Hill Rd. Turn left onto W. Snoqualmie Valley Rd. N.E. Turn right at N.E. 80th St. and then left at Carnation Farm Rd. N.E. Turn right onto very busy WA 203 and soon enter the city of Carnation. Turn right at the end of the bridge onto N.E. Tolt Hill Rd. Turn left at West Snoqualmie River Rd. N.E. and ride through the Carnation Golf Course. Turn left onto S.E. 24th St. and left again onto S.E. Redmond Fall City Rd. (**Caution:** Very busy, but you'll be on it for less than a mile.) Turn right at 336th Place S.E. into Fall City Family Market for snacks or drinks. Exiting the market, turn right onto 336th Place S.E. Turn right onto S.E. 43rd St. and right again at a stop sign on 334th Place S.E. Turn left at S.E. 42nd St. Take a left at 332nd Ave. S.E. Follow 332nd Ave., which turns into Issaquah–Fall City Rd. Turn left onto S.E. 40th St. for a 1-mile climb to Issaquah-Fall City Rd. Turn left at S.E. Duthie Hill Rd. and left at Issaquah–Fall City Rd. (You'll need to get in the center lane to make the left turn at this busy intersection.) Turn right onto S.E. 58th St. Take a left at S.E. 56th St. and right at E. Lake Sammamish Pkwy. Ride straight through several lights, finally through the Inglewood Hill Rd. light, and turn left at the stoplight at the Marymoor Park entrance.

Directions: To get to Marymoor Park from I-90, take exit 13 and go north along W. Lake Sammamish Pkwy. to the park. From I-5 or I-405, take WA 520 (exit 168B from I-5; exit 14 from 1-405) east to Redmond. Take the second Redmond exit and go south on W. Lake Sammamish Pkwy. to the park.

SNOHOMISH VALLEY

Location: 33 miles northeast of Seattle

Length: 29 miles

Difficulty: Easy to moderate

Book and map: *Bicycling the Backroads Around Puget Sound* describes this and many more Snohomish rides. *Washington Atlas and Gazetteer.*

Heads up: Country roads, lunch at Chuck's Seafood Grotto or City Deli in Snohomish

Description: There are many good rides in the rural Snohomish Valley. This one hits several parks and isn't overly challenging; it's a good way to get a feel for the place. The landscape is dairy farms, flower farms, and cornfields. Old town Snohomish is bursting with antique stores and cafés.

Route: Leaving Lewis Street Park, head south on WA 203 and across the Skykomish River. Turn right onto Tualco Rd. Ride straight past Swiss Hall onto Tualco Loop Rd. Turn right back onto Tualco Rd., which becomes Crescent Lake Rd. and ride past the Monroe State Dairy Farm. Cross the Snoqualmie River and turn right onto High Bridge Rd., which goes under WA 522 at mile 8; it becomes Elliott Rd. Bear right with Elliott at a stop sign. Turn right and uphill on Connelly Rd. Turn right and downhill onto Broadway. Turn right onto Springhetti Rd.—keep your eye out, it's halfway down a hill. Pass Abel Johnson Park. Snohomish Airport and The Buzz Inn restaurant are on the left. Cross the railroad tracks and the Snohomish River. Stop and explore the shops and restaurants here, then continue north on Ave. D. Turn right onto Ferguson Park Rd. to Ferguson Park. Continue through park to follow 74th St. S.E. down around a corner of Blackman's Lake. (If you want to visit another park here, turn left onto 13th St. and left again onto Park Ave. Turn left into Hill Park.) Turn left onto 13th St. Turn right onto Pine Ave. and right onto Center St.

Descend the hill to Center St. with caution—there is a ditch at the bottom of the hill on the right turn. Turn left onto Lincoln Ave. toward Monroe; it will become Old Snohomish–Monroe Road. Stay left at the Y intersection. Turn left onto Currie Rd., which becomes 171st Ave. S.E. Turn right onto 154th St. S.E. and ride under WA 522. The road's name changes to Blueberry Ln. Turn right onto N. Kelsey. Cross W. Main St. and continue on S. Kelsey. At the end of Kelsey, turn left onto Terrace St. At the end of Terrace turn right onto S. Sams St., then immediately left onto Sumac Drive. Cross WA 203 and turn right into the Lewis Street Park lot.

Directions: Take I-5 to exit 194 (US 2) to Monroe. Turn right toward WA 203 to Lewis Street Park on the south end of town, just before a bridge over the Skykomish. Park near the river.

Meccas

SAN JUAN ISLANDS: LOPEZ ISLAND

All of the ferry-accessible San Juans are great for bicycling. Ideally you'll have a few days to visit them all, staying at quaint inns, renting kayaks, and replenishing your fat stores at the many good restaurants. Orcas Island offers more hill challenges; San Juan is the farthest away by ferry. Both are busier than Lopez, which is the first ferry stop and therefore a reasonable day trip.

Location: The ferry launch at Anacortes is about 80 miles northwest of downtown Seattle.

Length: 20-mile loop with 10-mile loop option

Difficulty: Easy to moderate

Map and book: The "Map and Guide of Lopez Island" is

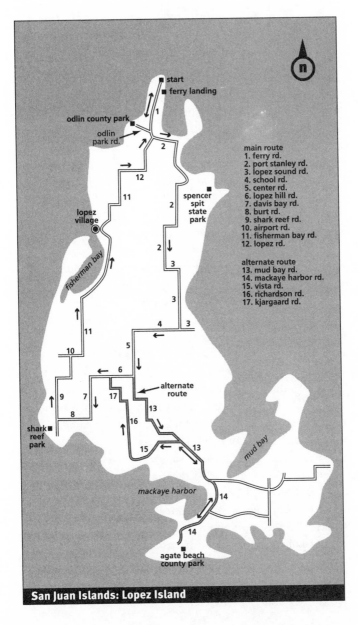

start
ferry landing
odlin county park
odlin
park rd.
lopez
village
fisherman bay
spencer
spit
state
park

main route
1. ferry rd.
2. port stanley rd.
3. lopez sound rd.
4. school rd.
5. center rd.
6. lopez hill rd.
7. davis bay rd.
8. burt rd.
9. shark reef rd.
10. airport rd.
11. fisherman bay rd.
12. lopez rd.

alternate route
13. mud bay rd.
14. mackaye harbor rd.
15. vista rd.
16. richardson rd.
17. kjargaard rd.

alternate
route

shark
reef
park

mud bay

mackaye harbor

agate beach
county park

San Juan Islands: Lopez Island

available on the island at the Odlin Park kiosk, or ask in Lopez Village, 4 miles from ferry dock. For other San Juan Islands rides, try *Short Bike Rides: Western Washington*.

Heads up: In Lopez Village, Vortex Juice Bar and Good Food lives up to its name. For takeout, Vita's Wildly Delicious is gourmet, and a beautiful shop to boot. Stay overnight if you can at a B&B, or camp at Odlin Park or Spencer Spit State Park. Lopez Bicycle Works has information and rentals.

Description: The place smells like rugosa roses, fir needles, and salt water. It sounds like the weird bleatings of sheep. And it looks like what I picture when I hear the word *bucolic*. This island, quiet on weekdays and some weekends, has rolling roads, stunning views, and a little town full of good snacks. It's pretty much perfect. I'm giving you a route to follow because I'm required to, but once you get off the ferry you're free to rip these pages out of the book and stuff them into your panniers. Then wander until you get tired and end up in Lopez Village eating fish tacos. If you'd rather have a route, save the pages, and follow the directions, which take you past several nice parks, up and down a few hills, and offer some nice vistas. If you ferry to the island around 10 A.M. you should have time to casually complete the main circuit and stop in for snacks before catching an early evening ferry home. I highly recommend visiting on a weekday, when you'll have the place to yourself.

Route: Leaving the ferry, ride straight up Ferry Rd. Stop at the Odlin Park Rd. intersection at 1.3 miles for a map at the kiosk. Turn left at this intersection onto Port Stanley Rd. At 3.7 miles, turn off for an optional sidetrip to Spencer Spit. At Lopez Sound Rd. (at intersection), turn left. At the School Rd. intersection, Lopez Sound Rd. turns left. Take School Rd. right uphill. Turn left at Center Rd. (See Mac-Kaye Harbor Loop, below, for an optional side trip.) Turn right onto Lopez Hill Rd., which becomes Fisherman Bay Rd. As it curves right, cross left onto Davis Bay Rd. (watch carefully for this one). Turn right onto Burt Rd. Turn left onto Shark Reef Rd. and immediately right into Shark Reef Park. After visiting the park, exit the way you came and take Shark Reef Rd. to Airport Rd. Turn right. Turn left onto Fisherman Bay Rd. Stay on this as it descends past Fisherman Bay on the left. Turn left at Lopez Rd. to visit Lopez Village. After your detour, return to Fisherman Bay Rd. Turn right onto Lopez Rd. Turn onto Ferry Rd. and take it to the ferry landing at the end.

MacKaye Harbor Loop: If you've left enough time, take this optional side trip to the southern end of the island. At the end of Center Rd. turn left onto Mud Bay Rd. Turn right onto MacKaye Harbor Rd. by the fire station. In about 2 miles, stop at Agate Beach County Park for a rest. Return to Mud Bay Rd. and turn left. Turn left onto Vista Rd., about halfway down the hill. At the end of Vista turn right onto Richardson Rd. Turn left onto Kjargaard Rd. at the fork, and left onto Fisherman Bay Rd.

Directions: Take I-5 north to exit 230 and head west, following signs for the ferry. This leg of the drive can take around 30 minutes, so plan accordingly. Park at one of the lots past the ticket windows for about $5 (you'll need to have small bills on hand or get change at the ticket window) and buy a walk-on ticket with bike supplement inside the ferry building. Then wait near the front of the ferry loading area until directed to board by the crew. Bicycles usually load first, so arrive early. For ferry schedules phone 800-84-FERRY or download a schedule from www.wsdot .wa.gov/ferries. Ferries run to Lopez from Anacortes seven or eight times a day; the crossing takes about 40 minutes. Avoid traveling here on holidays, but if you must, be sure to arrive early to get parking.

Hand-Crafted
Wheels

WHERE DO OLD CYCLING PROS go when their hamstrings give out? It may be awhile before we see about Lance, but for Giro d'Italia winner and Alpe d'Huez champ Andy Hampsten, we have the answer—design your own bikes. (Oh, and there's also that gig leading gourmet bike tours in Tuscany, but can one actually call that work?) While Hampsten generally does his work from Italy, his brother, Steve, runs their tiny bike company, Hampsten Cycles, right here in Seattle. They recently moved out of his garage and into a bigger space near the Burke-Gilman Trail. "They're bikes made by craftsmen who all ride bicycles," says Steve. "It's a labor of love." Hampsten is one of a few local cottage bike manufacturers who will custom-design a ride to your exact specifications. Once a company has a good bike design and quality parts, fitting bike to rider is all about finesse. If you love your old bike Hampsten can measure it and build one of similar dimensions, and if you hate it they'll take a look and find out what's not right. If they can (if you're local and available, that is), they'll even go out on a ride with you. One faraway customer sent them a video of himself cycling, for their diagnosis.

Besides fitting like a Milanese suit, these bikes look sharp. They're delicate, nimble, and painted in the bright colors of Italian syrups. Custom bikes are probably not for the beginning rider—a Hampsten, which is at the lower-end of the price scale for custom bikes, starts at over $2,000. But they're worth considering if you're ready to upgrade or have a difficult-to-size body. Seattle has a few custom manufacturers. Two others are Davidson, sold out of the Elliott Bay Bicycle store, and Erickson Bikes, available at R+E Cycles. To contact Hampsten Cycles, call Steve at (206) 524-6010, or check out their Web site, www .Hampsten.com

Where to Connect

Clubs and Organizations

- Bicycle Alliance (206-224-9252, www.bicyclealliance.org) makes sure you have safe places to ride. They participate in local transportation funding decisions, hold rallies, and promote bike commuting. If you love cycling, consider helping out this excellent grassroots advocacy organization.

- Boeing Employees Bicycle Club (206-657-9967)

- Cascade Bicycle Club (206-522-BIKE, www.cascade.org) is the city's (and the nation's) largest club and offers rides almost every day of the year. They organize many of the area's bike events.

- The Mountaineers (206-284-8484, 800-573-8484, www.mountaineers.org). Cycling outings and club.

- Northwest Women's Cycling (206-284-5407, www.nwwc.org) is a great group for women who want to learn how to get into bike racing. They offer casual weekly rides and more formal bike-skills workshops.

- Redmond Cycling Club (206-781-3903, www.redmondcyclingclub.org) offers many rides on the Eastside and sponsors the RAMROD, a grueling ride around Mt. Rainier "for the cyclist who aspires to a higher plane of endeavor."

- Seattle Bike Club (206-298-3722, www.seattlebicycle.com)

- Tacoma Wheelmen (253-759-2800, www.twbc.org)

- Washington State Department of Transportation (www.wsdot.wa.gov) has bike links to downloadable maps of Washington bike routes. Also gives updates on road closures and other cycling transportation issues.

Shops

There are heaps of bike shops in this city—drop in at your neighborhood shop and see what they can do for you. Or consult this list. Many places in the mountain bike chapter also sell road bikes, so if you don't see a nearby shop here, check there. Almost every shop will repair almost any kind of bike.

- Alki Bike and Board (2606 California Ave. S.W. in West Seattle, 206-938-3322). Sales, rentals, and repairs.

- All About Bike and Ski (3615 N.E. 45th St. in Laurelhurst, right off Burke-Gilman Trail, 206-524-2642). Rentals, sales, repair. Very nice people.

- BikeSmith (2309 N. 45th St. in Wallingford, 206-632-3102). This tiny shop is highly recommended for repairs, and they sell very cute new and reconstructed cruiser bikes.

- Elliott Bay Bicycles (2116 Western Ave. at the Pike Place Market, 206-441-8144). This higher-end shop specializes in road bikes and offers Davidson bikes hand-built on the premises. Repairs.

- Gregg's Greenlake Cycle (7007 Woodlawn Ave. N.E. in Greenlake, 206-523-1822) and Aurora Cycle (7401 Aurora Ave. N. in Greenlake, 206-783-1000) are two big shops owned by the same company with sales, rentals, and repair. They have a third location in Bellevue.

- Il Vecchio Bicycles (140 Lakeside Ave. in Leschi, 206-324-8148) is a swanky road bike shop.

- Lopez Bicycle Works on Lopez Island (360-468-2847, www.lopezbicycleworks.com) offers rentals and information.

- Montlake Bike Shop (2223 24th Ave. E. in Montlake, 206-329-7333; also shops in Bellevue and Kirkland)

- R+E Cycles (5627 University Way N.E. in the University District, 206-527-4822). Sales, custom frame building, repair. Specializes in road bikes.

- REI (222 Yale Ave. N., 206-223-1944, also shops in Lynnwood, Federal Way, Redmond). Sales, rental, repairs.

- Sammamish Valley Cycle (8451 164th Ave. N.E. in Redmond, 425-885-6363). Specializes in road bikes.

- Ti Cycles (2943 N.E. Blakeley, on the Burke-Gilman Trail near University Village, 206-522-7602 www.ticycles.com). Specializes in road bikes.

Events

This list is only a small sampling. Pick up copies of *Sports, Etc.* and the *Bicycle Paper* in bike and athletic shops around town—both have thorough event listings for upcoming months.

- Chilly Hilly, in February, is the classic opener of Seattle's cycling season, and has been around more than 30 years. Riders wait (the chilly part) in a big group at the ferry terminal. Camaraderie forms. Then you float over to Bainbridge Island and begin 33 miles of hilly. There are beautiful views all along the way. Contact the Cascade Bicycle Club (206-522-BIKE, www.cascade.org).

- Seattle International Bike Expo, in March, is a huge bike show with speakers, bike stunts, slide shows, and lots and lots of booths displaying the latest gadgetry. Once again, talk to the folks at Cascade Bicycle Club.

- The Daffodil Classic, in April, features a pretty ride through farmland south of Seattle. 20-, 50-, 70-, and 100-mile routes. Contact Tacoma Wheelmen (253-759-2800, www.twbc.org).

- The Boat Street Criterium, in April, is a great opportunity to watch fast cyclists race around a 0.6-mile loop right in the University District. Information at Recycled Cycles (206-547-4491).

- Bike to Work Month is May. If you never participate in anything else, bike to work. There's nothing like whizzing past a bunch of bored, cell-phone-yapping drivers on your gleaming steed. Think of it as reclaiming your youth. On this particular day there will be commuter support stations, T-shirts, a bike parade, and a lot of sexy calf muscles to gawk at.

- On Bicycle Saturdays and Sundays, May through September, about twice a month, the city blocks Lake Washington Boulevard to traffic so cyclists can ride peacefully. A glimpse at cycling utopia.

- The Flying Wheels Summer Century, in June, is the Eastside ride that features the Flying Wheels route, with 25- to 100-mile loop options. Gorgeous scenery (of course). Contact the Cascade Bicycle Club.

- The Seattle to Portland (STP), in July, is a 200-mile ride from one city to the next with a few thousand other people. Must be done once. Contact the Cascade Bicycle Club.

- The Ride Around Mount Rainier in One Day (RAMROD) is in July. Every year they actually have waiting lists of people desperate to participate in this grueling haul around the mountain. It's 154 miles long with 10,000 feet of elevation gain. (Slacker types have informally organized the NIMROD—Not Interested in Mt. Rainier in One Day—a more leisurely tour.) Contact the Redmond Cycling Club (206-781-3903, www.redmondcyclingclub.org).

- Ride Seattle to Vancouver, B.C., and Party (RSVP), in August, is another city-to-city ride, 183 miles long. Contact the Cascade Bicycle Club.

- Trek Tri-Island is in September. This Lung Association fund-raiser has been called the "love tour" for the number of relationships started during this 3-day, ferry-dependent ride up to Victoria, B.C., and back (800-732-9339, www.alaw.org).

- The Kitsap Color Classic, in October, features 14- to 64-mile loops on the Kitsap Peninsula north of Bainbridge Island. Contact the Cascade Bicycle Club.

Books

- Wagonfeld, Judy. *Short Bike Rides: Western Washington.* Guilford, CT: Globe Pequot Press, 2000.

- Woods, Erin, and Bill Woods. *Bicycling the Backroads Around Puget Sound.* Seattle: Mountaineers Books, 2000.

Link

www.bikeride.com for a cycling race calendar

NO MATTER HOW nicely they try to present
themselves, mountain bikers will always be
seen as rebellious younger siblings, while
road bikers (please, call them cyclists) are more
restrained and mature. Right? Hard to say 'round
here, where cyclists are advocates, no matter the
width of their wheels. Some, like Ben Spencer,
even advocate abolishing categories. "I discourage
an us-versus-them scenario," he says. After all,
both groups are aiming for the same goal—a little
more room on the roads and trails. Despite the outlaw image, I've found most local mountain bikers
incredibly generous with their skills and knowledge, and excited to connect with new riders.

Members of the Backcountry Bicycle Trails Club donate their time to maintain trails in state parks, and run a Boot Camp to help newbies learn the riding ropes. At many of our city's slew of small bike shops, you can find someone willing, on a slow day, to stop and talk about a worthwhile ride or rustle up a map.

Though you'll see mountain bikes (including mine) making short work of commutes, hooked on bus racks, and grinding up the city's steeper hills, you won't see mountain bikes on most dirt paths in Seattle. Within city limits there is almost nowhere to legally ride off-road—the Parks and Recreation Department has banned their use in nearly all urban parks. However, right in the urban backyard there are several excellent places to bust out the fat tires. Washington State Parks has worked with local bikers to include trails on their properties, including beautiful Saint Edward, just northeast of town.

Seasons can be a little tricky here. With all the precipitation, some trails, like those on mountain bike–favorite Tiger Mountain, are closed in winter to keep them from melting into the surrounding forest. Others aren't closed, but become so wrecked and mucky they probably should be avoided. Most of those described here are open year-round and those that aren't are indicated. If you love mountain biking be sure to join a local organization or help out in a work party now and then. Government officials are always impressed by elbow grease.

 City Limits

GREEN LAKE

Location: North of downtown

Trails: 4-mile dirt and gravel loop and less than a mile of hilly dirt trails

Season: Year-round

Difficulty: Beginner

Maps: Seattle Cycling Map; *Washington Atlas and Gazetteer*

Heads up: The only legal mountain bike adventure in the city

Contact: Seattle Parks and Recreation (206-684-4075)

Description: Joggers, strollers, and in-line skaters generally take to the paved path next to this popular urban lake. You head for the upper, unpaved path, and feel a little more radical in the act. Okay, okay, so you're just circling a city park on a dirt trail, trying to make the most of the occasional root and puddle. The main thing is, you're on your bike, beneath some really nice trees, and not far from home. Some people like Green Lake for the people-watching, but it's also a great place to watch birds, including bald eagles that have even been nesting in recent years in adjacent Woodland Park. Lower Woodland Park, just south of Green Lake, can also be visited by mountain bikes, though riding the paths through that park is illegal. Too bad, since this small but heavily wooded nook has steep hills and dirt footpaths that seem rarely occupied. If you follow the path to Lower Woodland on the map, you can dismount there and stroll. Occasionally you'll see signs of urban denizens camping behind the shrubbery.

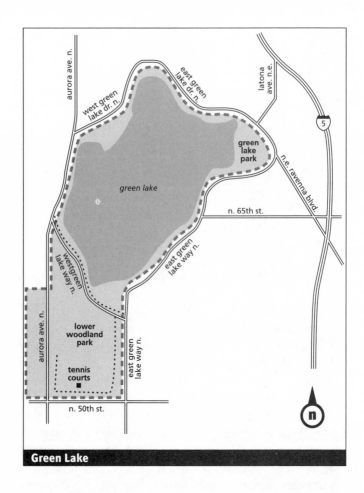

Green Lake

Route: The dirt trail circling Green Lake Park is on the park's outer edge. Lower Woodland Park is worth a visit—the map shows how to get there by bike via a path that runs parallel to East Green Lake Way N., then turns west (right) alongside N. 50th St. Enter Lower Woodland just past the tennis courts and before Aurora Ave. N.

Directions: Green Lake Park is easily accessed by bike via city streets. Check a city map or the Seattle Bicycle

Guide map for options. By car, take I-5 to exit 170 (Ravenna Blvd.) toward Ravenna Blvd/N.E. 65th St. Turn left onto N.E. Ravenna Blvd. continue straight onto E. Green Lake Dr. N. The park and entrance will be in less than a quarter mile on your left. Turn in at Latona Ave. N.E.

Backyard

SOUTH SEA-TAC

Location: About 17 miles southeast of Seattle.
Trails: Approximately 9 miles of dirt and pavement.
Season: Year-round
Difficulty: All levels
Heads up: Suburban ghost town
Contact: City of Sea-Tac (206-973-4670, www.seatac.wa .gov)

Description: Though the city of Sea-Tac Web site calls it Sunset Park, the biker nickname South Sea-Tac cuts right to the chase. This odd bit of open space is located right near the airport and feels gritty and urban despite the encroaching greenery. "You'll be riding along talking to your friend and all of a sudden you can't hear anything because of the deafening roar," says bike mechanic Andrew McColm. But that's not the weirdest thing about it. The park was created atop a neighborhood that became unlivable after Sea-Tac airport was built, and here and there you'll find yourself riding on a paved cul-de-sac, underneath a power line, or right past a house foundation. For practicing your tricks, there's an area with sandy hills, another with concrete blocks for an obstacle course, and a few miles of hard-packed dirt, all of which will get you ready for the cyclocross races organized here. Bikers recommend South Sea-Tac as a good place to go in

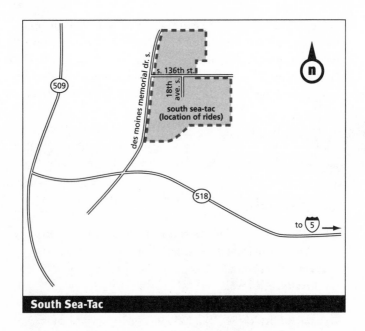

South Sea-Tac

winter, when it seems a little drier and more accessible than other nearby trails.

Location: Take I-5 south to exit 154A toward WA 518 and Sea-Tac Airport. Pass the airport exit and take the exit for Des Moines Memorial Dr. Turn right onto Des Moines Memorial Dr. S. Turn right onto S. 136th St., then right onto 18th Ave. S. Park next to the tennis courts.

TOLT-MACDONALD PARK

Location: About 25 miles southeast of Seattle
Trails: Over 10 miles of trails
Season: Year-round
Difficulty: All levels

Map: Trails change frequently; Andrew McColm at Second Ascent (see *Where to Connect*) will make you a copy of his latest map if you visit the shop.

Heads up: A local favorite

Contact: King County Parks (206-296-4232, www.metrokc .gov)

Description: This 450-acre park straddling the Snoqualmie River is a favorite of local bikers. Good drainage makes it great for not just summer but also for the off-season, when other options are inaccessible due to either conditions or seasonal closure. It's also wild and offers views of the area from high above. Speaking of ascents, prepare to grunt your way up, and to face some technical singletrack right out of the gate—it's the only way to get to the park's many rides. This initial slog can be surmounted even by confident beginners—just be willing to walk your bike if the way gets tough.

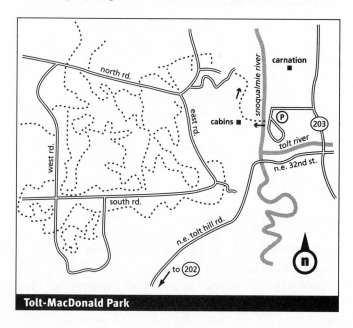

Tolt-MacDonald Park

Route: From the parking lot cross the suspension bridge over the Snoqualmie River and take the gravel road uphill, forking to the right up the hill and away from the river, walking if necessary. Up top stay on the main access roads for ease, or splinter off onto miles of twisty singletrack in adjacent woods.

Directions: Take I-5 to exit 168B (WA 520 east) and head over Lake Washington to Redmond. Turn right onto WA 202 (Redmond/Fall City Rd.). From here go south just over 7 miles to Tolt Hill Rd. and turn left. Cross the Snoqualmie River, and then turn left onto WA 203. Watch for signs for Tolt–John MacDonald Park on your left after the Christmas tree farm. Park in the gravel lot by the pedestrian bridge.

SNOQUALMIE VALLEY TRAIL

Location: About 27 miles southeast of Seattle

Trails: Gravel trail and paved roads, bridges

Distance: 22.8 miles out and back

Season: Year-round

Difficulty: Beginner—long but easily navigated

Maps and Book: USGS Carnation, Fall City, Snoqualmie maps; *Kissing the Trail*

Contact: King County Parks (206-296-4232, www .metrokc.gov). For more on the Rails-to-Trails Conservancy check out www.railtrails.org or call (202) 797-5400.

Description: This is one of several area trails created by the nonprofit Rails-to-Trails Conservancy; others include the Iron Horse and Burke-Gilman. All are public routes reclaimed from former railroad lines or rights-of-way. This one, on crushed gravel, is kind of a road bike–mountain bike outing, not requiring much skill but great for a long

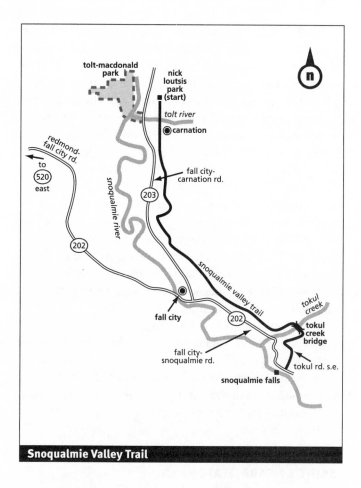

Snoqualmie Valley Trail

workout. Unlike the Burke-Gilman, the setting here is for the most part beautifully pastoral, with farms and views of surrounding mountains. The combination of bridges, gravel trails, wide dirt trails through woods, creeks, and a tunnel hold your interest for the entire ride. The trail can be accessed from several points, including McCormick Park, Nick Loutsis Park, and Rattlesnake Lake Recreation

Area. The trail also goes near Tolt-MacDonald Park, the previous bike outing. The route detailed here takes you all the way to Snoqualmie Falls, over 270 feet of roaring, crashing excitement that brings out the amateur photographer in the million or so tourists who visit them each year.

Route: Find the trail and begin riding south. At about 9 miles a bridge crosses Tokul Creek, with views of the area. In about 1.3 miles, the trail ends under the Tokul Rd. underpass. Take the singletrack trail on the left to 60th St. S.E. Turn left and ride to Tokul Road. Turn left onto Tokul Road and then right at the intersection with WA 202, at just over a mile. The parking lot for the Salish Lodge and Snoqualmie Falls is on your right. After you've taken in the view (and maybe a burger from the hotel's pub, whose prices are equally breathtaking), return the way you came.

If you'd like to know more about fishing the Snoqualmie, check "Fly-Fishing & Sportfishing," page 259.

Directions: To get to Nick Loutsis Park take I-5 to exit 168B (WA 520 east) and head over the bridge to Redmond. Take WA 202 southeast from here to Fall City. Follow the signs for left turns to WA 203 and drive north about 5 miles to Carnation. Turn right on Entwhistle St. and continue to Nick Loutsis Park, on your right.

SAINT EDWARD STATE PARK

Location: About 15 miles northeast of Seattle

Trails: 10-plus miles of trails, from gnarly dirt singletrack to genteel, Sunday-in-the-park options; most trails are labeled.

Season: Spring through fall. Best during the week or in shoulder seasons.

Difficulty: All levels

Map: The Saint Edward trail map is available at the park office.

Heads up: Lake Washington shoreline and plenty of amenities; also good for boating and trail running. This place gets very busy on summer weekends so plan around them or be extra cautious about watching out for pedestrians, children, joggers, and the like.

Contact: Washington State Parks (360-902-8844, www .parks.wa.gov). Backcountry Bicycle Trails Club (206-283-2995, www.bbtc.org) maintains trails here. Finn Hill Bikes (425-823-1215) is located nearby at 14130 Juanita Dr. N.E.

Description: Hang on to your hymnal. This former Catholic seminary on 316 acres is a beautiful place to ride under tall cedars along twisty paths, as long as you avoid the crowds on summer weekends. When you're done, or between rides, sun yourself on the park's wide lawns, visit the heated swimming pool, or walk down to the park's strip of rare undeveloped Lake Washington shoreline to check out views and watch for wildlife.

Route: Arrowhead Trail leads away from the parking lot and is great for beginners—stay on it for a mellow ride. In about 0.5 mile you can turn right onto the Juanita Trail for technical singletrack. This trail emerges at the park's entrance road and then crosses to more technical trail with lots of opportunity to practice skills. If you continue south you'll end up in adjacent Big Finn Hill County Park, with even more singletrack trails worth exploring. It's hard to get lost, even with all the branching trails, since you'll always hit Lake Washington on one side and Juanita Dr. on the other.

Directions: Take I-5 north to exit 171 (SR 522/Lake City Way). Continue on SR 522 about 7 miles to 68th Ave. N.E., which becomes Juanita Dr. N.E. Turn right (south). Continue about 2 miles to the park, on your right.

Short Hops

VICTOR FALLS

Location: About 40 miles southeast of Seattle

Trails: Hundreds of miles of trails with dirt, mud, wooden bridges, and more mud

Season: The parking lot is closed November through December for the owner's Christmas tree sales.

Difficulty: All levels, but best for intermediate to advanced riders

Map: Pick up a map at the Bonney Lake Bike Shop (253-863-5145) for around $2. You'll need it. The shop is located about 2 miles from the trails at 19102B WA 410. It's a great source of information—groups often meet there before going to the trailhead.

Contact: Bonney Lake Bike Shop

Description: If you're not entertained here, better double-check your inner tubes. This privately owned land is called "the Seattle area's biggest mountain bike mecca" by the folks at Aaron's Bicycle Repair. It's so big you can get away from crowds, even on a popular weekend, and find your own little ribbon of trail. Some trails are easy and offer views of Mount Rainier; on others you'll be wiping the mud from your eyes to see the next log or tree root.

Directions: Take I-5 south and exit toward Sea-Tac airport, exit 154B. Take exit 149 (WA 516) toward Kent/Des Moines. Turn left onto S. Kent Des Moines Rd./WA 516E. Merge onto WA 167S toward Auburn. Merge onto WA 410E toward Sumner/Yakima. In about 6 miles, watch for the Bonney Lake Bike Shop and get a map there. Continue to 214th Ave. E. and turn right. In just over a mile, turn right onto 120th St. Turn left onto 198th Ave. E. Park in the tree farm parking lot, a gravel lot on the right. The owners generously allow mountain bikers to park here; please be courteous.

TIGER MOUNTAIN

Location: About 22 miles east of Seattle

Trails: 12 miles of dirt trails

Season: Trails are closed October 15 to April 15; roads are open year-round.

Difficulty: Strong intermediate–advanced

Map: Department of Natural Resources State Forest Map, Tiger Mountain.

Heads up: Some of the sweetest technical trails near Seattle

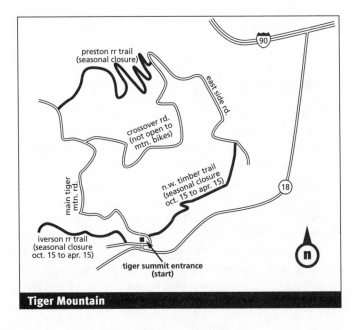

Tiger Mountain

Contact: Department of Natural Resources (360-825-1631)

Description: A member of the much-used but still lovely Issaquah Alps, that cluster of small peaks just east of Seattle, Tiger encompasses 13,000 acres of state forest land and is the only one of these mountains to offer trail access to mountain bikers. That means you'll be sharing. People come here because it's nearby but wild, sheltering an incredible amount of wildlife for a place that's shouldered up against suburban sprawl. You probably won't see them, but there are bears, bobcats, and coyotes in these woods— perhaps that fact alone will keep your wheels turning.

Route: Many of the mountain's trails are closed to mountain bikes, but you can still take off on the Northwest Timber Trail and the Iverson (Fat Hand) Trail, both accessed from this trailhead, and the nearby Preston Railroad Trail (see map for access).

Directions: Take I-90 east to exit 25 (WA 18). Turn south onto WA 18 and continue 5 miles to the East Tiger Summit parking on your right.

WHIDBEY ISLAND: FORT EBEY STATE PARK

Location: About 50 miles by car and ferry from Seattle

Trails: 30 miles of different trails

Season: Every one *but* summer, when hiker and camper use gets too heavy

Difficulty: All levels available but features great, knotty singletrack

Map: Pick one up at the park. Trails are marked, though be aware that there are more trails than have been mapped.

Heads up: Check the Washington State Ferries Web site for ferry routes, directions, and schedules (www.wsdot.wa.gov/ferries). Camping is available; see *Pitching Tent*, page 140.

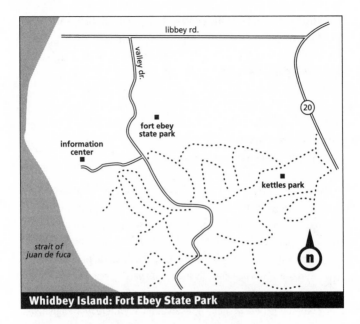

libbey rd.

valley dr.

20

fort ebey
state park

information
center

kettles park

strait of
juan de fuca

n

Whidbey Island: Fort Ebey State Park

Contact: Fort Ebey State Park (360-678-4636)

Description: This is the kind of island getaway that makes disgruntled Seattleites rethink their relocation plans. The park's 645 acres sprawl right on the Strait of Juan de Fuca, with amazing views and waves sloshing against a long strip of gravel beach. Whidbey, unlike Seattle, falls in the Olympic rain shadow (for more on this phenomenon, see "Hiking," page 187) and can often be balmy when the city is socked in and cranky. Thirty miles of trails mean you won't get bored all day long—or even two days long, if you take advantage of the camping. One very interesting feature of this park is the "kettles," sinkholes created several thousand years ago by the retreating glacier. Don't miss the views from the bluff trails.

Directions: From Seattle take I-5 north to exit 182 (WA 525). Take WA 525 north toward WA 99 (Alderwood Mall Blvd.). Follow signs for the ferry. Take the ferry to Clinton on Whidbey Island. Follow WA 525 north; it becomes WA 20. Two miles north of Coupeville, turn left onto Libbey Rd. and follow it 1.5 miles to Valley Dr., following signs for the park. Turn left and enter park.

fort ebey state park

THE RANGE OF FUN and bumpy trails here means you'll be broken down and saddle sore by the end of the day. Since it's best to visit in the off-season, you'll have a chance at the campsites that are choked up in the summer. The park is lovely, overlooking the Strait of Juan de Fuca, and there's a nice gravelly beach for walking out sore muscles.

Campsites are open year-round on a first-come, first-served basis. It is best to make a reservation anywhere near high season in summer. To reserve a state park campsite log on to www.parks.wa.gov or call 999-226-7688. Online you can see a map that shows campsite availability and location. Reservations cost around $7 on top of the use fees for each site. Group campsites are available.

Longer Hop

MOUNT SAINT HELENS: APE CANYON TRAIL

Location: About 180 miles southeast of Seattle
Distance: 16 miles one way
Trail: Maintained trail and old forest-service road
Season: Summer through fall, open after the snow level drops

Mountain Biking

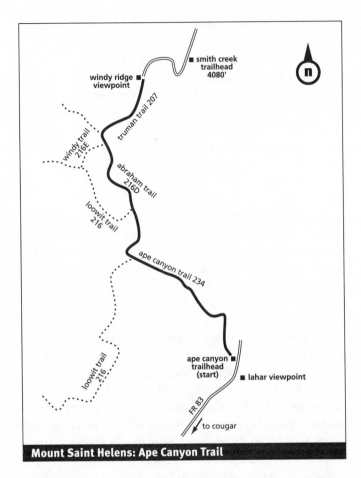

Mount Saint Helens: Ape Canyon Trail

Difficulty: Intermediate

Map: Gifford Pinchot National Forest Map.

Heads up: Volcanic vistas. You'll need a Northwest Forest Pass to park; they're available at various shops around Seattle (including REI) and some gas stations near the park.

Elevation Gain: 1,350 feet

Maximum elevation: 4,010 feet

Contact: Mount Saint Helens National Volcanic Monu-

ment (360-247-3900, www.fs.fed.us/gpnf/mshnvm/index
.shtml

Description: My family happened to be visiting a friend
in Roslyn, Washington, on the other side of the mountains,
when the eruption occurred. We hadn't turned on the news
that day, and hadn't a clue that Mt. St. Helens had come
alive. Driving back over the pass toward Seattle, we kids
craned our heads out the window, wondering why the sky
looked so murky. As my older brother tells it, we were one
of the last cars allowed back over the highway before they
shut it down. That's life under volcanoes.

If you wonder what it might be like when Mt. Rainier
erupts, or if you want to see how a landscape restores itself,
or if you just want a really fun ride, this is it. The route
begins at the edge of a lahar, or mud flow. Compare what
the volcano scoured out with the untouched sections of old
growth farther up the trail. The first 4 or 5 miles are parallel to the timber area and don't offer much in the way of
views, but you'll emerge at the more exposed Plains of
Abraham. From here you'll head right on the Abraham
Trail (216D) to the Windy Ridge Viewpoint for a partial
view of the crater and a really good view of Spirit Lake. You
can either return the way you came, or, if you've planned
carefully, you could arrange a shuttle with someone parked
at the Smith Creek trailhead. Ask at the ranger station
about how to coordinate this option.

Route: Take the Ape Canyon Trail (234) from the parking
lot 5.5 miles to trail 216 and turn right onto the Abraham
Trail (216D). (To the left is a very advanced section of trail.)
Watch out for loose rock in this area. In another 7.5 miles
is the junction with the Truman Trail (207). Turn right to
go to the Windy Ridge Viewpoint, another couple of miles.

Directions: Take I-5 south about 150 miles to exit 21
(Woodland and WA 503). Take WA 503 east for about 30
minutes to the town of Cougar. The road turns into FR 90

about 3 miles outside of town. Go 3 more miles. At the top of the road on the left is FR 83. Take this for 11 miles to a T intersection. Cross the bridge and go left to the Ape Canyon Trailhead parking Lot.

Meccas

GALBRAITH MOUNTAIN

Location: About 80 miles north of Seattle

Contact: www.galbraithmt.com, e-mail dude@ galbraithmt.com, www.astonisher.com/store/galbraithmt_ guide_store.html for their guidebook

Description: "Galbraith is king of the slimy root drop, the old-growth log crossing and the slash pile punch up" says the Galbraith Mountain guidebook page. Seattle bike mechanic Andrew McColm seconds that. "Galbraith? Um, the log rides are very slick—this place is much scarier than anything around here when it's raining." In other words, this is not, particularly in the wetter seasons, a destination for the timid, though there are a few trails that are fairly smooth, if the weather's cooperating. This is a working commercial forest into which mountain bikers with trail-building knowledge have put serious time and effort. They pride themselves on having used natural terrain to create the trails. The organization has a subscription service. For a fee you can sign up to get a guidebook and maps of the trails printed off the Web—they coyly offer a sampler on-line for free.

Or you can explore for yourself. Just a few miles from Bellingham, you can ride there right out of the city, spend the day on wild singletrack, and be back in B'ham for dinner. This college town has good brew, great music, and a beautiful location on Bellingham Bay, with Mount Baker as a backdrop. The folks at Fairhaven Bike and Mountain Sports (1103 11th St., 360-733-4433, www.fairhavenbike .com) or Kulshan Cycles (100 E. Chestnut St., 360-733-6440, www.kulshancycles.com) have more information on the mountain, history, routes, and other cycling in the area.

Directions: Take I-5 to Bellingham, about 80 miles north of Seattle, and take the North Lake Samish exit. Turn left on Samish and continue about 2 miles to the top of a hill and turn left into the Lake Padden parking lot. Park here, cross the road from the lot, and head up Galbraith Lane to the gate. Ride around it up logging roads to access the trails. There are maps on the Internet for these trails, but the most recent can be acquired from local bike shops, where they can also offer firsthand advice. To get to Kulshan Cycles, take the Lakeway exit in Bellingham and turn right (west) onto Lakeway. In a couple of blocks take a slight right onto Holly St. Merge into the left lane. Turn left onto Cornwall St. The shop is in 1 block on the left corner, at 100 E. Chestnut.

METHOW VALLEY

Location: About 200 miles northeast of Seattle

Contact: The Methow Valley Sport Trails Association (509-996-3287, www.mvsta.com) has helped develop and maintain many of the trails. Winthrop Mountain Sports (509-996-2886, www.winthropmountainsports.com) in downtown Winthrop manages to pack a rental shop and well-rounded outdoors store into one small space. Central Reservations (800-422-3048, www.extrabeds.com) will help you find local lodging in inns, hotels, or private cabins.

Description: First of all, everything smells different in the Methow. On the trails, it's the sweet scent of ponderosa pine mixed with the medicinal tang of sagebrush. In the restaurants it's the rich, smokey aroma of grilled beef, or the sweetness of nouveau ranch-house food, such as spare ribs glazed in blackberry sauce. Second, as you may have gathered, it looks different. From the faux-Western Winthrop storefronts to the hazy blue and tan of the surrounding mountains, this looks nothing like what we're used to in western Washington. When you're tired of living by water, this is the right place to clear your head, with low humidity and dime-bright sun.

It will also be paradise found for many mountain bikers. The Okanogan National Forest offers hundreds of miles of roads and trails, from gentle and wide to precipitous and knobby. October is an especially fun time to get your wheels here, when the area hosts a popular mountain bike festival during what is generally dazzling autumn weather.

Directions: Take I-5 N to Everett and then take Stevens Pass, US 2 East to Wenatchee. Turn left (north) at the junction with US 2/WA 97 to Okanogan Pateros. Continue on WA 97 and bear left at the junction with Orondo. About 60 miles past Wenatchee turn left at Pateros onto WA 153 to Twisp, then on WA 20 West to Winthrop. Winthrop has restaurants, lodging, and Winthrop Mountain Sports.

Summer Route: take I-5 N about 65 miles to North Cascades Highway (WA 20) east. Continue east approximately 132 miles to Winthrop. (Closed in winter due to avalanche danger.)

Bikestation

PICTURE THIS: One day, instead of driving to work and dumping your car in an overpriced lot where it acquires more dings than a New York cab, you rebel and ride your bike. Once downtown, you park in a glass-enclosed, high-tech bike storage facility, wash up in a clean, well-lit bathroom, and borrow an electric scooter, or maybe even an electric car, to get your errands done. While you're gone, the station technicians give the bike a tune-up; your tires are fat for the ride home. This isn't fiction, but Bikestation Seattle, the start of what will hopefully be a commuting revolution. Following in the tire tracks of successful bike stations in California, the station opened in Pioneer Square in May 2003. It is located at 311 Third Ave. S., across from the King Street Station in the Mottman Building. To learn how to use the station or become a member, check out www.bikestation.org or call (206) 332-9795.

Where to Connect

Clubs and Organizations

See "Road Biking" for additional clubs.

- Backcountry Bicycle Trails Club (206-283-2995, www.bbtc.com) is a mountain biking club that organizes rides, works on trails, and struggles for trail access. People rave that BBTC's Boot Camp, held at St. Edward State Park, is a great place to learn to ride or acquire new skills.

- Bicycle Alliance (206-224-9252, www.bicyclealliance.org) is the group that makes sure you have safe places to ride. They participate in local transportation funding decisions, hold rallies, and promote bike commuting. If you love cycling, consider helping out this excellent grassroots advocacy organization.

- Bike Works (206-725-9408, www.bikeworks.org) is a nonprofit organization that runs projects such as Earn-a-Bike, where kids learn bike repairs, then do volunteer repair in exchange for their own bike. More than 275 kids have earned bikes so far. Bike Works is also a bike repair shop that sells used bicycles. Donate, help out, or bring in your bike for a tune-up—it's a great organization.

- The Mountaineers (206-284-8484, 800-573-8484, www.mountaineers.org) has classes, club, and outings.

- Northwest Women's Cycling (206-284-5407, www.nwwc.org) is a great accessible club focused on (but not exclusive to) women.

- Seattle Bicycle Club (www.seattlebicycle.com) is a local club with regular rides and a monthly potluck and presentation night for members.

- Single Track Mind Cycling Club (www.stmcc.org) is based in Tacoma but rides all over.

Shops

- Aaron's Bicycle Repair (6400 California Ave. S.W. in West Seattle, 206-938-9795, www.rideyourbike.com)

- All About Bike and Ski (3615 N.E. 45th St. in Laurelhurst, 206-524-2642). Rentals (right off the Burke-Gilman Trail), sales, and repair. Very nice people.

- Alpine Hut (2215 15th Ave. W. a mile south of the Ballard bridge, 206-284-3575). Thirty years in business and the low-key owner still answers the phone himself. Sales, rental, repair.

- Angle Lake Cyclery (20804 Pacific Highway S. near Sea-Tac, 206-878-7457, www.anglelake.com). Sales, repair.

- Aurora Cycle (7401 Aurora Ave. N. in Greenlake, 206-783-1000) is a huge shop with sales, rentals and repair. (Also has a store in Bellevue, 206-523-1822.)

- BikeSmith (2309 N. 45th St. in Wallingford, 206-632-3102) is a tiny shop, especially good for repairs. They sell very cute new and reconstructed cruiser bikes.

- Bikesport (5601 24th Ave. N.W. in Ballard, 206-706-4700). Mountain bike sales, repair.

- Counterbalance Bicycles (2 W. Roy St. at the bottom of Queen Anne Hill, 206-352-3252, www.counterbalancebicycles .com). A small, full-service shop specializing in custom-built bikes for messengers and commuters.

- Free Range Cycles (3501 Phinney Ave. N., 206-547-8407) sells new and used road and mountain bikes. Repairs.

- Gregg's Greenlake Cycle (7007 Woodlawn Ave. N.E. in Greenlake, 206-523-1822) also has a sister shop, Aurora Cycle, nearby.

- Montlake Bike Shop (2223 24th Ave. E. in Montlake, 206-329-7333). Also has shops in Bellevue and Kirkland.

- Recycled Cycles (1007 Northeast Boat St. in the University District, 206-547-4491). Used-bike specialty. Sales, repairs.

- REI (222 Yale Ave. N., 206-223-1944, also shops in Lynnwood, Federal Way, and Redmond). Sales, rental, repairs.

- Second Ascent (5209 Ballard Ave. N.W. in Ballard, 206-545-8810) offers new and used outdoor gear, including bicycles and bike equipment.

- Velo Bike Shop (1535 11th Ave. on Capitol Hill, 206-352-3292)

- Wright Bros. Cycle Works (219 N. 36th St. in Fremont, 206-633-5132). Repairs and bike repair classes.

Events
- Bike to Work Day is in May. If you never participate in anything else, bike to work. There's nothing like whizzing past a bunch of bored, cell-phone-yapping drivers on your gleaming steed. Think of it as reclaiming your youth. On this particular day there will be commuter support sta-

tions, T-shirts, a bike parade, and a lot of sexy calf muscles to gawk at.

- Bicycle Saturdays and Sundays are May through September. Every summer, about twice a month, the city blocks Lake Washington Boulevard to traffic so cyclists can ride peacefully. A glimpse at cycling utopia.

- Boneshaker Mountain Bike Bash, in June, features downhill and cross-country mountain-bike racing in the Methow Valley.

- Chilly Hilly, in February, is the classic opener to Seattle's cycling season; this one's been around more than 30 years. Riders wait (the chilly part) in a big group at the ferry terminal. Camaraderie forms. Then you float over to Bainbridge Island and begin 33 miles of hilly. There are beautiful views all along the way. Contact Cascade Bicycle Club (206-522-BIKE, www.cascade.org).

- Boat Street Criterium, in April, is a great opportunity to watch fast cyclists race around a 0.6-mile loop right in the University District. Info at Recycled Cycles (206-547-4491).

- The Fremont Solstice Parade is, officially, a fun-filled introduction to summer in Seattle, with floats made by artists, samba dancers on platforms, unreconstructed flower children with painted faces, and a whole lot of people and food. Unofficially, it is an event in which crazy bicyclists get the parade started right by appearing from nowhere to lead the pack, naked but for helmet or identity-covering mask. This is an illegal activity, so you'd better know how to ride fast.

- Methow Valley Mountain Bike Festival, in October, features races, rides, and a bike rodeo. Contact the Methow Valley Sport Trails Association (509-996-3287, www.mvsta.com).

- The Seattle International Bike Expo, in March, is a huge bike show with speakers, bike stunts, slide shows, and lots and lots of booths displaying the latest gadgetry. Talk to the folks at the Cascade Bicycle Club.

- Seattle Bike Swap (www.pazzovelo.com) is just that. In 2003 it took place in mid-February; check the Web site for this year's date.

- Tour de Fat (www.newbelgium.com/) in August is a traveling festival sponsored by The New Belgium Brewing Company. It features wacky bike races and a vintage bike show, both of which benefit local nonprofits.

Books

- Poffenbarger, Amy. *Mountain Bike America Washington: An Atlas of Washington State's Greatest Off-Road Bicycle Rides.* 2d ed. Guilford, CT: Globe Pequot, 2001.

- Zilly, John. *Kissing the Trail: Greater Seattle Mountain Bike Adventures,* Seattle, WA: Sasquatch Books, 2003.

  ———. *Mountain Bike Northwest Washington.* Seattle, WA: Sasquatch Books, 1998.

  ———. *Mountain Bike Southwest Washington.* Seattle, WA: Sasquatch Books, 1998.

Links

www.bikeride.com lists cycling events and useful links to other sites as well as the latest biking news.

www.gorp.com offers planning guides and travel advice for outdoor adventure.

www.imba.com for the International Mountain Bicycling Association (IMBA), which works to create and preserve trail opportunities for mountain bikers.

www.wsdot.wa.gov, the Web site for the Washington State Department of Transportation, has links to downloadable maps of Washington bike routes. Also gives updates on road closures and other cycling transportation issues.

I MAGINE YOU LIVE within driving distance of several world-famous wilderness areas, complete with volcanoes, mountains, rivers, lakes, ocean, towering trees, glaciers, wildflowers, and many, many trails. Now, tell me where to go for my first 16 hikes. Actually, I don't need you to imagine this scenario, because I've suffered through it. Nearly every hike I've been on in Washington has been an absolute beauty in its own way, and I can hardly bring myself to recommend only a few. In order to limit things, I stuck fairly strictly to this guidebook's concept of near-urban outings. This chapter's sampling is focused on hikes within a 1½-hour drive, because those are the ones you'll be able to get to first. Another reason I gave extra attention to these is that they are mostly four-season hikes. Late July is typically when the majority of alpine hikes open up, and many are only accessible in August, September, and part of October. At least half of this chapter's hikes are accessible outside those narrow windows.

Three city "hikes" are probably better called walks, but they visit some of the wildest places right in Seattle, and they'll give you a chance to get outside when you've been too long at the office. There are many good Backyard hikes just east of the city, within 30 minutes of downtown. All are located in the Issaquah Alps, a string of attractive, scaled-down peaks hugging the skirts of the wilder and more imposing Alpine Lakes Wilderness. The Alps are considered the largest wilderness area within sprawling distance of a major U.S. city, and the fact that they have in some part been preserved is thanks to some very hard-working wilderness advocates, in particular the Issaquah Alps Trails Club, whose trip leader Fred Zeidler is a wealth of information about the area.

Alpine Lakes hikes, 15 or 20 minutes farther east on I-90, can be very popular in summer and fall, especially on the weekends, but are still quite beautiful, usually with more elevation gain and challenge than the Issaquah Alps. From here I branched out north and west, with a handful of options in the 1½- to 3-hour-drive range, longer hops I hope will introduce entirely new country, and get you started exploring it. So it's a "great nearby hikes" chapter, limited not by wilderness area or compass point but by drive time and desirability. For other nearby hike ideas, or even some places to walk, see the mountain biking, snowshoeing, skiing, and bird-watching chapters. If you're looking for something wheelchair friendly, or simply smooth and flat, the in-line skating and cycling chapters deliver a few gems.

When you're ready to go farther afield, consult *Wilderness Meccas*, which describes some of the wild places you just might have heard about already, Shangri-Las such as Mount Rainier and Olympic National Parks. I've included a couple of camping ideas in the Pitching Tent sidebars, but if you quickly sate yourself, you'd best stock up on more books. *Where to Connect* lists many choice titles. Also, consider joining a club, such as the Washington Trails Association, the Issaquah Alps Trails Club, or the Mountaineers, or visit their Web sites for further inspiration and advice. You're in world-class hiking country now, and it will take a lifetime to see it all.

City Limits

DISCOVERY PARK LOOP TRAIL

Location: Seattle
Length: 2.8-mile loop
Difficulty: Easy
Season: Year-round
Map and book: Map available at Discovery Park Visitor Center; *Nature in the City: Seattle*
Dogs: Yes, though not on park beaches
Permits: No
Heads-up: The park is open dawn to dusk, the Visitor Center Tuesday through Sunday, 8:30 to 5:00. See "Bird-Watching," page 232, for details on species to look for.
Description: Discovery Park is the city's largest, and a local favorite. Naturalists point out that this is one of the few parks in the city where you can find several different ecosystems side by side: saltwater beach, bluffs, meadows, and woods, to name a few. This makes for great bird-watching, and over 270 species have been spotted here, including several species of owls; a variety of warblers and other

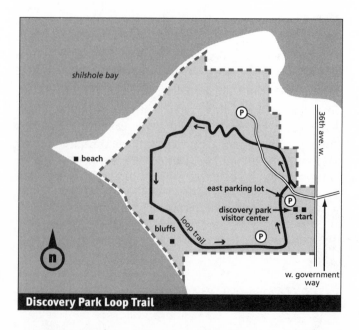

shilshole bay

■ beach

east parking lot

discovery park
visitor center

start

loop trail

bluffs

w. government
way

36th ave. w.

n

Discovery Park Loop Trail

passerines; grebes, wigeons, and other waterfowl; and hawks and eagles overhead. Bald eagles almost always nest in the park each year—ask at the visitors center for details. The park is visited by coyotes, foxes, and other mammals. It's big enough for all this and plenty of humans, too. The loop walk described takes you through most of the habitats mentioned except for the beach. It's about the same length as a walk around the city's favorite park, Green Lake, but feels longer and more strenuous because of the variety and a few good uphill climbs. Buy a map at the visitors center for a dollar if you want to explore, or wander on your own— there are plenty of signs, though it's possible to get lost. The beach is definitely worth a visit, with views west across Puget Sound to West Seattle, Bainbridge Island, and the Olympic Mountains. Very lucky souls have spotted orcas in the distance; seals and sea lions are more likely.

Route: Start at the north end of the Discovery Park Visitor

Center parking lot. From here, take a foot path, following the loop trail, which is well signed all the way through the park.

Directions: From the downtown Seattle waterfront area, take Elliott Ave. north, which quickly becomes 15th Ave. W. In about a quarter-mile, take the West Dravus St. exit, following signs for Daybreak Star Indian Cultural Center in Discovery Park. Turn left over the bridge onto Dravus St. After several blocks, turn right onto 20th Ave. W. Take 20th—which becomes Gilman Ave. W. and then W. Government Way—a little over 1 mile to Discovery Park's east entrance. Immediately to the left as you enter the park is the Discovery Park Visitor Center.

Trail
Running

IT SHOULD GO WITHOUT SAYING that many of the trails in this chapter are also great for picking up the pace. You'll see plenty of runners on Discovery Park trails, and all over Tiger, Squak, and Cougar Mountains. If you've got the lungs for elevation gain, you can't do much better nearby than running Mount Si, an Issaquah Alp that is frequented by runners and climbers training for Mount Rainier. For more on trail runs in the area there are two local guidebooks— *Trail Running Guide to Western Washington* by Mike McQuaide (Sasquatch Books) and *Fifty Trail Runs in Washington* by Cheri Pompeo Gillis (Mountaineers Books).

SCHMITZ PRESERVE PARK

Location: West Seattle
Length: A couple of miles
Difficulty: Easy to moderate
Season: Year-round

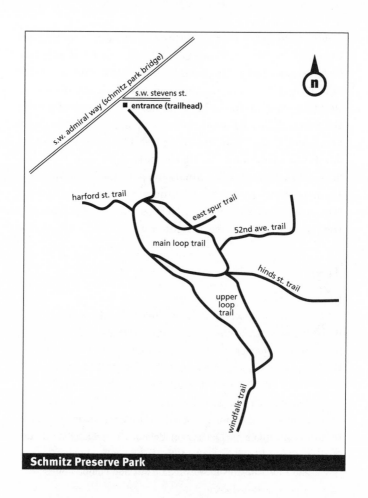

Schmitz Preserve Park

Book: *Nature in the City: Seattle*

Dogs: Yes, on a leash, but not in the stream

Permits: No

Heads up: Old growth in the city. If you'd like to help with park projects, Friends of Schmitz Park meets the last Saturday of each month, rain or shine, 9 A.M. to noon, in the park. Contact Ken Shaw (sppks2@yahoo.com) or Jefferson Saunders (JCSaunders@aol.com).

Description: Set aside as protected land by early Seattleites with vision, this 50-acre enclave of old growth is a balm for the cyber weary. The preserve has been adopted by members of Friends of Schmitz Park, who spend their free time keeping it wild. Like forest elves on a restoration mission, volunteers lovingly transplant native plants from Eastside forest–cum–building sites, including the duff or decaying organic matter that creates essential soil, to this majestic city forest. Although a major storm in the early 1990s made nurse logs of hundreds of trees, this is still a good place to see jaw-dropping, centuries-old specimens of western red cedar, Douglas fir and western hemlock, as well as many other native tree species. More than 30 species of birds have been counted, and it is a nesting site for ospreys and pileated woodpeckers. If you're lucky, you might hear great horned or screech owls calling. Look for red foxes, ensatina salamanders, and little brown bats hunting at dusk. The Friends of Schmitz Park have been compiling an impressive list of plants in the park, including 17 tree species, all kinds of native shrubs (vine maple, serviceberry, red osier dogwood, beaked hazlenut, red flowering currant, rhododendrons, and Nootka roses), and wildflowers (violets, goat's beard, fringecup, and western trillium). A recent daylighting project has also brought a creek back to the park's surface.

Route: Wander with map in hand—though trails are marked on the map, they aren't marked in the park, and the area is so small that trail names aren't necessary anyway.

Directions: From downtown, take I-5 south to exit 163A (Spokane Street/West Seattle Bridge). Take the West Seattle Bridge to the Admiral Way exit. Follow S.W. Admiral Way until you reach the park entrance at S.W. Stevens St. In 2002, the parking lot was removed to daylight the stream. Park on Admiral Way on the bridge west of the park entrance, or on S.W. Stevens St.

CARKEEK PARK

Location: Northwest Seattle
Length: Variable
Difficulty: Easy to moderate
Season: Year-round
Map and book: Park map available at the park's Environmental Learning Center and in kiosks; *Nature in the City: Seattle*
Dogs: Yes
Permits: No
Heads up: North Bluff and South Bluff Trails provide good access to the park's upper reaches. The park trails and environmental center were revamped in 2003; see www .cityofseattle.net/parks/parkspaces/carkeek.htm for updates.

Description: Carkeek Park, like many other city parks, was established in a steep ravine poorly suited for residential development. At the park's bottom is Piper's Creek, a restored salmon creek stocked with hatchery fish that return each fall. The Piper's Creek Trail leads beside the creek and up to the end of the park for over a mile; looming woods of maple, cedar, fir, and hemlock rise up each side of the ravine. The place feels damp and a bit wild. There are usually a few joggers and walkers on the trail, even in winter, and picnickers and families in the summer or during the fall salmon run. Answering the call of the wild, head up either the north or south slopes of the park. In recent years major trail refurbishment has taken place, but that hasn't brought any crowds. Hemlock nurse logs sprout seedlings and support licorice ferns, mountain beaver dig in the underbrush, and a variety of warblers, woodpeckers, and other birds visit or inhabit the area. You could probably link up 4 or 5 miles of hiking here if you visited both sides, and when you're done

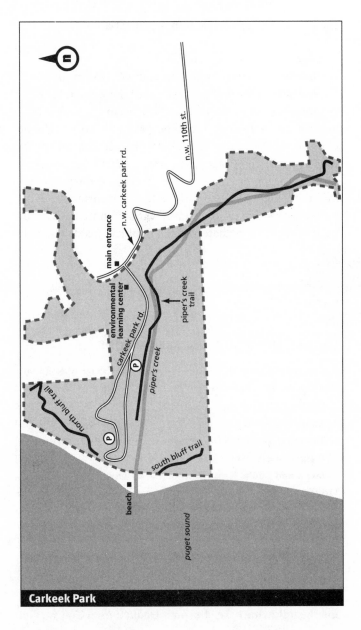

Carkeek Park

there's a beach accessible from a pedestrian walkway over train tracks.

Route: Grab the map and roam

Directions: Take I-5 north to exit 173. Continue north to Northgate Way and go west under the interstate. After crossing Meridian, Northgate Way becomes N.W. 105th St. and crosses Aurora Ave. N. (WA 99). Turn right on Greenwood Ave. N. and left on N.W. 110th St. (look for the crosswalk lights above the street). After 6 blocks, N.W. 110th St. becomes N.W. Carkeek Park Rd. and winds down into the valley for a half mile to the park entrance; watch for the park's sign on your left. The Environmental Center, with maps, is immediately to the right just inside the park.

Backyard

COUGAR MOUNTAIN: PERIMETER LOOP

Location: Issaquah, about 15 miles southeast of Seattle

Length: 10-mile loop

Difficulty: Moderate to difficult

Season: Year-round

Elevation gain: 2,000 feet over many ups and downs

Maximum elevation: 1,600 feet

Maps and Book: King County Parks Department Cougar Mountain map (available at trailhead); Green Trails map 203S: Cougar Mountain/Squak Mountain; *Authoritative Guide to the Hiking Trails of Cougar Mountain* (available from the Issaquah Alps Trails Club)

Dogs: Yes

Permits: No

Heads up: A round-the-mountain walk with views. This and the following hike offer an introduction to Cougar. Get

Hiking

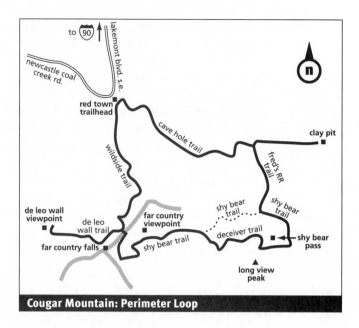

to (90) ↑

lakemont blvd. s.e.

newcastle coal creek rd.

red town trailhead

cave hole trail

clay pit

wildside trail

fred's RR trail

de leo wall viewpoint

de leo wall trail

far country viewpoint

shy bear trail

shy bear trail

far country falls

shy bear trail

deceiver trail

shy bear pass

long view peak

Cougar Mountain: Perimeter Loop

a trail map at most trailheads and you'll easily find your own favorite route.

Description: Cougar Mountain, at 4,000 acres, is considered the "largest wild park in an urban area in America." Of course, it's more accurately described as a suburban area, but that's just a quibble. The place is a boon for anyone in the Seattle-Bellevue corridor looking for a nearby break from clogged freeways and hipster cafés. A sign here explains that deer, porcupine, bobcat, cougar, and even black bear can be found at King County's largest park, and offers safety advice for close encounters. It's all part of the adventure at this something-for-everybody hot spot a short drive from Seattle. There are wide, gently sloping trails good for small children and other slow walkers, and gnarled stretches of hillier terrain off the beaten path suitable for trail runs. This lengthy perimeter-loop hike takes in some of the park's major areas and features.

Route: All of the trails here are well signed, and you're unlikely to get lost, particularly with map in hand. The route from the Red Town Trailhead looping the entire perimeter hooks up with multiple trails. Here are the major landmarks, as shown on the map: trailhead to DeLeo Wall, to Far Country, to Long View Peak, to Shy Bear and Fred's Railroad Trail, to Clay Pit, to Cave Hole Trail, to trailhead.

Directions: From downtown Seattle, take 90 east about 14 miles to exit 11A, bearing right on the exit ramp signed 150th Ave. S.E. Turn right and continue about 0.5 mile, going up a hill. Turn left at S.E. Newport Way. In about 1 mile turn right onto 164th Ave. S.E. Turn right in about 2 miles at Lakemont Blvd. At about 1.6 miles turn left into the Cougar Mountain entrance and Red Town trailhead.

COUGAR MOUNTAIN: BEAR RIDGE TRAIL

Location: About 16 miles southeast of Seattle

Length: 3-mile cherry-stem loop

Difficulty: Easy to moderate

Elevation gain: 800 feet

Maximum elevation: 1,260 feet

Season: Year-round

Map and book: Green Trails map 203S: Cougar Mountain/Squak Mountain; *Authoritative Guide to the Hiking Trails of Cougar Mountain* (available from the Issaquah Alps Trails Club)

Dogs: Yes

Permit: No

Heads up: Peaceful hike through deciduous forest. Beware of slippery and muddy stretches after rain.

Description: I came here with Issaquah Alps Trails Club hike leader Fred Zeitler, who says it's one of his favorite short loops, being both beautiful and surprisingly quiet,

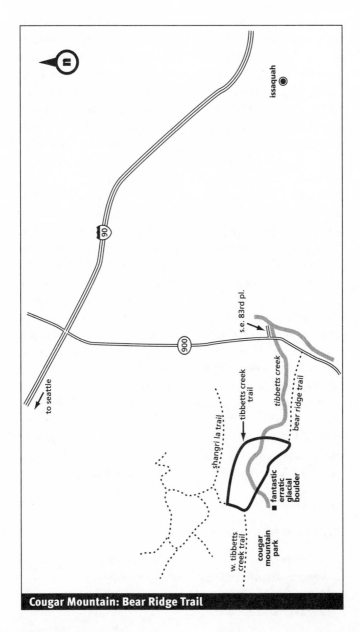

issaquah

90

to seattle

900

s.e. 83rd pl.

shangri la trail

tibbetts creek trail

tibbetts creek

bear ridge trail

fantastic erratic glacial boulder

w. tibbetts creek trail

cougar mountain park

Cougar Mountain: Bear Ridge Trail

though easily accessible off WA 900. The hike ambles up and down beneath alder canopy, sometimes beside Tibbetts Creek. In summer and fall watch for red huckleberry and salmonberry. This free picnic must be a feast for local bears and probably explains the trail name—I've heard no reports of sightings in years, but they may still pass by on occasion. About a mile in you'll pass the Fantastic Erratic, so named by the area's own hike aficionado Harvey Manning. It's a mighty big hunk of glacial debris (they say the largest in the Issaquah Alps), moss- and fern-speckled.

Route: Take the Bear Ridge Trail about 0.8 mile to where the trail forks. Veer left up onto a ridge, with obstructed views toward Tiger Mountain. At sign, continue right on Bear Ridge toward the Shangri La Trail. Follow this about 0.1 mile to the right-hand hairpin turnoff for the Tibbetts Creek Trail, which may or may not be signed. (It can sometimes be obscured by brush—if you get to the Shangri La Trail you've gone too far. Follow this trail down log steps and switchbacks through woods, eventually crossing a small bridge. After about 0.8 mile on this trail, turn right at the fork, go about 100 yards, and turn left, back onto the Bear Ridge Trail, returning to the parking area.

Directions: From downtown Seattle take I-90 about 15 miles to exit 15 (WA 900 West, Renton). Turn right on WA 900 and go just past S.E. 83rd Place (signed on the left) to the trailhead, which comes up quickly, on the right side of the road. There's parking for three or four cars.

SQUAK MOUNTAIN

Location: About 18 miles southeast of Seattle
Length: 10 miles out and back
Difficulty: Moderate to strenuous
Season: Year-round

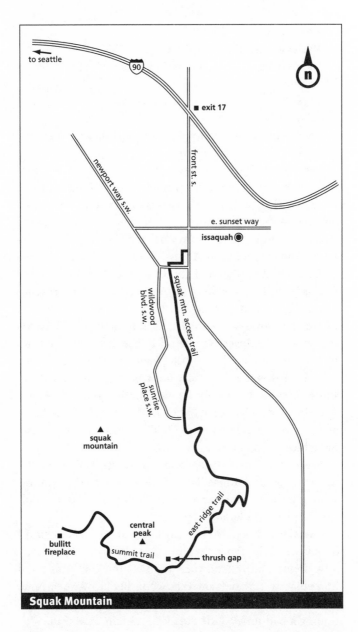

Squak Mountain

Elevation gain: 2,200 feet

Maximum elevation: 2,020 feet

Map: Green Trails map 203S: Cougar Mountain Squak Mountain

Dogs: Yes

Permits: No

Heads up: Good nearby year-round hike, woodsy and with plenty of ups and downs

Description: Squeezed between Cougar and Tiger Mountains, Squak is the least known and least visited of all the Issaquah Alps, perhaps because trails were once byzantine and access spotty. Volunteers have worked hard over the years to improve these conditions; one of their latest efforts is the Squak Mountain Access Trail, built in 2000. This rollercoaster trail dips and climbs as it leads from the town of Issaquah up the side of Squak. The hike first reaches Central Peak, with partially obstructed views from beneath microwave towers toward Lakes Sammamish and Washington and the Space Needle off in the distance. Continuing farther you hit the Bullitt Fireplace, which marks the site of a 1940s family retreat built here by attorney Stimson Bullitt, of the locally famous Bullitt family. His children donated 590 acres of Squak to Washington State Parks as permanent wildland in 1972. The chimney site has picnic tables and some sun exposure.

Route: Take the Squak Mountain Access Trail about 2.7 miles to the East Ridge Trail. Follow that to the Summit Trail and Central Peak. From here follow signs to the Bullitt Fireplace Trail and Fireplace.

Directions: Take I-90 east to Issaquah and take exit 17 (Front St.). Take Front St. through town to Newport Way S.W. about 1 mile, and turn right. Cross the bridge and immediately turn left on Wildwood Blvd. S.W. Continue about a half-mile to Sunrise Place S.W. and turn left, continuing a half-mile to the Squak Mountain Trailhead.

TIGER MOUNTAIN: TALUS ROCKS

Location: About 20 miles east of Seattle

Length: 4.5-mile loop

Difficulty: Easy to moderate

Season: Year-round

Elevation gain: 600 feet

Maximum elevation: 2,000 feet

Map: Green Trail map 204S: Tiger Mountain

Dogs: Yes

Permits: No

Heads up: Big trees, big rocks. The trip to Talus Rocks or to the boardwalk, done separately, are great with children.

Description: East of Cougar and Squak Mountains is Tiger Mountain, actually a cluster of peaks. Highlights on this trail, which starts at the High Point Entrance to the park, include a huge Douglas fir estimated to be 350 or 400 years old, a remnant of the immense forest that was here as recently as the turn of the 20th century. Weyerhaeuser acquired logging rights to much of the mountain early on and clear-cut much of the area. As they, joined by the Department of Natural Resources, returned for more timber in the 1970s, a movement began to save some of the land as wildlife habitat and recreational resource. Tiger is now known as "a working forest in an urban environment," a place where logging still occurs, but with regulation.

The Nook Trail is shaded by huge big leaf maple and vine maple, and leads to the junction for Talus Rocks. These large glacial erratics were deposited here during the last ice age. Near the end of the hike is a more popular area, the Swamp Trail, along whose boardwalks are storyboards with tales of swamp monsters and local history.

Route: Start at the Educational Shelter. Take the West Tiger Trail about 500 feet to the Bus Trail, hang a right, then turn left onto Nook Trail (the first left, unsigned) for

Tiger Mountain: Talus Rocks

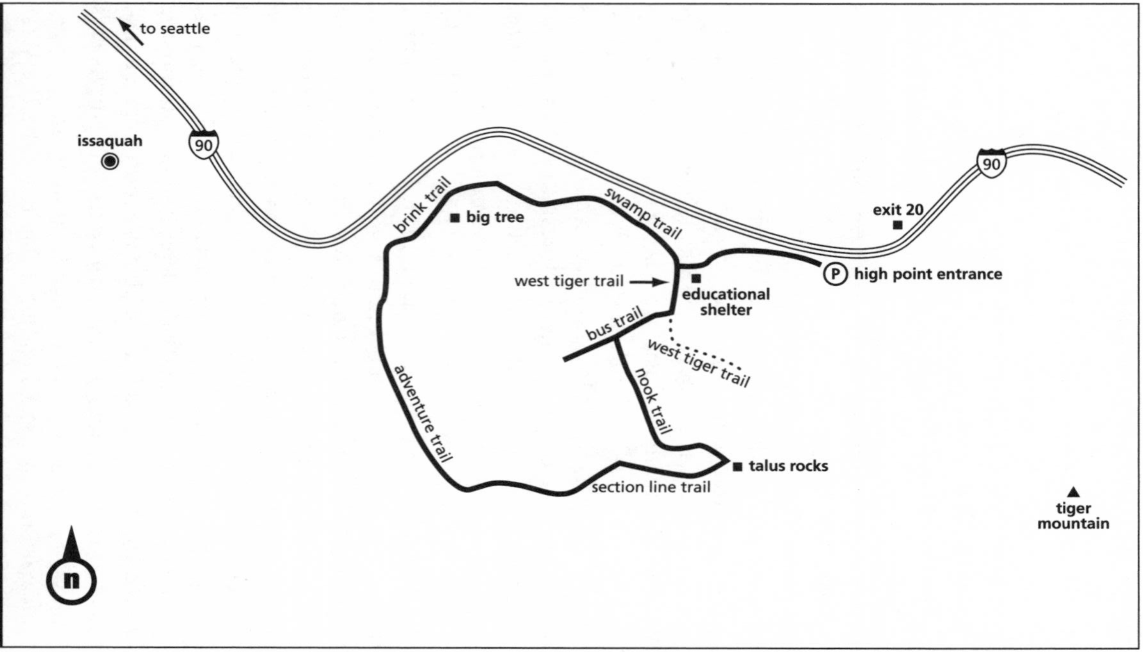

to seattle

issaquah

90

exit 20

P high point entrance

90

swamp trail

educational shelter

west tiger trail

bus trail

west tiger trail

nook trail

talus rocks

section line trail

big tree

brink trail

west tiger trail

adventure trail

tiger mountain

N

about 1.5 miles to Talus Rocks. Take a 0.2-mile side trip on a loop trail to see the Rocks, which provide shelter for bats. Returning to the Talus Rocks Trail junction, take the signed Connector Trail to the Section Line Trail and head right, west, 0.9 mile to the Adventure Trail, hooking north for another 0.9 mile to the Brink Trail. At the fork, follow the trail to the Big Tree and the Swamp Trail. Another 0.6 mile leads quickly back to the High Point entrance.

Directions: Take I-90 east of Issaquah to exit 20 (High Point). Turn right and then right again, taking a frontage road less than a mile past the West Tiger trailhead on a gravel road to the High Point trailhead parking lot. Beware—the big lot can get packed on a summer weekend.

RATTLESNAKE MOUNTAIN: LEDGE HIKE

Location: About 25 miles east of Seattle
Length: 4 miles out and back with option for 8 miles
Difficulty: Moderate
Elevation gain to ledge: 1,200 feet
Elevation at top ledge: 2,080 feet
Elevation at East Rattlesnake: 3,580 feet
Map: Green Trails 205S: Rattlesnake Mountain
Dogs: Yes
Permits: No
Heads up: Great views, good workout
Description: Rising from ledge to ledge on this mountain you'll get a great workout in a short distance, with spectacular views of Mount Si and the Snoqualmie Valley. A subalpine collection of flowers are scattered around in summer, including penstemon, phlox, and lupine. Those afraid of heights should stand back from the rock outcrops that form each ledge. (As should those afraid of losing their stuff. I once dropped my backpack down ahead of me onto

one of the ledges, and it slid on fine gravel about 8 feet before plummeting 100 more into some dense woods. It was recovered, pulverized bananas and all.) The lowest ledge is very popular in summer, but by the second and third ledges the crowds thin. If you want even more of a workout, climb to the summit at East Rattlesnake Tower.

Route: Get on the trail and go up.

Directions: Take I-90 east to exit 32. Turn right at the exit onto 436th Ave. S.E. and go uphill about 3 miles to the signed parking lot for the Rattlesnake Mountain East trailhead.

Safety Tips
and
Other Rules for the Trail

F YOU'VE BEEN out in the wild a few times, you probably know that things can go wrong. A wilderness education should be acquired through some combination of experience, talking to other backpackers, classes, and good books on backcountry travel. Two things that will surely be taught in any Seattle-area course are "The Ten Essentials" and "Leave No Trace Ethics." The former is a list of supplies you shouldn't be without, even for a day hike, and was created by that famous local club, The Mountaineers. The list: map, compass, flashlight, extra food and water, extra clothing, sunglasses, first-aid kit, pocketknife, waterproof matches, and candle and fire starter.

The ethics part is about doing what you can to preserve what is left of a diminishing wilderness and was developed by federal land management agencies, the National Outdoor Leadership School (NOLS), and thousands of conscientious hikers. Like the Ten Essentials, these commonsense rules are easily forgotten when city-folk go wild. Burn them into your brain, since you probably won't feel like carrying them around on a piece of paper, which might get lost anyway what with keeping track of the Ten Essentials. Maybe you could make them into a song. The lyrics might go something like this: O, limit the size of your party; stay on established trails; camp in established sites; and properly dispose of human waste away from water, trails, and campsites. Yes, people, use a stove, not a fire, (like those fools in the Southwest burning love letters). And soap, oh soap, don't use nonbiodegradable soap, or, for that matter, any soap near lakes or streams. Don't disturb flowers, rocks, or other natural features. Don't disturb wildlife. Pack out all your garbage. And don't forget the tent stakes.

Short Hops

SNOW LAKE

Location: Snoqualmie Pass, about 45 miles east of Seattle.

Length: 8 miles out and back

Difficulty: Moderate

Elevation gain: 1,700 feet

Maximum elevation: 4,400 feet

Map and book: Green Trails 207: Snoqualmie Pass; *100 Hikes in Washington's Alpine Lakes*

Dogs: Yes

Permits: A Northwest Forest Pass is required on all vehicles parked at the trailhead. A $5 day pass or $30 annual pass is available at forest service offices and vendors such as REI. They are not available at trailheads. The forest service Web site is www.fs.fed.us/r6/mbs.

Heads up: Popular in summer—try it in fall just before snow.

Description: A beautiful and accessible climb with a treat

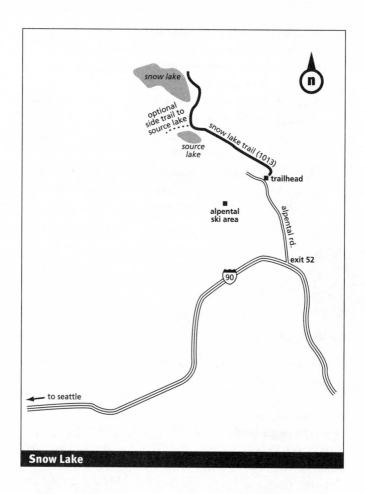

Snow Lake

for those who get to the top—a sparkling, more than 1-mile-long lake flanked by forest and cliffs that is a fantastic picnic spot. For this reason, and its proximity to Seattle, Snow is a very popular local hike. Scout around for a quiet corner at the top to call your own, and break out the cheese sandwiches.

Route: The hike starts at the Alpental Ski Resort. Drive through the ski area past cabins to the large, second-to-last parking lot where trail number 13 begins. Views of Denny Mountain and Chair Peak appear as you gain elevation. At 3,700 feet there's a marked junction for the Source Lake overlook, a half-mile detour each way if you want to bag both lakes on this hike. From here you'll switchback strenuously to the saddle at 4,400 feet, then descend a half-mile and about 400 feet to the lake's north shore.

Directions: Take I-90 east from Seattle to exit 52 and turn left, crossing under the freeway. Continue 2 miles on the Alpental Road through the ski area to the parking lot described above.

DENNY CREEK AND MELAKWA LAKE

Location: 40 miles east of Seattle

Length: 9-mile out and back

Difficulty: Moderate

Elevation gain: 2,300 feet

Maximum elevation: 4,909 feet

Map and book: Green Trail 207: Snoqualmie Pass; *100 Hikes in Washington's Alpine Lakes*

Dogs: Yes

Fee: A Northwest Forest Pass is required on all vehicles parked at the trailhead. A $5 day pass or $30 annual pass is available at forest service offices and vendors such as REI. They are not available at trailheads. The forest service Web site is www.fs.fed.us/r6/mbs.

Heads up: Waterfalls

Description: You won't be alone, at least for the first part of this hike—it's many people's favorite, with good reason. The first, moderate leg is through old forest, reaching a collection of bedrock slabs that are perfect for a snack break beside Denny Creek. Beware: On a hot day you can splash around in the water here for hours and forget to continue

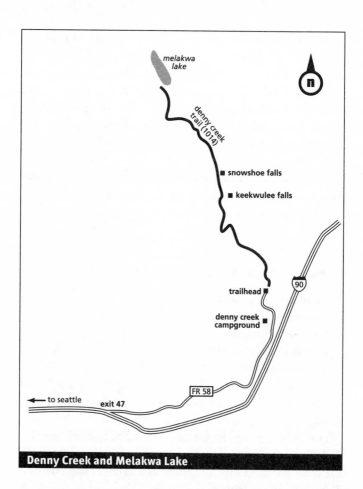

Denny Creek and Melakwa Lake

the hike. Ascending up the river valley, with views of nearby peaks, you'll pass a couple of waterfalls that provide an excuse to rest after steep switchbacks.

Route: Begin on Trail 1014 and follow it to the turn-around point at Melakwa Lake Basin, 4.5 miles in, with gorgeous views and a well-beaten camping area.

Directions: Take I-90 east from Seattle to exit 47. Turn north at the exit ramp, go over the interstate, and turn right at the T. In 0.25 mile turn left onto Denny Creek Road (FR 58). Go 2.5 miles, and just beyond the Denny Creek Campground turn left onto the paved road. Continue 0.25 mile to the end. Parking is limited; be sure to park off the right-of-way and do not block the driveways.

GRANITE MOUNTAIN

Location: 40 miles east of Seattle
Length: 8 miles out and back
Difficulty: Difficult, with steep switchbacks
Elevation gain: 3,800 feet
Maximum elevation: 5,629 feet

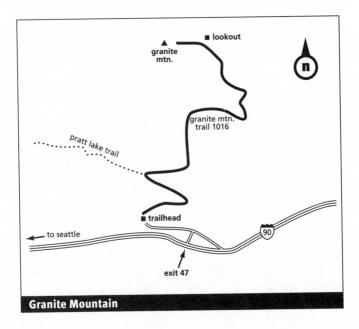

Granite Mountain

Map and book: Green Trails 207: Snoqualmie Pass; *100 Hikes in Washington's Alpine Lakes*

Dogs: Yes

Permits: A Northwest Forest Pass is required on all vehicles parked at the trailhead. A $5 day pass or $30 annual pass is available at forest service offices and vendors such as REI. They are not available at trailheads. The forest service Web site is www.fs.fed.us/r6/mbs. For the North Bend Ranger District call (425) 888-1421.

Heads up: A gorgeous trip to the top. Can be very hot on a sunny day.

Description: This is one of the more beautiful hikes in the I-90 corridor. After a forested beginning, the trail opens up onto a south slope that can be scorching on a sunny day. After every heart-pounding switchback, remind yourself that this is the price you pay to get high enough for the alpine flowers, the high meadows, and the wide open views of Mount Rainier, Mount Baker, and Glacier Peak from the fire lookout at the top. In the fall the flowers are replaced by the jewel colors of alpine shrubbery, scarlet blueberry bushes, and other native foliage. Rangers caution hikers to avoid hiking Granite early in the season, when avalanches are not uncommon. Call if you're unsure. Also, take care to stay on trail, as the alpine ecosystem is fragile.

Route: Take the Pratt Lake Trail about 1 mile to the junction with Granite Mountain Trail (1016) at 2,600 feet. Go right to the open south slope with switchbacks up to about 4,000 feet. The trail heads east and then climbs steeply to the summit ridge at 5,200 feet. Just over 400 feet of elevation gain brings you to the fire lookout, at 4 miles in.

Directions: Take I-90 east from Seattle to exit 47. Go north, crossing over the freeway, and turn west at 0.6 mile to the trailhead parking lot.

WALLACE FALLS

Location: Gold Bar, approximately 45 miles northeast of Seattle

Length: 4 miles out and back

Difficulty: Easy to moderate

Elevation gain: 880 feet

Maximum elevation: 1,120 feet

Dogs: Yes

Permits: Not needed for day hikes

Heads up: Fun for the whole family. Consult www.parks .wa.gov for more information about this state park, which is closed to day use October 7 to March 31.

Description: This hike is no secret—arrive by 11 A.M. on a summer weekend or there will be nowhere to park. On the other hand, it's a lot of fun on a weekday. It's also good during the shoulder seasons (when it's open) when you're snowed out elsewhere. Another thing to consider is its close proximity to the Index Town Walls, a rock climber's mecca, and the Skykomish River, renowned for both fly-fishing and white water. A family could make a day or two out of these pastimes, depending on skill level and interest. The hike itself is a pleasant wander along the scenic, boulder-strewn Wallace River beside lichen-speckled, moss-enrobed alder and maple trees; it rises slowly to a couple of spectacular overlooks. Wallace Falls plunges 265 feet into the river, and at the Middle Viewpoint you'll get a misty facial and go temporarily deaf from the river's roar.

Route: Start under the power lines on a service road. The trail forks at 0.25 mile. Take the right trail, the Woody, which continues beside the Wallace River for another mile to a wooden bridge overlook. From here the trail gets steeper until you reach the Middle Viewpoint and, 0.25 mile later, the Valley Overlook.

Directions: Take I-5 north from Seattle to US 2 and drive east to the town of Gold Bar. Turn left in town at the sign for Wallace Falls State Park, and continue following signs to the trailhead.

Longer Hops

GREEN MOUNTAIN

Location: About 110 miles northeast of Seattle
Length: About 8 miles out and back
Difficulty: Moderate to difficult
Elevation gain: 3,000 feet
Maximum elevation: 6,500 feet
Maps: Green Trails 79: Snowking, and 80: Cascade Pass
Dogs: Yes
Permits: A Northwest Forest Pass is required on all vehicles parked at the trailhead. A $5 day pass or $30 annual pass is available at forest service offices and vendors such as REI. They are not available at trailheads. The forest service Web site www.fs.fed.us/r6/mbs.

Heads up: Summit for big views; visit midsummer for wildflowers

Description: This is an excellent, strenuous day hike, though you might want to start early from Seattle as it's a bit of a drive. After a mile or so of moderately steep hiking through old growth you'll come to verdant subalpine meadows famous for flowers in mid- to late summer, depending on the year. Camping is available at sites in another mile or so, near a couple of small lakes. Rest up and eat—the upcoming switchbacks will burn off that burrito in no time. If it's a clear day you'll have panoramic views of the

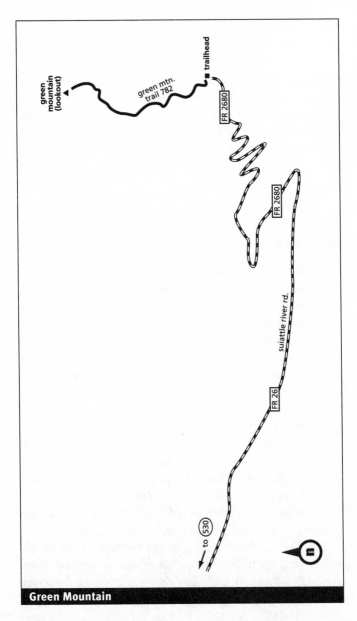

green
mountain
(lookout)

green mtn.
trail 782

■ trailhead

FR 2680

FR 2680

suiattle river rd.

FR 26

to 530

N

Green Mountain

Cascades from the top. Wildlife include deer and marmots, which will whistle at your approach.

Route: Take Green Mountain Trail (782) to the top.

Directions: Take I-5 north to exit 208 (WA 530, Arlington/Darrington). Go east on WA 530 approximately 30 miles through Arlington to Darrington. From Darrington drive north 7 miles on WA 530 toward Rockport to Suiattle River Road (FR 26). Take this 20.2 miles to road (FR 2680) on the left (north). Drive 5.9 miles to the trailhead, where there is limited parking.

MILLER PEAK

Location: About 90 miles northeast of Seattle

Length: About 8 miles out and back

Difficulty: Moderate to difficult

Elevation gain: 3,200 feet

Maximum elevation: 6,400 feet

Maps and book: USGS Blewett map; Green Trails 209: Liberty, and 210: Mount Stuart; *100 Hikes in Washington's Alpine Lakes*

Dogs: Yes

Permits: A Northwest Forest Pass is required on all vehicles parked at the trailhead. A $5 day pass or $30 annual pass is available at forest service offices and vendors such as REI. They are not available at trailheads. The forest service Web site is www.fs.fed.us/rb/mbs.

Heads up: ATVs are allowed here, though they are not always present. Midweek is best for avoiding them.

Description: Here's a hike on the arid side of the mountains, one good day hike among many around here, although almost all, including this one, have the drawback of being in unprotected land to which off-road vehicles have access. The good news is that the hike itself is a win-

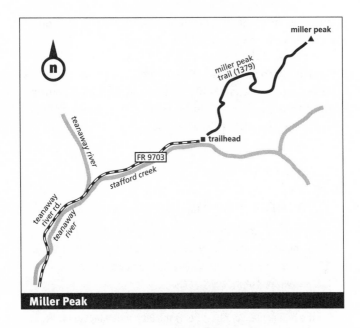

Miller Peak

ner, and if you go during the week you may not hear a single ATV the whole day. The trail begins easily enough along Miller Creek but soon begins to switchback until it reaches a saddle with impressive views. But this is merely a taste of what's to come. The trail gets very steep in the last leg to the summit, on a bootpath that takes off from the main trail, to a peak bursting with views. Look for Mounts Rainier and Adams, Goat Rocks, and the Stuart Range. In June the scree slopes on this hike can be spilling with red and purple wildflowers. For more trails in this area contact the Cle Elum Ranger Station (509-674-4411, www .fs.fed.us/r6/wenatchee/recreate/trails/cletr.htm)

Route: Head up Miller Peak Trail (1379), following the river for a ways, ascending slowly to the end of the valley at just over 2 miles. Switchback another 1.5 miles to the saddle and views. From here it's another half-mile or so, traversing the ridge and climbing another short section of switchbacks to the peak.

Directions: Take I-90 east about 75 miles to exit 85 (WA 970). Turn north, toward Wenatchee. After about 6 miles turn left onto Teanaway River Rd. and follow it approximately 15 miles. Turn right onto FR 9703. Go 3.5 miles to the end and the Miller Peak trailhead.

Getting to the Olympic Peninsula

ROM SEATTLE there are at least three ways to get to the peninsula. Two are by ferry, and one is not. Ferry routes, directions, and schedules are available online at www.wsdot.wa.gov/ferries.

Option 1: From the north end of Seattle to the northern part of the peninsula, your best bet is the Edmonds-Kingston ferry. Drive north on I-5 from Seattle about 8 miles to exit 177 and take WA 104 toward the Edmonds-Kingston ferry terminal. Follow signs for the ferry, getting onto 244th St. S.W. which becomes N.E. 205th St. and several other streets but always with signs for the ferry terminal. You will be directed into the line for the ferry ticket booths about 6 or 7 miles after exiting I-5. After taking the ferry from Edmonds to Kingston, follow signs to WA 104 and take this west to the Hood Canal Bridge. Turn right and cross the bridge. Follow specific directions to trailheads or other destinations.

Option 2: If you are downtown or in the south end of Seattle, you can take the Seattle-Bainbridge ferry. From Colman Dock (Pier 52) take the ferry to Bainbridge Island. Take WA 305 northwest about 13 miles to WA 3 north. Follow signs to the Hood Canal Bridge. Turn right across the bridge. Follow specific directions to trailheads or other destinations.

Option 3: From the Tacoma area you can take the Tacoma Narrows Bridge. From here continue on WA 104 about 10 miles. Turn left onto S. Keesling Rd. Continue on Center Rd./Griffith Rd. Get on US 101 and take it to your destination.

OLYMPIC PENINSULA: DUCKABUSH RIVER TRAIL

Location: Quilcene watershed about 100 miles by road from Seattle

Length: 5-plus miles out and back

Difficulty: Easy to 2.4 miles in, moderate to strenuous from this point on.

Elevation Gain: 700 feet for the first 2.4 miles, 1,300 feet to the national park boundary, at 6.7 miles

Maximum elevation: Big Hump is at 1,700 feet.

Map and Books: USGS Brothers map; *100 Hikes in Washington's South Cascades and Olympics; Olympic Mountains Trail Guide; Cascade-Olympic Natural History*

Dogs: Allowed on the first part of the trail but not in national park

Permits: A Northwest Forest Pass is required on all vehicles parked at the trailhead. A $5 day pass or $30 annual pass is available at forest service offices and vendors such as REI. They are not available at trailheads. The forest service Web site is www.fs.fed.us/r6/Olympic.

Heads up: This can be a moderate family hike or a strenuous backpack, depending on the length of your trip. Usually accessible May to November.

Description: This gorgeous hike, with towering firs and hemlocks and the promise of a gurgling river, is surprisingly accessible, an excellent low-elevation hike. The first section, to Big Hump, is a good day hike for the average walker. Continue farther to work up a sweat, with a 1,000-

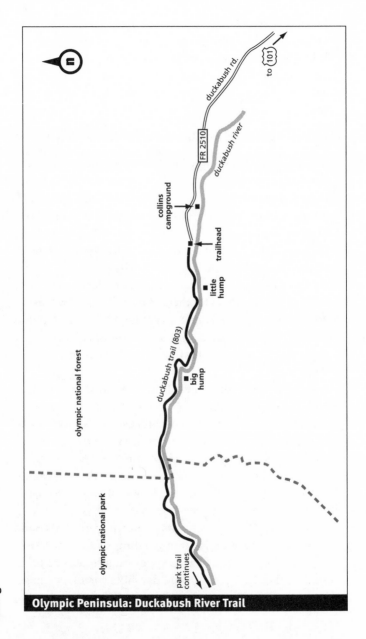

Olympic Peninsula: Duckabush River Trail

foot elevation gain on occasional loose rock over Big Hump before resuming a moderate pace to the Olympic National Park boundary at 6.7 miles. The farther you go the more opportunities to see wildlife, including deer and the occasional black bear.

Route: Take Duckabush Trail (803) 2.4 miles to the Duckabush River, where there is a rest area after Little Hump. To go farther, simply continue on the trail for as long as you like.

Directions: See *Getting to the Olympic Peninsula*, page 182. Once on the peninsula, take US 101 to the Duckabush Recreation Area, 22 miles north of Hoodsport. Turn west on Duckabush River Road and go 6 miles to FR 2510 and the trailhead.

PITCHING TENT
duckabush trail

HERE ARE SEVERAL good first-come, first-served camping areas established along the Duckabush Trail, including some near the river. They offer an opportunity for Olympic wilderness camping without a big hike.

Until you've gone 6.6 miles and see the Olympic National Park sign, you're on forest service property, and you don't need to pay to camp. You will need a Northwest Forest Pass on each vehicle parked at the trailhead. They are available at the Quilcene ranger office (360-765-2200) on US 101. Hours there are variable, but Peninsula Foods Grocery, a quarter mile north of the station, has more generous hours and also sells the pass. If you do choose to camp in Olympic National Park you will need both the parking pass and a National Park Wilderness permit, which is available at the trailhead.

OLYMPIC PENINSULA: MOUNT TOWNSEND TRAIL

Location: Quilcene watershed, about 100 miles by road from Seattle

Length: 11 miles out and back

Difficulty: Strenuous

Elevation gain: 3,350 feet

Maximum elevation: 6,280 feet

Map and books: Custom Correct: The Brothers—Mount Anderson, Washington; *100 Hikes in Washington's South Cascades and Olympics; Olympic Mountains Trail Guide; Cascade-Olympic Natural History*

Dogs: Yes

Permits: A Northwest Forest Pass is required on all vehicles parked at the trailhead. A $5 day pass or $30 annual pass is available at forest service offices, such as the Quilcene Ranger Station on US 101, and vendors such as REI. They are not available at trailheads. The forest service Web site is www.fs.fed.us/r6/Olympic.

Heads up: Rain-shadow hiking into the alpine with views.

Description: There aren't a lot of Olympic Peninsula hikes near the city that can give you big views, including a sense of the entire peninsula, the Strait of Juan de Fuca, Puget Sound, and mountains to the east. This is one of them. Located in the Olympic rain shadow, this hike is often snow-free early, particularly on the southeast slopes, which usually clear sometime in mid-June. Rhododendron and wildflower displays can be spectacular, with dusky blue delphiniums, penstemon, and Piper's bellflower on the list. The top of the mountain is exposed to the west wind, which is exhilarating or chilling, depending on the day.

Route: Take Mt. Townsend Trail (839) about 5.3 miles to the summit.

Directions: See *Getting to the Olympic Peninsula*. Once

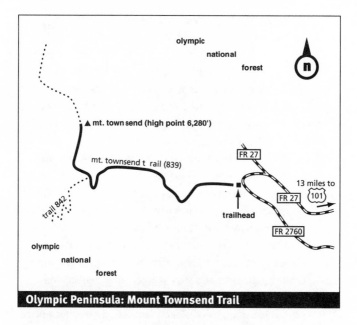

Olympic Peninsula: Mount Townsend Trail

on the peninsula, take US 101 to 1 mile south of Quilcene and turn right (west) onto Penny Creek Road for 1.4 miles, staying left at the Y. Continue on to the forest service boundary and paved FR 27. Proceed on FR 27 10.6 miles to FR 2760. Follow this 0.7 mile to the lower trailhead.

Olympic Peninsula Rain Shadow

WHILE THE WORDS "Olympic Peninsula" generally conjure up a demulcent atmosphere of moss, lichen, and ferns, like something out of Tolkien, there's another side to the picture.

Specifically, the leeward side. On the north and east slopes of the Olympics winds come in from the southwest, not the ocean, and the land is fairly well protected from the Pacific storms that dump rain on the south and west. Towns in this rain shadow, such as Port Angeles and Sequim, have been able to lure retirees to the area with the results of their rain gauges. "Welcome to Sunny Sequim" trumpets that town's Web site, claiming an annual rainfall of only 14 to 17 inches. (If you ever go to their annual Irrigation Festival, held in May, I'd certainly like to hear about it.)

The leeward side is also the one closest to Seattle, and therefore more accessible for short trips. You'll also be more likely to see other travelers, especially in summer. Hikers wishing to take advantage of this rain-shadow effect have plenty of outings to choose from, as almost 40 percent of the Olympic Mountains are in this region. Both Olympic Peninsula day hikes described are in the rain shadow, though they are unlikely to be quite as dry as weather-proud Sequim, which claims to have more sun than anywhere else in western Washington. Something to consider when you're looking for a place to dry out your tent.

Wilderness Meccas

After getting in shape on the trails in and around Seattle, and maybe even snatching a few after-work overnights close to home, you may be ready for several days of thigh-busting, backcountry backpacking. For this, consider going farther into the Cascades or the Olympics, both of which contain forest service and national park lands with various degrees of wilderness protection. I have chosen to highlight only two meccas below, because there are dozens of wilderness areas within visiting range, and it would take another book to cover them all. To the east, the Cascade Range, with its string of volcanoes, stretches south and north. High alpine mountaineering, camping, river running, hiking, rock climbing, and all kinds of other activities take place in this immense space. Up north, North Cascades National Park is one of the lesser-visited wild places in the Lower Forty-eight, and offers a chance to get away from crowds, even in high summer. Consult forest service and national park Web sites to gather information on backcountry trips in these areas. Local clubs, such as the Mountaineers and the Washington Trails Association, are also great resources.

I have offered details for two of the most revered wild areas in our state—Mount Rainier and Olympic National Parks. You'll need to plan ahead for backcountry adventures in either. You might want to decide first how many days you have, and if you're okay with an out and back trip or if you demand a loop, which will limit your options. Then it's time to gather maps and hike ideas, call for permits (sometimes, for a very popular route, you'll need to reserve months in advance), and maybe even break out a dehydrator and get going on the dehydrated grub.

MOUNT RAINIER NATIONAL PARK

Location: Just over 2 hours south of Seattle

Contact: The park service Web site is www.nps.gov/mora /recreation/wic.htm. The number for the Wilderness Information Center at the ranger station at Wilkeson, one of the closest to Seattle, is (360) 829-5127. More contact info is listed under *Pitching Tent* for Mount Rainier National Park.

Maps and books: See specific Green Trails and Park Service Maps for your chosen hike; *50 Hikes in Mount Rainier National Park; Hiking Mount Rainier National Park; Sunrise to Paradise*

Dogs: No

Description: It's our state's second most famous volcano; Mount St. Helens claimed the first-place title in 1980 with her spectacular eruption. Known simply as "the Mountain" to most Seattle-area residents, this snow-capped 14,410-foot ice cream sundae is not only a climbing destination but also a place for mind-blowing day hikes—and overnights, if you can get a permit. The mountain hasn't let off steam since the 1840s, but some say it's coming in the near future. Don't worry—you won't be melted by hot lava. Just steam-rolled by glacial debris and mud flows that would likely pave over surrounding lowlands, but stop short of Seattle itself.

This threat hasn't stopped people from waxing rhapsodic about the mountain, and about the surrounding park, established over a hundred years ago. A park publication from 1919 quotes various experts. John Muir: "Of all the fire-mountains which, like beacons, once blazed along the Pacific Coast, Mount Rainier is the noblest." F. E. Mathes, of the U.S. Geological Survey: "Easily King of all is Mount Rainier." The good press has obviously done its work, since nearly two million people visit here each year. When they arrive, they find a mix of forest, subalpine, and alpine landscapes, including huge glaciers. Permanent snow and ice cover almost 20 percent of the park, which encompasses not only the Mountain herself, but surrounding lowlands. Some old growth here is more than 1,000 years old. Even on a day hike you can visit one of these stands of ancient forest, or climb a lesser peak in the park and get a view of Rainier. Several areas are famous for wildflower meadows with hundreds of different plant species.

The park's popularity means high season can be very tough for getting backcountry permits. Rangers also report that the park gets incredibly busy anytime it's sunny and people spot the mountain from the city. If you're going to be doing technical climbing, snow camping, or skiing you can visit almost year-round, but hikers have a more limited window of opportunity. Access to most trails begins in June or July, and even then there can be hazardous conditions. Sometime in October most trails become inaccessible without snow equipment of some sort. There is technically no limit on the number of people day hiking on trails in the park, but access is limited by the number of cars allowed at each trailhead—no overflow parking is allowed.

Directions: Directions to Mount Rainier National Park vary by trailhead. Visit the park's Web site or consult guidebooks for specific directions.

PITCHING TENT

mount rainier national park

THE LARGE NUMBER of visitors to this park, combined with a much smaller backcountry area than, say, Olympic National Park, means you won't always be able to get away from other people, and you will need to plan well in advance. For this reason many local backpackers make the longer trek to the lesser-beaten paths of the Olympic Peninsula or to often overlooked North Cascades National Park for a wilderness experience. But sometimes only Rainier will do, particularly if you have come from across the country to see it.

A free Wilderness Camping Permit, required for camping in the park, is available at the Wilderness Information Centers at Longmire and White River, and any ranger station during the summer. There are limits for nearly all wilderness areas between May 1 and October 31. Three types of backcountry camping exist. Trailside camping is at designated trailside locations, with one to eight individual sites, a primitive toilet, and a nearby, untreated water supply, as well as a storage pole for hanging food and garbage away from bears. Cross-country camping, outside trail areas, can be done in certain park zones and is for the backcountry expert. Various rules apply. Alpine camping is generally for mountain climbers on the slopes of Rainier itself. Limits are placed on party size and number of parties, as well as locations.

Reservations are available starting April 1 for backpackers and climbers for camping any time from May 1 to September 30. They are optional and not always needed, according to the park, but on summer weekends it might be near impossible to camp without them. About 60 percent of the wilderness campsites and zones are reservable; the others are first-come, first served and disappear quickly. Reservations are available by fax or snail mail only. You can print out the reservation form from the park service Web site (www.nps.gov/mora/recreation/rsvpform.htm) and follow the fax or snail mail directions given. You can also make a reservation in person at the Longmire Wilderness Information Center. For more information call (360) 569-HIKE beginning Memorial Day weekend, but be aware that they may not be able to answer your call.

The Wonderland Trail

MOUNT RAINIER'S RENOWNED Wonderland Trail (see map, page 405) is a 93-mile loop around the park, rambling through lowland forests, wildflower meadows, and just about everything else the area has to offer, short of summitting the mountain itself. Hikers have done it in a few short days, but that seems to miss the point. The park recommends 10 to 14 days to enjoy it without succumbing to complete exhaustion; some suggest several years of visits. To make sure the trip is indeed wonderful, you will probably need to cache food and supplies at ranger stations along the trail, or have a good friend hike in on a designated day to restock your supply. And understand that the weather can be unpredictable. My friend Kathryn True was turned back two-thirds of the way through by an early October snowstorm. Despite that, she emerged from the woods entranced, and has vowed to return and complete it all. Here's what she told me:

"I will never forget swimming in an aqua glacial pool near Summerland and then sitting on the sandy edge to dry in the sun, or watching bears eating berries at Spray Park. Emilie saw elk and was amazed at their size. It's amazing to hear the crack of glaciers and see boulders tumbling down as something shifts. There are some of the most scenic outhouse views in the state. You feel like you could touch the top of the mountain from many of the high points. It's like walking a big roller-coaster, because you go up and down into and out of the valleys and over and alongside glaciers. It is very challenging, especially with a full pack. We had near-perfect weather. There are several impressive waterfalls. You feel like you are really getting under Rainier's skin. It is an intimate experience with the mountain, something more personal than scaling her heights—like you are getting to know her."

OLYMPIC NATIONAL PARK

Location: Olympic Peninsula, west of Seattle

Contact: To plan a trip, particularly into the backcountry, get in touch with the Wilderness Information Center (WIC) in Port Angeles (360-565-3100, e-mail olymwic@nps.gov). To get there take US 101 on the Olympic Peninsula to Port Angeles. Once in town follow signs to the Olympic National Park Visitor Center. WIC is behind the center. They can assist with permits, trip planning, and advance reservations for restricted areas. The park also has numerous visitors centers around the peninsula. For a full list and quite a bit more information see www.nps.gov/olym/home.htm.

Maps and books: Consult USGS topographic maps; *Olympic Mountains Trail Guide; 100 Hikes in Washington's South Cascades and Olympics.* Many maps and books can be ordered from the park's store at www.nps.gov/mora/NWIA/nwia.htm#maps.

Dogs: No

Description: One of the most accessible temperate rain forests in the world starts just a couple of hours from Seattle. Spectacular alpine scenery combined with the surreal, moss-draped wonderland of the park's old-growth forest make a visit one of the backpacking experiences of a lifetime.

If at all possible, give yourself time to really explore. A multiday trip is ideal. Go deep into the rain forest to encounter huge Western red cedar, Douglas fir, and hemlock and, most likely, a variety of wildlife. Black bear, cougar, coyote, Roosevelt elk, the Olympic marmot, and many other mammals, birds, and other creatures have found homes in this protected place. No roads lead through the heart of the park, so you'll have to pick one of the access points and head in from there. Rain forest areas adjoin several rivers, including the Hoh, Queets, and Quinault. Access to higher alpine areas is at Hurricane Ridge, where you can head out for a beautiful day hike and get a bigger view of the area.

Another trip could focus on the coast. The park encompasses large strips of Olympic Peninsula beach, which lend themselves to overnights or even week-long hikes if you arrange for a shuttle. Some of the richest tide pools in the world are here. Huge rock formations called sea stacks jut out of a crashing ocean, seabirds hang like kites in the wind, and the Pacific lends a sense of infinity.

Wherever you go on the peninsula, be prepared for it to be wet. The rain shadow side of the mountains (see page 187) is somewhat drier, but in the rain forest and on the coast you'll need good raingear and a psyche prepared for boots squish-squishing, rain beading on your eyelashes, and a gentle but perhaps clammy end to the day in your moss-covered rain-forest campsite. Ask a local backpacker for their best-drenched tale—several days of nonstop precip are certainly possible. But for the right person, this is the only way they'd have it. As one hiker said, "It's like hiking in Alice's Wonderland. Everything is outsized—big trees, incredible moss—and all startlingly green."

Directions: Directions to Olympic National Park vary by trailhead. To get to the Olympic Peninsula, see page 182. To get to specific trailheads visit the park's Web site or consult guidebooks for directions.

PITCHING TENT
olympic national park

THERE ARE HUNDREDS of spectacular places to camp within park boundaries. Unlike forest service areas, these places tend to be restricted, and many require reservations and advance planning.

You'll need a Wilderness Camping Permit for any overnight stay in the backcountry. Get one at the Wilderness Information Center in Port Angeles or year-round at the Information Center in Forks. In summer some of the park's other visitors centers and ranger stations also provide them. Some remote trailheads offer self-registration. Several high-use areas have quotas, and reservations need to be made (though no more than 30 days beforehand) by calling the WIC (360-565-3100). Visit the WIC Web site at www.nps.gov/olym/wic/index.html for more information. Wilderness use fees are currently $5 registration plus $2 per person, per night. Annual passes are available.

Where to Connect

Clubs and Organizations

- Issaquah Alps Trails Club (www.issaquahalps.org, for general inquiries e-mail david_langrock@yahoo.com) was founded in 1979 to preserve open space on Cougar, Squak, Tiger, Taylor, and Rattlesnake Mountains, and on Grand Ridge. They continue to advocate for these areas, and to organize free outings to members and the general public.

- The Mountaineers (206-284-6310, www.mountaineers.org) offers classes in mountaineering, skiing, climbing, and all kinds of outdoor activity, as well as extensive information on trails and other resources.

- Washington Trails Association (1305 4th Ave. Suite 512, 206-625-1367, www.wta.org) is a volunteer-driven, nonprofit that has been around since 1966. They have contributed countless hours to trail maintenance and advocacy, and maintain a phenomenal Web site that offers trip reports from hundreds of trails all over the area.

Shops and Outfitters

- Feathered Friends (119 Yale Ave. N., 206-292-2210) is just across the street from the flagship REI, but smaller and with attitude. They built a reputation for down gear (in the damp Northwest, no less), but sell and rent a variety of equipment.

- Marmot Mountain Works (827 Bellevue Way N.E. in Bellevue, 425-453-1515, www.marmotmountain.com) offers backpacking, climbing, cross-country skiing, and ski mountaineering gear. The staff is very knowledgeable and has a great reputation.

- Recreation Equipment Outfitters (REI) (222 Yale Ave. N., 206-223-1944, www.rei.com) sells and rents just about everything. This famous store is as much amusement park as hardware emporium. REI has shops in Federal Way, Lynnwood, Redmond, Tukwila, and Tacoma.

- Second Ascent (5209 Ballard Ave. N.W., 206-545-8810) sells new and used outdoors equipment. [See page 210.]

Books

- Barchi, Peggy. *Eastside Family Hikes.* Issaquah, WA: Issaquah Alps Trails Club,* 2001.

- Dolan, Maria, and Kathryn True. *Nature in the City: Seattle.* Seattle, WA: Mountaineers Books, 2003.

- Graydon, Don, and Kurt Hanson, eds. *The Freedom of the Hills.* 6th ed. Seattle, WA: Mountaineers Books, 1997. Essential guide to the outdoors, including safety, weather, geology, climbing techniques, building snow caves.

- Judd, Ron C. *Day Hike! Mount Rainier.* Seattle, WA: Sasquatch Books, 2002.

- Kirk, Ruth. *Sunrise to Paradise: The Story of Mount Rainier National Park.* Seattle: University of Washington Press, 1999.

- Longwell, Bill. *Guide to Trails of Tiger Mountain.* Issaquah, WA: Issaquah Alps Trails Club, 1995. Useful map included.

- Manning, Harvey. *55 Hikes Around Snoqualmie Pass: Mountains-to-Sound Greenway.* 2d ed. Seattle, WA: Mountaineers Books, 2001.

- Manning, Harvey, and Ira Spring. *50 Hikes in Mount Rainier National Park.* 4th ed. Seattle, WA: Mountaineers Books, 1999.

———. *100 Classic Hikes in Washington.* Seattle, WA: Mountaineers Books, 2001.

———. *100 Hikes in Washington's South Cascades and Olympics.* Seattle, WA: Mountaineers Books, 1992.

*All Issaquah Alps Trails Club books are available by mail order. Check www.issaquahalps.org for more information.

- Mathews, Daniel. *Cascade-Olympic Natural History: A Trailside Reference.* Portland, OR: Raven Editions, 1999. A knockout field guide that's actually too big to carry on a trail. Regional, natural, and human history, with notes on specific species.

- McCrone, Charles. *The Authoritative Guide to the Hiking Trails of Cougar Mountain Regional Wildland Park and Surrounds.* Issaquah, WA: Issaquah Alps Trails Club, 2001. Anecdotes as well as facts and a useful map.

- McDonald, Cathy M. and Stephen R. Whitney. *Nature Walks in and Around Seattle.* Seattle, WA: Mountaineers Books, 1998.

- Schneider, Heidi. *Hiking Mount Rainier National Park.* Helena, MT: Falcon Books, 1999.

- Suiter, John. *Poets on the Peaks: Gary Snyder, Philip Whalen and Jack Kerouac in the North Cascades.* New York: Counterpoint Press, 2002. Beatnik mountain men.

- Weinmann, Fred, Ann Weinmann, and Harvey Manning. *The Flowering of the Issaquah Alps.* Issaquah, WA: Issaquah Alps Trails Club, 1996.

- Wood, Robert L. *Olympic Mountains Trail Guide: National Park and National Forest.* Seattle, WA: Mountaineers Books, 2000.

Links

www.gorp.com offers planning guides and travel advice for outdoor adventure.

www.wta.org for Washington Trails Association

www.eskimo.com/~pc22/WWW/wilderness-without-wheels.html for Washington Wilderness Without Wheels, devoted to ways to get to trailheads without bringing a car. The Mountaineers Web site also discusses this.

THE GOOD NEWS is that Seattle is remarkably close to some excellent climbing. If you knock off work early, or only have a small window of playtime one weekend, you will still have the chance to climb outside. Farther afield, the state is blessed with a variety of great rock, from the cliffs in Index, northeast of Seattle, to the granite and sandstone in Leavenworth on the east side of the Cascade Mountain range.

The bad news, as you might have guessed, is the weather. "People from California, Wyoming think we're crazy," says climber Maria Lee. "We're out on rocks that have moss on them. Half the time I get spit off the rock because of the weather." Rock climbers here must resign themselves to spending the damper seasons at indoor gyms or picking up ice climbing or some other winter sport to tide them over. Come summer, though, most climbers will find much to occupy their days, including some satisfying nearby destinations and some really nice (and dry) climbing hubs on the east side of the mountains.

The climbing community may have a few more challenges to overcome than in true rock meccas, but that makes our climbers the intrepid sort. If you're new to the sport, don't try to figure it out on your own. Hook up with locals and be sure to take some classes—this isn't a danger-free sport, and falling from even a smallish boulder can be lethal under the right circumstances. A good place to meet like-minded people is at one of the area's indoor climbing gyms, which tend to be friendly and very busy, especially in the aforementioned wet season. The gym will get your fingers and mind ready for the outdoors, and the classes will help with technique. Another option is to take an outdoor class from a local climbing club; these usually happen in spring and summer. One choice is the Washington Alpine Club, whose small, multiweek classes on rock climbing, backcountry travel, and telemark skiing are popular and rumored to be serious fun.

There's not room in this chapter, or this book, for a comprehensive guide to all available rock. I've picked out a combination of the best nearby climbing mixed with a couple of great climbing meccas to give a taste of what's out there. I don't describe routes or offer very technical information—for this seek out the guidebooks listed and visit the Web sites mentioned. For the same reasons, this is not a chapter on bagging major peaks or anything else that might be called serious mountaineering.

Climbers are always developing new areas or finding new routes in old ones, so you probably won't run out of things to do. More information can be found at the climbing shops and in local guidebooks. *Selected Climbs in the Cascades* and Jeff Smoot's *Rock Climbing Washington* are both well known. Be aware that the latter guide gets mixed reviews from climbers, a picky lot, some of whom claim it's best for advanced climbers, or that it leaves out some areas or isn't quite accurate. Lesson: Don't expect any one book to give you the complete climbing beta. Use each resource as one tool in your gear rack. Talking to local climbers and doing some exploring is half the fun.

Mastering the Lingo

R OCK CLIMBING, like many sports, has its own language. "Don't go there, that's chossy rock," they'll say, or "I was spit off the wall." Some is just jargon and fun to throw out over a beer—try *chossy* (crumbly or soft) three times fast. Other terms you'll actually need to know to get anywhere. A few of them are defined below. Fling them about like Mardi Gras beads to get in the spirit.

Trad climbing: If you're going trad (traditional) climbing you (or your partner) will be using your own gear, placing it as you go up the rock. You will need to know exactly how to do this. The gear itself can include hexes, cams, stoppers, slings, and the like. A basic set of gear is called a "standard rack."

Sport climbing: Sport climbing, such as what is offered at Deception Crags, involves rock that already has gear bolted to it. You attach yourself into the gear as you climb the rock. Theoretically (though not in all instances), this requires less training than trad, since the protection has already been placed. Some sport climbs, especially on older routes, may contain run-outs, where the spaces between bolts are too long. In those cases you'll have to place your own gear.

Top rope/top roping: Rope anchors have been set at the top of the climb. Most gym climbing involves top roping.

Multipitch: This kind of climb on bigger walls requires more than one length of rope. You probably won't be doing this if you don't know what it means.

The **Yosemite decimal system** is commonly used to rate rock climbing difficulty. The scale is generally 5.0 to 5.14 c/d. Higher is harder.

Backyard

LITTLE SI

Location: North Bend, about 30 miles east of Seattle
Book: *Rock Climbing Washington*
Heads up: Sport climbing heaven
Description: Little Si (1,576 feet) is the sidekick to the ever-popular North Bend hiking and trail running destination Big Si, neglected by many of those folks because it's shorter and less demanding. That's good news for rock climbers, giving them more room among the conifers, boulders, and sometimes even mountain goats. World Wall I, with routes from 5.9 to 5.13, is considered by some to be the best sport climbing wall in Washington. It is almost entirely overhung, and some climbs are two pitches. Also recommended is Reptiles and Amphetamines, 5.9, and Rainy Day Women, 5.11d or 5.12a.

Directions: Go east on I-90 to North Bend, exit 31. One mile from the east edge of town, turn left on S.E. Mount Si Rd. past the North Bend Ranger Station. Cross the bridge over the Middle Fork of the Snoqualmie River. Take a right a few hundred feet down the road and locate the large parking area for Little Si on your left. After parking, follow the trail off the lot signed for Little Si and climbing areas.

DECEPTION CRAGS—EXIT 38

Location: Off I-90 between North Bend and Snoqualmie Pass

Books: *Exit 38 Rock Climbing Guide; Selected Climbs in the Cascades; Rock Climbing Washington*

Heads up: An after-work destination; check out www .deceptioncrags.com to see panoramic views of the different areas.

Description: The Deception Crags Web site describes it as "one of the newest and best single-pitch bolted rock climbing areas in Washington," while Jeff Smoot in *Rock Climbing Washington* mentions loose rock and some poor climbing routes. The truth lies somewhere in the middle. This is a very popular sport-climbing destination for urbanites looking for some after-work adventure. There is no trad climbing. The beginner and intermediate routes make this the place many local climbers go to learn solid skills before heading to one of the farther-off climbing hubs. Bryan Burdo has written an entire book on climbing and helped develop many of the routes—look to his guide (updated by Garth Bruce) for details. Nevermind Wall in the Trestle area is recommended for great routes and for staying dry in the shoulder seasons. Amazonia Wall, accessible from the Mt. Washington trail, has routes between 5.9 and 5.10. We Did Rock, on top of the trestle, is especially good for first-time visitors.

Directions: Take exit 38 off I-90 and turn right. Park in Mount Washington parking, beside the Mount Washington trailhead. Hike in a few minutes to the climbing area. If you are climbing in the Trestle area, you can continue on the road past the first parking lot 0.5 mile to Change Creek. Park and cross the road, taking an obvious trail to the right of the creek to the climbing areas.

Washington Alpine Club

A LOCAL INSTITUTION, the WAC has been around since 1916. One of its founders, the aptly named Anna Louise Strong, was the original Riot Grrl. A tough, adventurous, and well-educated woman, she led the first winter climb of Mount Hood, guided on Mount Rainier, and became a social pariah for decades because of her socialist views and agitation against the U.S. entry into World War I. She eventually became tight with Mao Tse-Tung and was buried in Beijing with state honors. The club outlasted the political controversy. WAC membership gets you access to classes and a club-owned cabin at Snoqualmie Pass, and a chance to meet the people you'll be climbing with for the next 40 years—or at least until you take off for Cuba or plot a military coup. The WAC is one of the best places to sign up for a beginning or intermediate rock climbing class. "We all love to hang out with each other," says climber Maria Lee, "so usually there are almost too many instructors for each student. It becomes a social event." Check out www.wacweb.org or call (206) 467-3042.

Short Hops

INDEX TOWN WALLS

Location: 1 to 1½ hours northeast of Seattle

Book: *Sky Valley Rock*

Heads up: Popular, with many advanced routes. Check out the Bush House Country Inn Restaurant in Index for a decent meal or lodging.

Description: Index Town Walls are some of the most

popular climbing in Washington, and one of the few easily accessible aid-climbing areas—that is, wall—that require gear to ascend. There's sport climbing here, but it's not particularly popular—Index is best known for trad routes with up to six pitches. The American Alpine Institute, which teaches classes here, hails the place for having a larger concentration of clean, steep cracks than just about anywhere else in the United States. Located behind the tiny town of Index and above the scenic Skykomish River, this destination is known for the challenging climbing and for its beautiful setting. The main black-and-white granite walls are steep, with hundreds of routes, including quite a few 5.10 to 5.12s. Keep in mind that ratings for these routes are often "sandbagged," meaning you'll probably find them harder than their ratings suggest. As with most other western Washington areas, this one is too damp for comfort for most of the winter and spring. However, the walls offer a good alternative to the heat of Leavenworth (see page 208) in late summer. City Park, a 5.13, is a notorious climb, and for a short time was known as the hardest free climb in America—to date only two people have free-climbed it.

Directions: From Seattle take I-5 north about 30 miles to Everett, then go east on US 2. As you enter the town of Index, turn left at Index-Galena Rd. (watch for the Mount Index Café). Take a left at a bridge over the Skykomish. Go straight past the Index General Store and make a left at the T intersection with Bush House on your right. Follow the river down until you get to a small parking lot on the right. The walls are in front of you.

MOUNT ERIE

Location: About 70 miles north of Seattle
Heads up: If it's a weekend, a climbing group or club may

have plans to bring their students here. To avoid disappointment you can call ahead to the City of Anacortes Parks and Recreation (360-293-1918) and see if any groups have scheduled such a trip.

Description: Erie, a mountain with a road to the top, is a destination for tourists seeking views as well as climbers and those out for light day hikes. With reason—it's easily accessible and capped by scenic splendor. Bald eagles soar and swoop in front of the cliffs, while everyone gapes at the Cascades, the San Juan Islands, and the sweep of Puget Sound. Some fairly easy routes draw rock-climbing classes, but the mountain offers variety. Student Wall has several beginner routes, including the aptly named Top Roping. There's both sport and trad climbing, as well as bouldering near the bottom, which is growing in popularity, especially since a bouldering competition has sprung up.

Directions: Take I-5 north to exit 230, just past Mount Vernon. Follow signs for WA 20. Turn left at the fork, staying on WA 20 toward Deception Pass rather than going right to Anacortes. Turn right on Campbell Lake Rd. Take the next right (the cliffs, are now visible on the right) and continue 1 mile to the park entrance. Continue on Ray Auld Dr. from the entrance gate to the summit. There are individual parking spots along the way, and various trails leading to the walls.

Meccas

VANTAGE AND FRENCHMAN COULEE

Location: Central Washington, about 150 miles east of Seattle

Book: *Frenchman Coulee: A Rock Climber's Guide*

Heads up: Hot in summer, loose rocks, rattlesnakes. If you have extra time, check out the nearby Ginkgo Petrified Forest State Park. Good food at the Valley Café in Ellensburg, 28 miles before Vantage on I-90.

Description: Just beside the Columbia River is the hottest climbing destination in Washington—temperature, that is. The basalt columns, folded like an accordion, that rise up at Frenchman Coulee are a destination for many climbers in spring and fall, when western Washington is socked in and even Leavenworth might be experiencing wet weather. This fact and the presence of some great, challenging climbs counterbalance the many caveats shared by climbers: Summer heat will sear you like Angus beef. If you're not avoiding heat stroke, it may be because you've taken a knock to the head. The climbs are on basalt that can be quite flaky, so particular attention needs to be paid to how you belay, where you walk, and where you park your dog. You must wear a helmet. (Consult books and Web resources for more details on the rock before you go.) This is a desert, so watch out for rattlesnakes. And finally, Frenchman Coulee is located within listening distance of the Gorge Amphitheater. If it is a summer weekend, you may very well enjoy the Motley Crüe revival tour and the all-night parking lot revelry that follows. Camping is primitive and not too appealing, and there is no water—bring your own. Use the trails, since this is a very fragile desert environment.

The Feathers is known as a popular spot for beginners. Sunshine Wall also draws climbers—it's got good sport climbs but is rated moderate to difficult.

Directions: Take I-90 east about 140 miles to exit 143 (Silica Rd.). Go north on Silica Rd. and turn left onto the old Vantage Hwy., the first paved road on the left. Continue a little over a mile to parking for the Feathers, and a jot farther for Agatha Tower parking.

LEAVENWORTH

Location: About 120 miles northeast of Seattle

Books: *Leavenworth Rock; Rock Climbing Washington*

Heads up: Watch out for sudden afternoon rain and thunderstorms in summer. Also, the town of Leavenworth fancies itself a Bavarian village. Do not be alarmed by lederhosen, yodeling, polka bands, and Wiener schnitzel. It may be hard to find the right grub. There are a couple of supermarkets on the main highway, and a restaurant called Gustav's that is both loved and vilified by the climbing set—loved for its good beer and pub food, and decried by some as a sellout because of a post-fire remodel that removed some of its quirky character. Worth a visit.

Description: A favorite of Washington climbers for its diversity, gorgeous location, and sunny weather, Leavenworth is worth the drive. (Consider turning your trip into a multisport adventure. In the same area you'll find day and backcountry hiking, whitewater kayaking and rafting on the Wenatchee River, and fishing. See the appropriate chapters in this book.) Known as the birthplace of Washington rock climbing, it was scouted out as early as the 1940s by such legendary climbers as Fred Beckey. The climbing is in four major areas: Icicle Creek Canyon, Snow Creek Wall, Tumwater Canyon and—technically just outside the Leavenworth area—Peshastin Pinnacles. Climbing ranges from crack, face, and slab routes on the solid granite and gneiss of Tumwater and Icicle Creek to the sandstone of Peshastin Pinnacles to the east. (There's more sun here than just about anywhere else in the state, which in late summer can mean it's too hot for some.) At this point, head back across the mountains to the Index Town Walls.

Specific rock recommendations include the great views of Snow Creek Wall, which is accessible after an hour or so of hiking—get the beta from someone at the campground or trailhead. The multipitch routes on this wall will take all day. Classics include Outerspace and Orbit. This is not beginner climbing and will require route finding. It's mostly trad, with occasional bolts. Icicle Creek Canyon has many buttresses, with trad, sport, and even top-roping options. Many classes climb at Mountaineers Dome and Barney's Rubble. Also popular are Careno Crag, Icicle Buttress, 8-mile Buttress, and Alphabet Rock. If you are willing to hike up and off the road away from the most accessible climbs you can escape the crowds.

Peshastin Pinnacles, which can be even drier than Leavenworth itself, is slabby and flaky, with some easy beginner routes.

Directions: Take I-5 north toward Everett, turning off onto US 2. Head east about 85 miles over Stevens Pass to Leavenworth. At the west end of Leavenworth is Icicle Creek Road. Turn right here. Most of the climbing areas are within the next ten miles.

PITCHING TENT

leavenworth

THERE ARE PLENTY of hotels, motels, and Bavarian inns in Leavenworth, but they tend to be pricey, and, in most seasons, stuffed with tourists. If you want to avoid this, plan to camp near the climbing areas. Camaraderie is a side benefit to camping when you climb, and you might net some new companions. The favorite sites are either the Eightmile or Bridge Creek Campgrounds, both in Icicle Creek Canyon along Icicle Creek Road. Bear in mind that busy summer weekends and holidays can completely obliterate camping opportunities. Plan ahead and try to get there early.

Both Bridge Creek and Eightmile Campgrounds are in the

Leavenworth Ranger District: the forest service can provide details on other campground availability (509-548-6977). Bridge Creek has 45 sites, including one that can be reserved for a group (800-274-6104). Prices are around $11 for the first car and $8 for the second, with a group rate of $86. The group reservation can be made a week to six months in advance. Bridge Creek has six sites with one reservation group site. Prices are comparable to Eightmile. All other sites are first come, first to get a decent spot. Eightmile is 8 miles up Icicle Creek Road from US 2, and Bridge Creek is 9.4 miles.

Second Ascent

DOUBT MOST 30-SOMETHING customers rummaging for equipment in this 5,000-square-foot outdoors store are aware of the adventurous history that surrounds them. Does Mr. Geek Chic, pillaging the box of used gaiters, realize he's standing under Ed Viesturs's Mount Everest snowsuit? Does the woman fingering that gaudy Aloha shirt emblazoned with carabiners and pickaxes recognize it as one of Yvon Chouinard's early forays into clothing design? Above a rack of ski pants is a wall decorated with antique wooden ice axes. In another spot hangs a lineup of worn out backpacks, each with a history. Be sure to get a look at the one that belonged to a well-known nudist mountaineer—maybe the staff will let you try it on for a special thrill?

When last visiting the store, I suggested posting some museum-type plaques to alert others to the legendary leftovers they were browsing under, but owner Greg Shaw was sanguine about the anonymity of his gear museum. He's more concerned about pressure from the people who *do* know. "I don't want to sell most of this stuff, and some people who come in want to buy it from me. They get frustrated seeing it hanging there all the time."

The store is more likely to satisfy than provoke its customers. SA sells new and used outdoors equipment and offers something, at a decent price, for just about everyone who goes outside. There are new and used fleece jackets for every man, woman, and child; mountain bikes; camp stoves; climbing ropes; snowboards; guidebooks; and boots and shoes of all stripes. They rent snowshoes and repair bikes. You can drop $200 on a new Marmot parka, or dig up parts for your 1970s Optimus 8R camp stove. And if you happen to be looking for an early pair of clipless bike pedals? The kind you have to unclip manually, or be forever wedded to your bike? Well, you're in luck.

The people who work here—mostly guys with hair in various states of dishevelment—are laid-back and welcoming to whomever walks in the door, from people who just want a cheap fleece vest to hard-core athletes. Mountaineer Greg Child, climber Lynn Hill, and plenty of other local and national bigwigs have dropped in to sell or buy equipment. Shaw, age 31, who describes himself as a jack-of-all-trades when it comes to his own outdoor interests, worked at mainstream ski and sporting goods stores before he bought into Second Ascent and, over the last seven years or so, made it his own. He wanted the place to be an alternative to typical outdoors stores, a place where some products are at thrift-store prices and used equipment is recycled instead of getting tossed into a landfill. Shaw guesses that they've got a larger variety of stock than just about any other Seattle shop, since they carry not just a few lines of, say, backpacks, but lots of different models, from different years, both new and used. It's a good place to come if you're avoiding the high-priced gear meccas, since you won't find any chocolate-covered cherries or $300 sunglasses here. Of course, if you're interested in some old ice-screw prototypes, drop in—they're on the wall. Just don't ask if they're for sale.

Where to Connect

Clubs and Schools

- American Alpine Institute (1515 12th St. in Bellingham, 360-671-1505, www.mtnguide.com/default.asp). Teaches beginning, intermediate, and advanced rock climbing.

- Boeing Alpine Society (www.boealps.org). Classes, group outings. Membership for non-Boeing employees is limited.

- The Mountaineers (300 Third Ave. W., 206-284-8484, 800-573-8484, www.mountaineers.org). This famous and all-encompassing outdoors club has a long climbing history. They offer basic to advanced climbing courses, seminars, and outings around Puget Sound.

- University of Washington Climbing Club (www.students.washington.edu/climb). Membership open to UW students, faculty, and staff.

- Washington Alpine Club (P.O. Box 352, 206-467-3042, www.wacweb.org). Classes, outings, and a cabin on Snoqualmie Pass for members.

Shops

- Backpacker's Supply (5206 S. Tacoma Way in Tacoma, 253-472-4402)

- Der Sportsman (837 Front St. in Leavenworth, 509-548-5623). If you can scramble your way through the tourists, you'll find some respite here.

- Feathered Friends (119 Yale Ave. N., 206-292-2210). Just across the street from the flagship REI, but smaller and with attitude. They built a reputation for down gear (in the damp Northwest, no less), but sell and rent a variety of equipment. Knowledgeable about climbing.

- Marmot Mountain Works (827 Bellevue Way N.E. in Bellevue, 425-453-1515, www.marmotmountain.com). Just east of Seattle in Bellevue, this store has backpacking, climbing, and cross-country and ski mountaineering gear. Staff is very knowledgeable with a great reputation.

- Pro Mountain Sports (5625 University Way N.E., 206-522-1627). Owner Jim Nelson is up on all things climbing. The store's hours are irregular; call to check.

- Recreation Equipment Inc. (222 Yale Ave. N., 206-223-1944). The famous REI's flagship store is as much amusement park as hardware store. They sell and rent just about everything, and you can try out the climbing pinnacle while you're there. Additional shops in Federal Way, Lynnwood, Redmond, Tukwila, and Tacoma.

- Second Ascent (5209 Ballard Ave. N.W., 206-545-8810). A great store with new climbing gear and new and used outdoors equipment. (See page 210.)

Books

- Beckey, Fred. *Cascade Alpine Guide: Climbing and High Routes. Volume 1: Columbia River to Stevens Pass.* 3rd ed. Seattle, WA: Mountaineers Books, 2000. More about mountaineering than rock climbing, this is a classic, combining practical advice with the geology and history of the Cascades. There are three Beckey volumes, and they are essential reading for anyone who wants to delve into the local mountain detail. They're also expensive and overwhelming, so prepare yourself.

- Bruce, Garth. *Exit 38 Rock Climbing Guide.* North Bend, WA: Free Solo Publishing, 2002.

- Cramer, Darryl. *Sky Valley Rock: A Guide to the Rock Climbs of the Skykomish River Valley.* Bishop, CA: Spotted Dog Press, 2000.

- Ford, Marlene, and Jim Yoder. *Frenchman Coulee: A Rock Climber's Guide.* Homepress, 1998.

- Kramar, Viktor. *Leavenworth Rock.* Leavenworth, WA: Snowcreek Design, 1996.

- Nelson, Jim, and Peter Potterfield. *Selected Climbs in the Cascades.* 2 vols. Seattle, WA: Mountaineers Books, 2000.

- Smoot, Jeff. *Rock Climbing Washington.* Guilford, CT: Globe Pequot, 1999

Links

www.nwac.noaa.gov for Northwest Weather and Avalanche Center

www.wsdot.wa.gov/Rweather has real-time road and weather information from the Washington State Department of Transportation.

www.ClimbingWashington.com is Jeff Smoot's Web site, with great stories and links.

www.cascadeclimbers.com is a resource for Northwest climbing.

www.users.owt.com/wrobins covers Vantage and Frenchman Coulee.

www.accessfund.org for info on a nonprofit dedicated to climbing access and conservation.

http://students.wahington.edu/dbb/uw_buildering/index.html is an outlaw guide to building climbs on the University of Washington campus. For armchair reading only!

I N SEATTLE, MANY people retreat to health club cardio machines to make it from hiking season to serious snow season, or from the snow season to dry summer weather. There's just too much dank out there for many folks, fly-fishing junkies excepted. Despite the fact that this book has given a hundred other things to do outside during those frustrating shoulder seasons, I understand the desire to stay warm and dry on occasion. An alternative to stepping monotonously to nowhere under fluorescent lights can be found at a local climbing gym. Once you find your way to one of these dens of agility, you are unlikely to return to regular gym-going ever again. My first experience was like that. Instead of repetition, climbing was about trying something new each time. In addition to firing up my deltoids, this sport kept my mind working, my courage challenged, and my fingers, toes, and spine involved. Like dancing or playing basketball, it engages the whole body. It feels more like playing than anything else. There's camaraderie, too, since, unless you're bouldering, you'll need someone on belay. And there are always experts to stand and gawk at while you're taking a break.

Seattle is home to one of the first climbing gyms in the country and to a gym with the biggest artificial walls for bouldering on the entire West Coast. This chapter covers these and several others. The gyms have weight rooms, pro shops for buying and renting gear, and classes to get you started. I've also listed three outdoor artificial walls, where you'll be on your own for lessons and gear but can show up for free anytime you're ready. Get off that treadmill and climb.

City Limits

REI PINNACLE

222 Yale Ave. N.
(206) 223-1944, 888-873-1938
www.rei.com/stores/seattle/pinnacle.html
Location: Just north of downtown Seattle off I-5
Description: You're sure to have seen people scrambling all over this edifice if you've ever visited the REI flagship store. It's the largest freestanding indoor pinnacle of its kind, 65 feet of steel and concrete with routes from 5.4 to 5.12. Everyone, from exacting experts to rank novices, has come in to try it out, says manager Pat Jouppy, but most are just dropping in for the novelty.

Aside from the ropes, handholds, and air of sweaty intensity, this place differs in a few important ways from a climbing gym. For one thing, only Pinnacle staff, all experienced climbers, are allowed to belay. This will discourage those who want to pair up, but for many offers a good alternative when there's no one around to chalk up with. At only $3 per route, it's a pretty sweet deal, especially compared to the investment you'd make trying out most technical sports.

Unlike most climbing gyms, there's no weight-lifting area, locker room, or stretch class. And you may have to push through a crowd of tourists to find your spot. The Pinnacle has challenged everyone from the Seattle Police SWAT team to the Girls' School of Seattle (Jouppy's favorite visitors). The place can be reserved for group climbs—up to five people can ascend at once.

The Redmond REI has a climbing wall half this height, and the Lynnwood store has a smaller wall. Those REIs have different rules—call for more information.

Directions: From downtown Seattle drive north on I-5 to the Olive Way exit. Follow Olive Way to Bellevue Ave. Turn left onto Bellevue and left onto Denny Way. Cross over the freeway, turn right onto Pontius Ave. and right again onto Thomas St. REI is on the right at 222 Yale Ave.

STONE GARDENS

2839 N.E. Market St.

(206) 781-9828, www.stonegardens.com

Location: Ballard, northwest of downtown

Description: You'll feel like you've ratcheted up your sexy hipster quotient about 50 percent just by hanging out here. Lithe men lean back on belay, their rippled thighs not even straining under the weight of burly and buff women descending from towering pillars. This place is welcoming, professional, and quite established, open since 1995. I took my first indoor climbing lesson here and learned the ropes from Becky Bradshaw, who also got her start at this gym. I would recommend her to any climbing novice—she was patient, funny, and extremely encouraging as I sweated my way from one stingy handhold to the next. Stone Gardens recently added 6,000 square feet of space, and they've now got a 30-foot pillar and dome for more top-roping and lead climbing. With 3,500 square feet of bouldering space, manager Bruce Andresen says they now offer more bouldering wall than any other climbing gym on the West Coast. They also have the tallest outdoor climbing wall in Seattle—40 feet high with routes from 5.6 to 5.14. The outside wall is open during the "non-rainy months," which they claim are from March to October. I like their optimism. The gym caters to all levels, and Bruce says they pride themselves on being "the friendly gym." Youth programs, summer climbing camps, group climbing events, and a comprehensive class series are available.

Directions: From downtown Seattle, head north on I-5 to exit 169 (45th St.). Turn left (west) and continue several miles on 45th until it becomes N.W. Market St. Continue through the Ballard neighborhood. Stone Gardens is located on the left (south) side of the road just east of the Ballard Locks.

Stone Gardens Bouldering Competition

OULDERERS FROM ALL OVER the West come to town for this one-day event at Seattle's bouldering hotbed. Even if not participating you can come check out the talent—if, that is, you can get in the door. The event draws teen climbers as well as adults, and is wildly popular and fun for all levels. The atmosphere is supportive, and it's a great place to meet other climbers.

VERTICAL WORLD

2123 W. Elmore St.

(206) 283-4497, www.verticalworld.com

Location: Interbay/Magnolia, northwest of downtown

Description: Although I've also seen a gym in Denver claim this title, Vertical World insists they are "America's First Climbing Gym." The original Seattle gym was opened by rock climbers Rich Johnston and Dan Cauthorn in 1987, and the chain now has three outlets—one each in Ballard, Redmond, and Bremerton. The Ballard gym boasts 14,000 square feet of wall space, about 35 feet high, with leading, top-roping, bouldering, and a cardio machine and weight area. Dustin, the manager, says the gym is visited more by intermediate and beginning climbers, but some well-known mountaineering types also train there—drop in and look sharp, since he won't name names. There are more than 200 routes available, with 60 percent at 10B and below. Novices have plenty to work with. Some local climbers claim this place is less of a scene than Stone Gardens.

Directions: From Seattle take I-5 to exit 169 (45th St.). Turn left (west) onto 45th and drive several miles until it becomes N.W. Market St. Turn left at 15th Ave. N.W. and cross the Ballard Bridge. Take the first exit, Fisherman's Terminal/Emerson St. At the second traffic light turn right onto 21st and then left onto W. Elmore. The gym is on your right.

UNIVERSITY OF WASHINGTON CLIMBING ROCK

Location: Next to Husky Stadium on the University of Washington campus

Description: The second-oldest climbing structure in the United States, this campus climbing rock is officially for students and faculty. Unofficially, it is frequented by many people not wearing purple and yellow Husky regalia, who take advantage of free access to a great training wall with lots of cracks for practicing technique. Right next to the Montlake Cut, it's nicely located and visited by all levels of climbers—you'll even see kids. Like all the other outdoor climbing around here, it becomes dicey during the damp season.

Directions: From downtown take I-5 north about three miles to exit 169 toward N.E. 45th St./N.E. 50th St. Take the ramp toward N.E. 45th St./University of Washington. Turn right onto 45th. In several blocks turn right onto 50th Ave. N.E. Turn left onto N.E. Pacific St. Get in the turning lane at N.E. Pacific Place, just across from the University of Washington medical center and before the Montlake Bridge. Turn left onto N.E. Pacific Place. Continue straight at the next light, cross Montlake Blvd., and drive into the parking lot for Husky Stadium. Park in the lot to the right (south) of the stadium. Parking rates vary—if you don't want to pay, you'll need to seek parking elsewhere. Or come by bike—the wall is just off the Burke-Gilman Trail.

MARYMOOR PARK CLIMBING WALL

6046 W. Lake Sammamish Pkwy N.E., Redmond
(206) 296-8687, www.metrokc.gov/parks
Location: Redmond, just east of Seattle

Description: The triangles at Marymoor rival the bra cups of pop-star Madonna for pointy projection. Reaching 45 feet, this combination pinnacle and wall offers lots of bouldering opportunities as well as lead rope climbing from 5.5 to 5.12. There are slabs, pockets, roof routes, cracks, and whatever else you can dream up, along with a group of enthusiastic climbers on any sunny day. The place is especially popular with novices and children, but hardcore climbers show up, too.

Directions: Take I-5 to exit 168B, then WA 520 east toward Bellevue/Kirkland. Take the W. Lake Sammamish Pkwy. exit. At the bottom of the ramp, go right (south) on W. Lake Sammamish Pkwy. N.E. The park entrance is the next left at the traffic light.

SCHURMAN ROCK

Camp Long, Dawson Street, West Seattle
(206) 684-7434
www.cityofseattle.net/parks/environment/camplong
Location: West Seattle
Description: The first man made climbing rock in the United States may still be undergoing renovation by the time this book comes out. One of the city's favorite places to try out skills since the 1930s, set in the midst of woodsy Camp Long, a city park, it was closed in 1999 because of deterioration. The local climbing and parks communities have been working to restore this legendary 20-foot pile of stone.

Directions: Take I-5 to the West Seattle Bridge, exit 163A. Merge onto the bridge. At the first light after the bridge, turn left on 35th Ave. S.W. Go nearly a mile to Dawson St. Turn left here to enter the park.

Backyard

VERTICAL WORLD

15036-B 95th St., Redmond
(425) 881-8826, www.verticalworld.com
Location: Several miles east of Seattle
Description: A spin-off of Seattle's Vertical World, this gym is smaller, at 8,500 square feet, with more of an emphasis on bouldering. There is also a new, full-sized Vertical World in Bremerton.
Directions: From Seattle take I-520 east. Exit on 51st St., and go left. Turn right onto 148th St. Turn left onto Willows Rd. Turn right onto 95th St. The gym is the sixth driveway on your left.

Short Hop

CASCADE CRAGS

2820 Rucker Ave., Everett
(425) 258-3431, www.cascadecrags.com
Location: Everett, about 30 miles north of Seattle
Description: This place boasts some special features, such as the only indoor ice wall in the western United States (and instruction to go with it), free yoga classes (a limited number) with membership, and 10,000 square feet of climbing wall. There are hundreds of lead and top-rope routes and a separate bouldering area. The 30-foot-high ice wall (complete with small roof and icicle section) isn't

Climbing Gyms & Walls

actually ice—it's a foam substance that mimics ice and can take the punishment of crampons and ice axes. The gym also supports a junior climbing team and youth climbing series. Employees have a refreshing attitude toward beginners. Novices can take a class or just start climbing on their own. "We're all born to do this," says employee Jason Brasfield. "People think this is so hard, but it's a joke we play on ourselves. This is an ancestral ability—we once did it on trees."

Directions: Take I-5 to exit 192 (Broadway/Port of Everett). Go north on Broadway to Pacific Ave. Turn left onto Pacific. After several blocks, turn right onto Rucker. Cascade Crags is on the left.

Bird-Watching

OutsidePix.com

IF IT HAS at some point occurred to you that rock climbing, whitewater kayaking, and even in-line skating are difficult to combine with the geek chic aesthetic so popular in urban areas today; if you wonder where on earth you can fit in to this outdoor adventure picture and still pay homage to your inner nerd, look no further than bird-watching. As with sideburns, glasses, and polyester, the answer to the question Are birds hot, or not? has been decidedly answered: Birds are hot. According to Audubon Washington, 71 million Americans describe themselves as "interested in bird-watching."

Our state's citizens are no exception.

"We've got a very active birding community

225

here—a lot of people of an environmental bent who appreciate it that the city has wild places," says architect, bird-watcher, and Seattle Audubon past-president Richard Youel. Like many birders, he got hooked when a friend took him out with a pair of binoculars and helped him see dozens of species he'd been completely unaware of. "I thought for a while that what we'd seen were rare birds," he says, "but I soon realized these birds were all around me—I'd just never noticed them before."

And there were, and are, a lot of birds to be overlooked. Seattle is naturally well sited, with salt- and freshwater habitat in abundance, a position near the continent's West Coast, a temperate climate, and mountains on either side. The city is also graced with an extensive park system, courtesy of some forward-thinking early citizens, which encompasses remnant old-growth forests, waterfront, and several creeks. It has become very common to see people with binoculars and even spotting scopes trained on trees, lakes, and telephone poles, not only at hot spots, such as the Montlake Fill, Discovery Park, and Seward Park, but at any nearby patch of green. Even downtown has become a sky-watching place, with peregrine falcons nesting on the side of a bank building and hawks hunting pigeons on the waterfront. Bald eagles fledge their young in Discovery and Seward Parks, and in Green Lake evergreens; their courting and hunting can be observed all over town, from Queen Anne viewpoints to the shoreline of West Seattle.

Seasons here in temperate Puget Sound are less severe than in most U.S. cities, but the bird migration schedule maintains a fairly regular pattern. In general, winter is the time for waterfowl, including a huge diversity of duck species that dabble and dive in on our local lakes and ponds. In summer there are far fewer such birds, and more terrestrial types pay a visit. Birders look forward to spring, particularly late April and May, when the males of many species fluff up their best, most colorful feathers and summon songs to melt the most unsentimental heart.

More than just about any other chapter in this book, the outings here are in or not more than an hour from the city, though a few range farther afield. The mountain ranges and eastern plains offer seasonal variation and a whole different list of birds to be "had," in bird-watching parlance, and several of the bird books listed can offer direction. One exciting new source for destination ideas is "The Great Washington State Birding Trail," a free map (get one quickly) available from Audubon Washington (866-922-4737, www.wa.audubon.org). The trail directs the reader to 68 prime birding spots on what they're calling the Cascade Loop, which starts north of Seattle and travels across WA 20 to the Methow Valley, south to Wenatchee, and then back on US 2 to Everett.

Ms. Birding Manners

WE'VE ALREADY ESTABLISHED that birds are experiencing the kind of popularity usually reserved for homecoming queens. Alas, this sort of population-wide crush does not come without a price. Birds are trying to go about their lives while under our scrutiny, and if we don't give them the space to do it, they may just up and leave. In the city this is especially true, since we're already in close quarters. Here are a few rules of conduct, gleaned from birders and the birds themselves:

1. Keep your distance. It can be very tempting to get up close to a wild bird—they're usually small. Don't do it. They are likely to be busy breeding, foraging, or serving up a snack to their young, and too many disruptions can be hazardous to their health. Get the best binoculars you can find so you

can view the birds from a decent distance. Rule of thumb: If the birds look agitated, like they might want to take flight, you're getting too close.

2. Dogs and birds don't mix. This should be obvious to anyone who has ever owned a dog, but it bears repeating. If you happen to spot birds while you're out walking your dog, that's fine. But bringing your dog along with you on a bird-watching outing can upset birds and will likely prevent you from ever spotting more nervous species. Be forewarned, many bird areas do not allow pets.

3. Birds in migration are very vulnerable. They need every calorie they can retain for the long journey, and repeated lift-offs can endanger their survival. The rules above are doubly important for long-distance migrants.

4. During the breeding season, generally May through mid-summer, make an extra effort to stay on trails. Ground-nesting birds sometimes roost in the middle of meadows or even on mowed grass.

City Limits

MONTLAKE FILL

Location: Northeast of downtown, near the University of Washington campus

Books: *Nature in the City: Seattle; A Guide to Bird Finding in Washington*

Heads up: Seattle's little birding jewel. Birds are very vulnerable during nesting season, spring through summer. Be sure to stay on the trail at this time, and follow birding etiquette (see *Ms. Birding Manners*, page 227).

Description: "This is my favorite urban site," says veteran birder and author Lyanda Haupt. "It's exciting in all seasons, and anything goes in migration." The Fill, more formally known as the Union Bay Natural Area (UBNA) is a wetland and prairie area on top of clay that caps a former garbage dump. That dump filled in what was once one of the city's flourishing ecosystems, a rich wetland near the mouth of Ravenna Creek. Now, in more enlightened times, all kinds of restoration projects bring native vegetation back to this disturbed site. The birds don't seem to mind the Fill's checkered history—one reason you'll see binoculars raised here every season of the year is the diverse range of habitats, including prairie/meadow, freshwater ponds, and lake shoreline. A large variety of birds common to distinct areas of Seattle come here, including winter shorebirds, waterfowl such as cinnamon teals, and ruddy ducks, warblers, woodpeckers, peregrine falcons in the snags (dead trees) next to the lake, and bald eagles cruising overhead. American goldfinches, Washington State's official bird, flit happily about the thistle.

The Fill is also known in the bird-watching community as a place to find the one bird (or birds) you never thought you'd catch sight of within view of the Space Needle. Haupt mentions solitary sandpipers, palm warblers, and Say's phoebe. "We expect surprises here." My personal surprise was the sleek American bittern, doing its best to look inconspicuous among the cattails in the swampy area at the Fill's southeast corner. The wide-open, grassy expanses provide great views of Mount Rainier on clear days and a fine dose of sunshine. UBNA shares a campus with the Center for Urban Horticulture (206-543-8616, www.urbanhort.org), whose grounds and garden are also a great place for bird spotting—you'll see the center when you park. Also part of the University of Washington, the center has a renowned horticultural library and participates in managing the area.

Directions: From I-5 take the N.E. 45th St. exit and head east through the University District, past the campus, and down the hill (viaduct). At the stoplight at the bottom of the viaduct, turn left to stay on N.E. 45th. At the next stoplight, a five-way intersection, turn right (south) onto Mary Gates Memorial Dr. Continue south to the bend in the road, where Mary Gates Dr. becomes N.E. 41st St. The entrance to the Center for Urban Horticulture is on your right.

ALKI BEACH

Location: West Seattle

Heads up: Cappuccino birding

Description: A visit to Alki goes something like this: Stroll along the waterfront path, suck the foam off your cappuccino . . . Hey, is that a phalarope? Let's warm up with some scones at the Alki Bakery and take a look in the field guide, shall we?

It's a busy stretch of beach, with pizza joints, fish-and-chips shops, and waterfront condos, but it also happens to be a great place for winter seabirds and gulls. Watch for rock sandpipers, scoters, loons, western and horned grebes, and harlequin and other duck species. Brants come through during migration. Look out over the water to spy seals or California sea lions, or, with great luck and good binoculars, an orca. South of here in West Seattle, Lincoln Park, next to the Fauntleroy ferry dock, offers similar waterfront birding possibilities, along with a forested area above the water that attracts woodland birds.

Directions: From I-5 or WA 99 (Aurora Avenue), take the West Seattle Bridge to West Seattle. Take the Harbor Ave. Avalon Way off-ramp. Turn right onto Harbor Ave. S.W. Bear left onto Alki Ave. S.W. Alki Beach Park is on your right for a couple of miles, coffee shops and restaurants on your left.

Seattle
Audubon

OCAL BIRD-WATCHERS are lucky to have a remarkable bird-ing resource right in the city. The Seattle Audubon Society (SAS) is one of the National Audubon Society's largest chap-ters, with more than 5,000 members and at least 700 active volunteers. A thumb through the monthly newsletter suggests an organized hive of activity: bird walks for new members, an annual Christmas bird count, and a campaign to decide the offi-cial bird for this avian- mad city. Volunteers are working on the shade-grown coffee campaign to protect migrating songbirds, and about 20 field trips are offered per month. If you're new to the city and interested in birds, you're in luck. SAS has always offered field trips to Washington birding hot spots, but these are often out of town and half- or all-day ventures. Starting in 2003, however, the organization has begun a project called Neighborhood Bird Walks, outings that take place in city parks and help members learn more about the birds in their own backyard. "It helps connect you a little more to the bigger pic-ture," says Audubon's Shelly Ross. These urban excursions are part of an effort to involve members who might not have time for longer trips, or who are just getting started bird-watching. Of course, if you're just looking for some tips on getting a good bird feeder, there's room for you, too. SAS runs a Nature Shop in Seattle's Wedgwood neighborhood (8050 35th NE; 206-523-4483), staffed by members and stuffed with birdseed, bird books, binoculars, feeders, and free advice.

DISCOVERY PARK

Location: West of downtown in the Magnolia neighborhood
Map and Books: Map available at Discovery Park Visitor

Center; *A Guide to Bird Finding in Washington; Nature in the City: Seattle*

Heads Up: The Discovery Park Visitor Center (206-386-4236, www.cityofseattle.net/parks) has loads of information on what to see at the park and offers naturalist outings for children and adults throughout the year, including birdwatching classes.

Description: If it's not one habitat it's another. The city's largest park, 534-acre Discovery has, hands down, the most diverse range of bird habitats in one place in the entire city. Perched on the edge of ancient bluffs overlooking Puget Sound, on a former military site, the park encompasses woodlands, grasslands, saltwater shoreline, sand dunes, and cliffs, each of which attracts a different range of birds. Over 260 species have been seen here over the years, over half the total for the state. Grassland sparrows such as savannah, golden-crowned, and Lincoln's make use of park meadows, and this is also where you'll find raptors, including American kestrels, northern harriers and red-tailed hawks. Several species of owls have been seen in the park's woods, some visiting, some nesting.

The two beaches, and the West Point peninsula between them (easily recognized by the lighthouse), are a fantastic place in winter to watch for loons and a variety of ducks, or perhaps a flotilla of thousands of western grebes, decked out in their black and white tuxedos. Come regularly for a chance at spotting members of the alcid family, including ancient murrelets, marbled murrelets, common murres, and rhinoceros auklets. Pigeon guillemots nest in holes in the South Bluff strata, just above South Beach.

If you're tired of searching for rarities and ready for big game there are two other bird phenomena in the area worth a mention. One is a bald eagle nest site, located in most recent years in late winter and early spring near Discovery's east entrance. Call or drop in at the visitors center for directions to look at that year's nest. The naturalists will often set up a spotting scope so visitors can view the birds as they go about nest-building or feeding their young. This is a particularly good outing for kids. As long as you're in the area, be sure to visit the Kiwanis Ravine, a few blocks southeast of the park above the Chittenden Locks. This 9-acre sanctuary is home to one of the largest great blue heron nesting grounds in the Seattle area. From February through May the herons will be courting and raising young. The Discovery Park Visitor Center can offer directions and more information.

Directions: From downtown, go north on Western to Elliott, which becomes 15th Ave. W. Follow 15th to the Dravus St. exit. At the stoplight turn left onto Dravus. Take a right onto 20th Ave. W., which becomes Gilman Ave. W. at a four-way stop. Gilman Ave. W. then becomes W. Government Way. Follow this until you come to the Park's east entrance. The visitors center will be on the left.

SEWARD PARK

Location: Southeast of downtown on Lake Washington

Book: *Nature in the City: Seattle*

Heads up: Old-growth forest on the lake. Seattle Parks and Recreation (www.cityofseattle.net/parks) has more on Seward. For a bird checklist and more on the park's natural history visit the Friends of Seward Park site at www.sewardpark.net.

Description: If ever there was a green thumb, this is it. The jutting digit of the Bailey Peninsula, on which Seward Park lies, is a little patch of pre-Seattle in an urbanized section of the city. The Magnificent Forest at the center of the park is the largest stand of old growth left in Seattle, with some trees more than 250 years old, skirted by an understory of native plants. Birds seen in this woodland are often unexpected in an urban environment, like the varied, Swainson's, and hermit thrushes that sing the forest alive. Only about 120 acres, the forest has recently hosted six kinds of woodpeckers, winter wrens, warblers, a variety of sparrows, Western screech owls, and a range of other species. Raptors include Cooper's, sharp-shinned and red-tailed hawks; merlins; peregrine falcons; and bald eagles, a pair of which have taken to nesting in the area.

To better understand how the forest and birdlife intertwine, head to the Native Plant Garden just off the parking lots, next to the bathrooms. Here at the edge of the forest volunteers have posted signs identifying the plants, and a board that explains how certain native animals and plants benefit one another. Cedar waxwings, for instance, gorge on serviceberries in late summer, while rufous-sided towhees take refuge in the camouflage of red-flowering currant. The red-breasted nuthatch, which you might catch walking up a Douglas fir, harvests seeds from the fir's cones. The park is good for two different types of visits— one trip takes you through the forest to wander the trails; the other along 3 miles of Seward Park shoreline, where you can make your own game of duck, duck, goose. Watch for loons, grebes (five kinds have been seen here), and a variety of ducks including bufflehead and goldeneye, and hooded, common, and red-breasted mergansers.

Directions: Head south on I-5. Take exit 163A (W. Seattle Bridge/Columbian Way). Stay left at the fork in the ramp. Merge onto Columbian. Make a slight right onto 15th Ave. S. Turn slight left onto S. Columbian Way. Make a slight right onto S. Alaska St. Turn right onto Rainier Ave. S./WA 167. Turn left onto S. Orcas St., which becomes Lake Washington Blvd. S., which leads into Seward Park.

Backyard

KVI BEACH

Location: Vashon Island, just west of Seattle across Puget Sound

Map and Books: Vashon–Maury Island map (free at island realtors and parks office) for other island sights; *Nature in the City: Seattle; A Guide to Bird Finding in Washington*

Heads up: This is also a great beach to explore at low tide when a sandbar reaches far out into the harbor, or visit in summer for some of the warmer saltwater swimming around. For more information on birding try the Vashon-Maury Island Audubon Society (463-3153, e-mail raynaholtz @aol.com). Ferries from Seattle run every 20 minutes to an hour, depending on the time of day, for a 15-minute trip (www.wsdot.wa.gov/ferries/schedules/current).

Description: Don't be put off by the commercial-sounding name, or the radio tower presiding over this otherwise beautiful sweep of south-facing beach. A true local's strand, it's not even marked on the island map, and is only crowded on hot weekend days and the 4th of July. Visit in mid-July to catch the beginning of fall migration, when otherwise rare birds stop over for a rest before continuing south. Walking down the path toward the radio tower, look for least and western sandpipers in the estuary to your left. Ospreys and kingfishers fish nearby. After the fall equinox, scan Tramp Harbor, the open water to the southwest, to see shorebirds such as pectoral sandpipers, semipalmated plovers, and greater yellowlegs. You might see common loons and red-necked grebes, still decked out in their "pick me" feathers, breeding plumage they've been making use of farther north. In the fall and winter, Vashon hosts more than 35 species of waterbirds, including harlequin ducks, surf scoters, common goldeneyes, and brants. Many of these can be spotted in Tramp Harbor or in nearby Quartermaster Harbor, which was named an Important Bird Area by the National Audubon Society because of its essential western grebe habitat.

Directions: To get to the Vashon ferry, take US 99 south to the West Seattle Bridge exit (don't go to Harbor Island) and cross the bridge. The road becomes Fauntleroy Way. Stay in the left two lanes. Follow Fauntleroy as it turns left (south) at Alaska St. Continue just over 3 miles to the Vashon ferry terminal on your right. After disembarking at Vashon, take the Vashon Highway (follow the main flow of traffic) uphill about 3.5 miles to the town of Vashon. At the four-way stop (Bank Rd.), turn left. Follow this about 0.5 mile to Beall Rd., a T intersection. Turn right. Drive for 0.5 mile to S.W. 184th St. Turn left. 184th curves right into Ridge Rd. Follow Ridge about 1.5 miles to a four-way stop at Chautauqua Beach Rd. S.W. Go straight. At the bottom of the hill you will see the path to the beach. To park, continue up the hill to your left and pull off on the left side of the road.

Birding
by
Boat

P ERHAPS THE BEST WAY to see pelagic bird species in Washington is to get out on a boat, and few outfitters can boast the professional expertise of Westport Seabirds (360-268-5222, www.westportseabirds.com), a bird-watching venture based on the Central Washington coast. Well-known seabird biologist and regular trip leader Terry Wahl, for instance, has been studying the same waters since 1966, censusing them since 1971. (He's also the coauthor with Dennis Paulson of *A Guide to Bird Finding in Washington,* one of the essential reference guides in our area.)

The 50-foot *Monte Carlo* sets out on day trips to Grays Canyon, a submarine canyon 35 nautical miles west of Gray's Harbor on the edge of the North American continental shelf, a location rich with marine life. Westport Seabirds also offers two deepwater trips even farther offshore. If you're looking for a luxurious day cruise complete with cheese platter, look elsewhere—here it's strictly bring your own lunches, binoculars, and seasickness remedies. But if it's birds you're after, you'll be too distracted to notice the lack of amenities. Sightings the outfitter boasts for nearly all trips April through October include black-footed albatross, northern fulmar, sooty shearwater, fork-tailed storm-petrel, phalaropes, jaegers, black-legged kittiwakes, and a variety of unusual gull species and alcids. They also have a list of incredible rarities that have come their way, including, for the lucky tour-goer, other albatross species. Trips focus on seabird biology, bird identification, marine mammals, and oceanography. Trips leave from Westport.

Short Hops

SPENCER ISLAND

Location: Everett, about 30 miles north of Seattle

Maps and Book: The Snohomish River Estuary Recreation Guide contains maps and descriptions (425-388-6600, co.Snohomish.wa.us/parks/spencer.htm); *Nature in the City: Seattle*

Heads up: Estuarine abundance. No dogs are allowed on

the south side of the island, which is owned by Snohomish County. The north side of the island is managed by the Department of Fish and Wildlife, where hunting is allowed in season. Nearby in the port of Everett is another bird haven, Jetty Island, managed by the Everett Parks Department. See "Sea Kayaking," page 50, for a description of paddling in the Snohomish River Estuary sloughs.

Description: The port of Everett has been the site of heavy industry, but some parts of the estuary, formed where the salt water of Possession Sound and Snohomish River's freshwater meet, have retained a feeling of relative sanctuary. One of these is Spencer Island, preserved in the form of agricultural farmland for decades until its conversion into a park teeming with birdish abundance. Approaching the island you walk through the Everett Sewage Treatment lagoons. If you're not a regular bird-watcher you may not realize that sewage ponds are a hot foraging ground, where birders swing their binoculars about like treasure hunters with metal detectors. The Everett lagoons are as much a destination for bird-watchers as the island itself. They're known for waterfowl in the late fall through early spring, with a huge variety and a number of rarities seen each year that set pencils ticking down birding lists. Gulls can fill the place on the right day, or hawks might have dropped in for a snack. Ducks often congregate here during hunting season, says bird-watcher and former Seattle Audubon president Richard Youel, to avoid the unrestricted north end of Spencer Island. "It's uncanny how they seem to know the timing of the season."

As you walk over a short bridge to Spencer, the atmosphere quickly turns parklike. A short, wheelchair-accessible boardwalk offers views of the island. A 3.5-mile trail follows a dike around the perimeter, which is bordered by estuarine sloughs that make a great kayaking destination, as well as wonderful shelter for herons and other marsh-loving water-fowl. From the thickets emerge the sounds of chickadees, bushtits, vireos, and warblers; woodpeckers tic-tac holes into snags. Five kinds of swallows have been seen here, snatching at the abundant insect life. In winter, merlins and peregrine falcons come foraging. Near Spencer huge osprey nests top old pilings around the estuary. All told, over 200 species of birds have been spotted plus mammals such as river otter, deer, and coyote. During hunting season you may or may not want to avoid the island's north end, where hunting is legal. Some birders, such as Youel, don't avoid the area, while others dislike the disruption. If you plan to visit then, it's best, of course, to don your orange plumage. Check with the Department of Fish and Wildlife for open season dates.

Directions: Drive I-5 north to Everett and take exit 195 (Marine View Dr./Port of Everett). Turn left (west) onto E. Marine View Dr. In about 1.5 miles turn left (north) onto WA 529N ramp and drive over the bridge. Turn right (east) onto 28th Place N.E. Turn right onto 35th Ave. N.E. Turn left onto Ross Ave. Drive 1.2 miles and turn left onto 4th St. S.E. Continue to City of Everett Water Pollution Control Facility parking lot. From here it is a 0.3 mile walk to the bridge to Spencer Island.

NISQUALLY NATIONAL WILDLIFE REFUGE

Location: About 65 miles south of Seattle

Map and book: Map available at refuge headquarters; *A Guide to Bird Finding in Washington*

Heads up: The Tahoma Audubon chapter (Pierce County chapter of Audubon, 253-565-9278) has been involved in the refuge for years. Nisqually National Wildlife Refuge Headquarters (360-753-9467, www.nisqually.fws.gov) has bird checklists and other information. The Nisqually Reach Nature Center (360-459-0387, www.nisquallyestuary.org) provides information on the delta and has aquariums with estuarine sea life. They are open Saturday and Sunday 12–4, also Wednesday in summer.

Description: The rich estuary of the Nisqually River delta is one of the largest protected estuaries in our region. For that reason, and because it packs a large variety of habitats into a small space, it is beloved of naturalists and rewards multiple visits. The 7 miles of trails take you through or near the entire range of habitats, including mud flats, freshwater ponds, woodlands, and bluffs. The main 5.5-mile loop trail has been created with an eye toward unobtrusive observation, offering several overlooks and photo blinds along the way. Migratory birds are at Nisqually in every season, with songbirds in spring and shorebirds, ducks, and geese in fall and winter. A checklist, available from the refuge office, lists over 200 species, including 40 species of swans, geese, and ducks and a huge variety of sandpipers. Nine species of warblers, many more sparrow species, and numerous other passerines have been seen in the woods and grasslands. These entice raptors, such as northern harriers and short-eared owls, which hunt over the meadows in the afternoons. This is also the rare western Washington location for spotting purple martins (see *On the Wing*, page 241).

Directions: To get to the Refuge, take I-5 south 60 miles to exit 114 near Olympia. From here follow signs to the refuge. To get to the Nisqually Reach Nature Center, take exit 114 up, left, and over freeway. At the traffic signal go uphill on Martin Way E.; in 1 mile turn right onto Meridian Rd. N.E. In 2.5 miles turn right onto 46th Ave. N.E. Take first left onto D'Milluhr Dr. Follow it to the nature center, located to the right of the boat launch.

On the Wing

A SWALLOW'S GRACE and aerodynamic shape make it a bird of childhood fantasy. An elegantly forked tail on which to hang your hopes of flying, a dream of loop-de-loops and airplane wing-walking. Their aerial artistry has its practical aspect: swallows survive almost solely on insects gleaned in flight. Five swallow species regularly visit greater Seattle: the early arriving (usually in March) tree swallow; the violet-green, cliff, and barn swallows; and—largest and least common—the purple martin. All of these birds migrate south by late summer or fall, some to the Amazon River Basin and even to the southern reaches of South America.

Long revered for their flying skill, swallows were once used like pigeons to carry messages. In ancient Rome, Pliny wrote:

One Roman gentleman who was particularly fond of chariot racing would catch swallows from a nest at his country home and take them to the races in Rome. To give his friends advance results, he would paint the birds with the color of the winning team and release them to fly back to their nest. Swallows were excellent carriers, as their speed meant they were rarely caught by predators.

Closer to home, visit Green Lake at dusk in the summer to catch sight of thousands of tree, violet-green, and barn swallows swooping over the water for an evening meal. The latter two may be tough to distinguish in flight—both have beautifully colored backs and moderately forked tails.

Cliff swallows are readily seen in summer at the 16th Ave. bridge over the Duwamish River. Look for their broad, rounded wings and short, square, unforked tails. You can see the cliff swallows' mud nests at the base of the Aurora Ave. Bridge on the north shore, but they are sometimes appropriated by house sparrows.

Though swallows seem to adjust well to human development, you're still more likely to see them in wilder environs.
The Nisqually National Wildlife Refuge is the place to visit in
early summer for a chance at all six species. The nearby
Nisqually Reach Nature Center has several purple martin nest
boxes where busy parents can be seen bringing meals of
dragonflies and wasps to their hungry young.

The number of martins nesting in the city dropped to zero
for nearly a decade, but currently has recovered to 13 pairs.
Martins have a long history of nesting near people. East Coast
Native Americans hung hollowed-out gourds near their fields to
attract the birds, which were renowned for their song, aerial
displays, ability to keep crows away from crops, and controlling
insects. Since the 20th century, the entire eastern subspecies
of purple martin nests only in human-constructed homes. Only
in the Pacific Northwest and the Southwest do martins continue to nest in the wild. Driven out of their natural nest sites
by house sparrows and European starlings, the martins' affinity
for manmade houses has helped reestablish them in western
Washington. Local Audubon chapter volunteers have hung and
monitored nest boxes to establish 35 colonies. The Purple Martin Conservation Association is a clearing house for information
on the species (814-734-4420, www.purplemartin.org).

Purple martin nest-box sites in Seattle include Shilshole
Bay (the public-access beach behind the Ballard Elks Club),
Port of Seattle's Jack Block Park on Elliott Bay (off Harbor
Avenue near Salty's Restaurant), and Herring's House Park/
Kellogg Island off West Marginal Way.

To get to the Nisqually Reach Nature Center, see directions
under Nisqually National Wildlife Refuge outing, page 239.

Meccas

SKAGIT RIVER DELTA

Location: About 60 miles north of Seattle

Map: Great Washington State Birding Trail map from Audubon Washington

Heads up: Nearby, tourist-oriented La Conner has picnic fixings, pizza, and even gourmet restaurants.

Description: If the image of thousands of snow geese achieving lift-off over a grassy field in evening light sounds enticing, look no further. The immense Skagit River, which starts in Canada and flows south and west through the Cascades, meets the saltwater of Skagit Bay here, creating a maze of wetlands that are incredible bird habitat, visited by migrating snow geese, wintering waterfowl, trumpeter swans, and shorebirds. This area (which is not one park but a variety of preserved lands and agricultural fields) is also the best place for winter raptors anywhere near Seattle; aficionados seek out peregrine falcons, gyrfalcons, merlins, prairie falcons, rough-legged hawks, and short-eared owls. From Fir Island Rd., you are most likely to see snow geese, and trumpeter and tundra swans; Skagit Wildlife Area, a Washington Department of Fish and Wildlife site, has prime raptor viewing. One other note: East, on the Skagit River proper, one of the largest concentrations of bald eagles in the United States occurs each January when the birds gather to feed on spawned-out salmon carcasses. See *Floating with the Big Birds*, page 86.

Directions: Take I-5 north about 60 miles to exit 221 (Lake McMurray/Conway) and head west 0.1 mile. Turn right onto Fir Island Rd. Drive west 3.2 miles. Turn left at the Washington Department of Fish and Wildlife (WDFW) sign. Park in the designated area, 0.5 miles ahead. To get to the Skagit Wildlife Area–Samish Unit, drive north from the first destination to WA 20 and turn west. At milepost 53.2 turn north onto Bayview-Edison Rd. Drive 7.7 miles. Turn left at the T onto Samish Island Rd. Drive 0.7 mile to the WDFW parking lot.

DUNGENESS SPIT

Location: On the Olympic Peninsula, about an hour and a half from the Seattle ferry

Books: *A Guide to Bird Finding in Washington; Shorebirds of the Pacific Northwest*

Heads up: The refuge (www.dungeness.com/refuge) charges a daily entrance fee, currently around $3. Fires, camping, and pets are prohibited. The trailhead is located within the Dungeness Recreation Area, a county park, which allows both camping and pets (360-683-5847, www.portangeles.org).

Description: The longest natural sand spit in the United States, this beckoning finger of sand and gravel attracts all kinds of shorebirds and other species. With 5 miles to walk from one end to the other, you probably won't see the entire thing at a go, which is fine—this is a fantastic day trip from the city, worth doing many more times. As a side benefit to your bird search, you may very well find yourself soaking in some much-needed sun, since Dungeness lies within the Olympics' rain shadow and is more likely than Seattle to be cloud-free in winter (see *Olympic Peninsula Rain Shadow*, page 187). This has been a National Wildlife Refuge since 1915, and the number of bird species visiting or nesting here is remarkable. According to the Department of Ecology, over 250 species of birds have been seen here, 91 of which are known to nest in the refuge. For the best sightings, walk the estuary side. It's a great place to see shorebirds, including good numbers of dowitchers, whimbrels, dunlins, black-bellied plovers, western and least sandpipers, and terns. The black brant, a true sea goose that can drink salt water, was part of the impetus for establishing the refuge—up to 8,000 migrate through in March and April. Keep an eye out for unusual waterfowl, such as the colorful harlequin duck and threatened marbled murrelet. Bird-watcher Lyanda Haupt also advises you to watch for jaegers prowling over the water. Near the end of the spit, should you somehow get that far, is a haul-out and pupping site for harbor seals. Up to 600 have been recorded here in recent years. Enjoy the sounds and take a look through your binoculars, but stay a good distance away and do not disturb the animals.

Directions: The Dungeness Spit is located just west of the town of Sequim off US 101 on the Olympic Peninsula. Once you've gotten to the peninsula by either the Bainbridge or Edmonds-Kingston ferries, get on US 101. Continue past Sequim and turn north onto Kitchen-Dick Road for 3 miles, continuing to the refuge parking lot.

Protection Island

WHERE THE STRAIT OF JUAN DE FUCA approaches Puget Sound, Protection Island lounges like a singing siren, drawing seabirds, and local birders, to its shores. The Port Townsend Marine Science Center (360-385-5582, www.ptmsc.org) offers 3-hour boat cruises around this island refuge during the spring and fall migrations, an amazing opportunity to see a huge variety of unusual birds. The island's sand dunes and prairie support breeding, nesting, and visiting populations of over 85 bird species, including loons, phalaropes, mergansers, harlequin ducks, murrelets, rhinoceros auklets, and tufted puffins, as well as a huge nesting colony of glaucous-winged gulls.

GRAYS HARBOR

Location: About 115 miles southwest of Seattle on the central Washington coast

Books: *A Birder's Guide to Coastal Washington; Rare Encounters with Ordinary Birds* (see especially the essay "One-Eyed Dunlin")

Heads up: The million shorebird march, late April and early May. For maps and more information go to the U.S. Fish and Wildlife Service Web site (www.graysharbor .fws.gov), call the Nisqually National Wildlife Refuge (360-753-9467), or contact Grays Harbor Audubon Society (360-495-3289, www.ghas.org). Pay close attention to birding etiquette—migrating birds can't afford extra calorie expenditure, so don't startle them into flight.

Description: Arctic-bound from as far south as Argentina, hundreds of thousands of shorebirds congregate at Grays Harbor in spring, one of the largest such concentrations on the West Coast south of Alaska. The birds are attracted to the 1,500 acres of intertidal mud flats, salt marsh, and uplands protected as a National Wildlife Refuge. One of the best places to view the migrants is in Hoquiam, just beside the airport, perhaps an appropriate location considering the birds are here for their own refueling. In season sandpipers, dowitchers, plovers, dunlins, and red knots stand on delicate legs poking and prodding at the muck, gathering fortification for the flight north. This is hunting season for birds of prey such as the peregrine falcon—when one dive-bombs into a flock, thousands of shorebirds burst into the air,

Bird-Watching

twirling and dipping like Sufi mystics, before settling back to their supper. The best birding time is in the hours around the high tide, which herds the birds in near shore and each other. At the refuge a mile-long boardwalk, the Sandpiper Trail, provides good access. Come for the Grays Harbor Shorebird Festival (www.blackhillsaudubon.org /bowerman/ or www.ghas.org) in late April for birding and naturalist-led field trips, lectures, and exhibits.

Directions: Take I-5 south past Tacoma to exit 104 (US 101, Aberdeen/Port Angeles). Take WA 8W toward Montesano/Aberdeen. WA 8 becomes US 12W. US12 W becomes US 101N. Turn right onto Levee St./US 101N. Stay on 101, then turn left onto Emerson St./WA 109W toward Ocean Shores. About a mile after leaving town you will see the Hoquiam High School on your right. Take the next left, Paulson Rd., to a T at the sewage pond. Turn right and follow the road into the airport until you reach the National Wildlife Refuge. Park across from Lana's Café and follow the trail to the boardwalk out on the mudflats.

Important Bird Areas

WHILE THE BIRD FEEDER hanging from your back porch probably qualifies as an important bird area to you, the Audubon Society has something more specific in mind. Audubon Washington is participating in a worldwide mapping of sites that provide what is considered essential habitat for one or more species of birds. So far 53 places in our state have earned the Important Bird Area (IBA) designation. Criteria for selection include places that shelter rare species, a significant number of one species, or have particularly good native habitat. Nisqually Delta, for example, has been chosen as an IBA because it offers estuarine habitat for a large number of migrating waterfowl and shorebirds, and harbors a mineral springs used by many of the state's native band-tailed pigeons, a declining species. The goal of mapping these IBAs is to identify and protect a network of sites that will promote the health of wild bird populations. To learn more contact Audubon Washington.

Where to Connect

Clubs and Organizations

- Audubon Washington (206-652-2444, www.wa.audubon.org /new/audubon) is the state branch of the National Audubon Society. AW has developed local Audubon centers and is in charge of the Washington Birding Trail and Important Bird Areas. A few of the local Audubon chapters are listed below. Visit the Web site for additional contact information.

- East Lake Washington Audubon (425-576-8805, www .elwas.org) is the Eastside chapter.

- Rainier Audubon (253-939-6411, www.rainieraudubon.org /index.html) is the South King County chapter. The Web site has great descriptions of local bird-watching destinations.

- Seattle Audubon (206-523-4483, www.seattleaudubon.org) is one of the country's largest Audubon chapters and is very active in local conservation issues. They lead tours, classes, and workshops for members and the general public.

- Skagit Audubon (www.fidalgo.net/-audubon) is the Skagit County chapter; they organize many field trips in the area.

- The Washington Department of Fish and Wildlife's Backyard Sanctuary Program (www.wa.gov/wdfw

/wlm/byw_prog.htm) offers instructions on how to create habitat for birds and other animals around your home.

- The Washington Ornithological Society (www.wos.org) is open to anyone interested in Washington birds and offers an annual journal, a bimonthly newsletter, field trips, and conferences. WOS runs the Washington Bird Box, where birders report notable bird sightings.

Shops

- Anacortes Telescope and Wild Bird (360-588-9000, www .BuyTelescopes.com) is a well-regarded store with online shopping.

- Flora and Fauna Books (121 1st Ave. S., 206-623-4727, www.abebooks.com/home/FFBOOK) is an excellent Pioneer Square bookstore specializing in natural history and science. Lots of bird books.

- Seattle Audubon Nature Shop (8050 35th N.E. 206-523-4483) sells birdseed, feeders, books, binoculars, and other equipment.

Books

This is only a sampling of good birding books, and new regional bird books come out every couple of years. Visit the Audubon Nature Shop or Flora and Fauna Books in Pioneer Square for more.

- Dolan, Maria, and Kathryn True. *Nature in the City: Seattle.* Seattle, WA: Mountaineers Books, 2003.

- Fisher, Chris C. *Birds of Seattle and Puget Sound.* Renton, WA: Lone Pine Publishing, 1996.

- Haupt, Lyanda Lynn. *Rare Encounters with Ordinary Birds: Notes From a Northwest Year.* Seattle, WA: Sasquatch Books, 2001.

- Hunn, Eugene. *Birding in Seattle and King County*. Seattle, WA: Seattle Audubon Society, 1983. An old book but still useful if you can find it.

- MacRae, Diann. *Birders Guide to Washington*. Houston, TX: Gulf Publishing Co., 1995

- Morse, Bob. *A Birders' Guide to Coastal Washington*. Olympia, WA: R.W. Morse and Co., 2001

- Paulson, Dennis. *Shorebirds of the Pacific Northwest*. Reprint. Seattle, WA: University of Washington Press, 1998.

- Pilchuck Audubon Society. *Birding in Snohomish County*. Everett, WA: Pilchuck Audubon Society, 1997.

- Sibley, David Allen. *The Sibley Guide to Birds*. New York: Alfred A. Knopf, 2000.

- Wahl, T.R., and Dennis R. Paulson. *A Guide to Bird Finding in Washington*. Bellingham, WA: T.R. Wahl, 1991.

Links

www.birdweb.org is Seattle Audubon's online guide to the birds of Washington state.

www.scn.org/earth/tweeters/index.html. If you haven't heard of Tweeters yet, you may not be ready for them. But if you find yourself unable to detach from your binoculars, there's a Listserv out there for you. Tweeters is a Northwest birding e-mail list that has been around since 1992 and shares messages about bird sightings and the like. Take a look at the digests or subscribe at the Web site, which also offers a massive list of Northwest birding links.

WESTERN WASHINGTON—the part of the state west of the Cascade Mountains— has an abundance and variety of waters that sustain a robust fishery. Turquoise alpine lakes hold brightly colored native cutthroat trout. Rivers fed by the glaciers and rain forests of the Cascades and the Olympics support runs of migratory fish that spend much of their lives in salt water. Some, such as the sea-run cutthroat, live out much of their adult lives feeding in or near the estuary of their home stream. Others, such as the Chinook salmon and steelhead, have been known to migrate as far as eastern Russia. In many cases, the rivers and lakes and the bodies of salt water into which they empty offer great opportunities for sport fisherman to catch large fish in large quantities. Salmon, steelhead, and several other salmonids are probably what most people think of when they visualize fishing the Great Northwest. It is still possible on a given morning to wake up in Seattle at 4 A.M. on a drizzly January morning, put your boat into a river by 6 A.M., and be home with two 30-pound salmon by noon. When the coho salmon run peaks in September, "sick days" are taken and, in a good year, freezers are filled with fish caught in Shilshole Bay, 15 minutes from downtown Seattle.

In particularly good years, at just the right time, the waters described in this chapter can provide such opportunities. But they aren't necessarily what everyone would call the "best"—that is, if you define your finest fishing days as the ones when you can catch your limit. You are most likely to do this in government-managed waters: Rainbow trout are planted in lakes periodically throughout the year so you can pick them off with a few flicks of the wrist. Hatcheries release young salmon and steelhead into rivers and in two or three years, many, sometimes hordes, return, full grown. When the word gets out that there's been a hatchery return, people line the banks as close to the hatchery as they are allowed to fish. If a hatchery is too successful—more fish make it back than are needed to sustain the run—the excess fish are trucked back downstream and dropped back into the river to provide more opportunities for anglers. Some are even released into local lakes. It is, on occasion, possible to catch a 15-pound hatchery steelhead that spent three years migrating to Kamchatka and back in the local trout pond. Information about such opportunities aren't especially closely guarded secrets and a bit of casual research will unearth them.

This chapter is weighted heavily toward wild fly-fishing, and the methods for doing that in our waters may seem relatively unsophisticated compared to many fisheries in the

West. The fly-fishing enthusiast who has spent time in Idaho, Oregon, Montana, Wyoming, or Colorado will find that, for the most part, the fish of western Washington are far less "educated." The west slope cutthroat native to our rivers and lakes tends to be less selective than the rainbows and browns found throughout the West. Nonspecific patterns—stimulators, humpies, spider patterns, wooly buggers—that imitate something buggy and filling often are all that is needed. Methods for catching the fish that migrate from fresh to salt water and back vary greatly. One generality that can be made with some confidence is this: When fishing for salmon and steelhead that are returning to the rivers to spawn, you are trying to take advantage of a fish's territorial instinct rather than its feeding instinct.

Each body of water discussed here was chosen for some reason in addition to the fact that it is sometimes a great place to catch fish. Most are surrounded by spectacular scenery. Some are remote enough to seem unmanaged. And the rare opportunity still exists to catch a fish in a place that looks just like it did 200 years ago.

I have tried to include all the current information about local fishing regulations, but keep in mind that fishing openings and closings change rapidly, as do license fees and rules, and you'll need to check with the Washington Department of Fish and Wildlife (www.wa.gov/wdfw /fish/regs/fishregs.htm).

Saltwater Fly-Fishing

About the only aspect of recreational fishing that has actually been increasing its ranks lately is saltwater fly-fishing. "Freshwater fly-fishing rivers are so inundated," says guide Keith Robbins, "that people are fleeing to bigger waters for solitude." A handful of charter companies have begun taking out anglers for catch-and-release fly-fishing on boats, both on the Sound and on the Pacific coast. Robbins adds that the sport keeps you on your toes. "Every time I go I learn something new," he says. "We probably know 10 percent now of what we'll eventually know about saltwater fly-fishing." Casting from shore (or in your backyard) is a good way to get a feel for this sport before taking off on a charter. You'll need to know a little about casting to have much fun, since the combination of waves and wind make fly-fishing from a boat more challenging. Fish tend to pull a lot harder in salt water.

Backyard

PUGET SOUND

Location: Charters leave from Shilshole Bay in Seattle and from Olympia

Fish: Salmon

Season: Nearly year-round

Outfitters: Keith Robbins at Spot Tail Salmon Guide (206-283-6680, www.salmonguide.com) covers mid-Sound— "Vashon to Whidbey and all spots in-between"—using top-of-the-line gear. For Olympia, try Tom Wolf at Puget Sound Fly Fishing Saltwater Guide Service (253-863-0711, e-mail capttwolf@earthlink.net)

Heads up: If you fish from shore be sure to get a license. Spot Tail Salmon Guide provides licenses and fishing gear. Seasickness is not terribly common on Puget Sound, which has few swells and is often relatively placid.

Description: The deep, protected basin of Puget Sound

Fly-Fishing & Sportfishing

and its many bays and harbors make it a beautiful place to get out on a boat, and this is a good way to do it. There are plenty of fish coming through at different seasons of the year, including the salmon that are Robbins's specialty. Possibilities include Chinook salmon from June through early September, coho salmon from mid-August to the beginning of October, a run of pink (humpback) salmon every other year from August to early September, and chum salmon in October and November. Anything over 20 pounds in Puget Sound is considered big, and over 30 pounds ranks as a heavyweight. Robbins practices catch-and-release fishing only and offers fly-fishing as well as mooching, a technique that involves long fishing rods, bait, and a slow-motion fishing style. Trips are six hours and may visit such destinations as Point-no-Point, Jefferson Head, Bainbridge, Vashon and Whidbey Islands, Possession Bar, Kingston, and other parts of Puget Sound depending on season. He provides all bait, tackle, and nonalcoholic beverages.

Farther south, Captain Tom Wolf runs saltwater fly trips out of Olympia for salmon and cutthroat. He can take two anglers at a time, and offers full-day (10 hours with deli lunch) and half-day options with tackle and instruction provided.

As with much river fishing, a benefit to being out on Puget Sound is that even if the fish are scarce, you'll be getting a first-class nature outing. Waterfowl are common, as well as bald eagles, ospreys, and various gull species. Robbins reports many sightings of orcas, sea lions, Dall's porpoise, river otters, and, usually some time in March, gray whales.

There are various shoreline areas worth a try if you're going it alone. Try Seacrest Marina on Elliott Bay in West Seattle, Lincoln Park in West Seattle, or Point-no-Point north of Seattle for coho and Chinook.

Directions: *To get to Seacrest,* take I-5 to exit 163A (West Seattle Bridge). Continue across the bridge and take the Harbor Ave. S.W. exit. Turn right at the light onto Harbor, then continue to Alki. You will pass Salty's Restaurant on your right. Park just past Salty's, where there is a fishing pier and bait shop.

Mecca

NEAH BAY

Location: The northwest tip of the Olympic Peninsula, 4–5 hours from Seattle by road or ferry and road.

Fish: Salmon, rockfish (sea bass), and lingcod.

Season: Year-round for bottom fish, fall for coho, late summer every other year for pink salmon

Outfitters: Chris Bellows at Topwater Charters offers saltwater fly-fishing out of Neah Bay (360-460-7479 year-round, 360-663-2682 in the winter months; www .fly-fishing-neahbay.com). He provides rods and flies.

Heads up: Bigger fish, wilder waters. This is also a destination for halibut fishing—more on this below.

Description: The northwest coast of the peninsula is one of the wildest spots around. Salmon out here are still storing up for the return to their natal streams, and the area off this coast is a major feeding ground. The fishing mainstay here is coho salmon, sought in the offshore tide rips and banks. Recent salmon seasons have been exceptional, after about a decade of decline. There are pink salmon in odd-numbered years. Bottom fish, including black rockfish and lingcod, are best in spring and early summer. Rockfish are considered especially aggressive and receptive to flies. Larger lingcod can be 5 to 15 pounds, and require bigger

Fly-Fishing & Sportfishing

flies sunk lower into the water, where they usually feed. The catch-and-keep limit is two hatchery coho per angler.

If you're coming all the way out here to fish, you should definitely make plans to visit Olympic National Park for hiking, camping, or beach walks. And right in Neah Bay you'll want to do some cultural research. This is the home of the Makah Nation, a group that became famous in recent years when it reinstituted a whale hunt. The Makah Cultural and Research Center (360-645-2711, www.makah .com) is a tribal museum with artifacts, a longhouse replica, and cedar dugout canoes. There are examples here of traditional whaling, sealing, and fishing gear.

Directions: There are several ways to get to the Olympic Peninsula from Seattle. For options, see *Getting to the Olympic Peninsula*, page 182. Once on the Peninsula, take US 101 west from Port Angeles to WA 113. Turn north and follow to WA 112, which takes you into Neah Bay.

Sea Monster

F PEOPLE OUT BUYING a pound of tender halibut cheeks to go with their chardonnay ever actually saw a full-grown specimen, they might avoid the fish counter altogether. As the cute baby halibut grows toward adulthood, it turns into a big lug, a Quasimodo, a—well, there's no way around it—a real bottom-feeder. The halibut gets huge and flat and white on one side, and its eyes kind of bunch up together on the top side like Picasso's wildest Guernica moment. The less squeamish Washington angler can check this out for herself by heading out to one of the state's halibut hotspots—La Push, Neah Bay, or Port Angeles.

Halibut are among the Northwest's burliest fish. They can grow to 400 pounds or more, but the state record for catching one is currently closer to 300 pounds. One fisherman described hauling in a big one this way: "It's like pulling up a refrigerator full of water, and the door's occasionally opening and closing." Charters are pretty crucial, at least your first time out, for locating the fish in their deep-water habitat: plateaus and sloping drop-offs. Also, reeling in a full-sized halibut can be dangerous, and you'll need to learn the rather brutal tactics used to dispatch something this large. If you're already at Neah Bay for saltwater fly-fishing, Gordy Bentler at the Cape Motel (360-645-2250) is a good source of halibut information.

Freshwater Fly-Fishing

Short Hops

SKYKOMISH RIVER

Location: About 40 miles northeast of Seattle
Fish: Coho, steelhead
Season: June through October for steelhead, fall for coho
Outfitters: Emerald Water Anglers (206-545-2197, www.emeraldwateranglers.com); Mike Kinney (360-435-3778, www.mikekinney.com); Ron's Guide Service (425-222-7654).
Map: *Washington Atlas and Gazetteer*
Heads up: Stunning setting, very popular
Description: The scenic "Sky" is especially gorgeous in winter, when the snowcapped Cascades jut up in the distance like something from a Swiss tale. These waters are

Fly-Fishing & Sportfishing

legendary in the Northwest for steelhead, and there's even a fly named after the river. Loved half to death, the Sky can be congested and difficult to fish. On a busy day you'll see lots of people up to the tops of their waders in the section near the town of Sultan, wrists flicking to and fro. For the hardcore angler who doesn't mind some bushwhacking, it is sometimes possible to find a beautiful stretch to call your own upriver, perhaps 10 to 15 miles past Sultan. "Higher up it can be gin clear, wadeable, and intimate," says Dave McCoy of Emerald Water Anglers.

Directions: Take I-5 north to Everett and the exit for US 2 toward Wenatchee. Continue east to the town of Sultan. You'll see the river on your right.

SNOQUALMIE RIVER

Location: About 25 miles east of Seattle

Fish: Rainbow and cutthroat trout, and winter and summer steelhead.

Outfitter: Creekside Angling Company in Issaquah is a nearby fly-fishing shop.

Map and book: *Washington Atlas and Gazetteer; Washington Fishing*

Description: Right off I-90, this is the closest river to Seattle. If you're traveling with people who don't appreciate your enthusiasm for fishing—say, the husband and kids—the Snoqualmie is the perfect destination. This kind of accessibility comes with a price: You're sure to have company, particularly on the weekends. When word gets out that the fish are there, the place mobs up—Gary at Kauffmann's Streamborn has seen 100 boats floating by in a day. He suggests waiting it out for a few days, to let the riff-raff disperse.

The Snoqualmie offers good fishing for rainbow, native cutthroat trout, and steelhead. To fish for trout, explore the three forks of the Snoqualmie in the immediate vicinity of North Bend. Which fork you choose depends on how determined you are to be alone, and how the waters are running. The South Fork is hemmed in by lots of private property, and you'll have to search out a good spot. The North Fork offers the easiest access, which means sharing space. The Middle Fork, unlike the proverbial bowl of porridge in the three bears story, is not "just right," but has some good things going for it. There will be more solitude here because there is less shoreline access, but this is also the best place to come when water volumes are low, since it's most likely to be fishable. The Middle Fork can be explored by following Middle Fork Road east from North Bend. The trout fishery is open from late spring until early fall. Park at an exit off-ramp and walk until you find a good spot.

If you have nonfishing companions, Snoqualmie Falls is a great place to leave them. The 268-foot falls are a spectacular sight. A hike to the bottom of the falls and back up, followed by a meal at the ritzy Salish Lodge (and possibly a trip to the heavenly Asian-style spa, complete with soaking pools) could easily keep your companions occupied for an entire afternoon. Meanwhile, fishing for steelhead is possible almost immediately below the falls.

Directions: A good jumping-off point for fishing the Snoqualmie is the town of Fall City. Take I-90 east from Seattle about 25 miles to Preston. Drive north on Preston–Fall City Rd. S.E. to Fall City. Cross the Snoqualmie River and turn right on WA 202 to go upstream toward Snoqualmie Falls and North Bend, where the Middle Fork is located. Turn left on WA 203 to go downstream.

Meccas

THE SKAGIT AND SAUK RIVERS

Location: The Skagit River and its principal tributary, the Sauk, are accessed an hour and a half north of Seattle on I-5.

Book: *Steelhead River Journal: Skagit-Sauk*

Contact: Emerald Water Anglers (206-545-2197, www .emeraldwateranglers.com) guides all-day floats here with gourmet meals included. Mike Kinney (360-435-3778, www .mikekinney.com) is the in-house guide for the well-known shop Creekside Angling Company, and has over 25 years of experience. Dennis Dickson specializes in guiding the Skagit and Sauk (360-435-6499, www.flyfishsteelhead.com).

Description: The Skagit is a big river. It has broad, sweeping runs that can be difficult to access effectively without a boat. On the other hand, the Sauk—the Skagit's biggest tributary—although untamed and fast flowing at times, is very accessible by foot. Approach the Skagit system this way: If you want to prospect for fish on foot, fish the Sauk. If you want to float, fish either.

The rivers support healthy runs of several species of salmon and trout, but are probably best known for spring steelhead. Some of the biggest native steelhead caught in Washington State, fish in excess of 30 pounds, come out of the Skagit. February through April is the prime time for catching native Skagit steelhead.

To fish the Skagit, follow I-5 about 80 miles north to Mount Vernon. It's not a bad idea to hire a guide for this river, to make sense of it your first time through. An added incentive to fish the Skagit is the fact that it hosts a large population of bald eagles that migrate south from Alaska and Canada to spend the winter. (See *Floating with the Big Birds*, page 86, for more information on eagle-watching float trips.)

The river above Darrington is closed to fishing after February 28. In most years, this comes before the bulk of the steelhead run has entered the river. If there are enough fish in the early part of the run, however, angling can be an exciting prospect. The river is smaller, because many tributaries have yet to enter it. Boat traffic is almost nonexistent so the wader has the river to him- or herself. Access to the upper river can be gained by following the Mountain Loop Highway (WA 20) south from Darrington. Following an extension of the highway, which crosses the Sauk where the White Chuck River joins it, allows access to the east side of the river. Four-wheel-drive vehicles are recommended for exploring much of the Sauk upstream of Darrington, particularly in winter. One suggestion for the boatless: Start the day on the North Fork of the Stillaguamish River, profiled below, and, after lunch, try the Sauk. Good water on the Stilly is only about fifteen minutes from Darrington. The rivers contrast nicely; the Stillaguamish is smaller and tamer as it wanders through farmland, while the Sauk is a brawling mountain stream. Also, if fish aren't in one, they may be in the other, since the timing of steelhead runs will vary greatly from river to river.

Directions: To fish the Skagit, follow I-5 about 80 miles north to Mount Vernon. From there, take WA 20 east. Most fishing activity happens around the towns of Concrete, Rockport, and Marblemount. If you're looking for a place to put your boat in the water, the Howard Miller Steelhead Park in Rockport is decent. To fish the Sauk, head north on I-5 to Arlington. Follow WA 530 east past Arlington and up the Stillaguamish River valley. The town of Darrington marks your arrival at the Sauk River. The most popular water to fish is between Darrington and the confluence with the Skagit; WA 530 follows this section. Access points are numerous. Several boat ramps can be found along the way as well—keep an eye out for trucks with trailers attached.

STILLAGUAMISH RIVER

Location: About an hour north of Seattle

Contact: Ted's Sport's Center (425-743-9505) in Lynnwood is a good resource.

Description: The Stillaguamish, or "Stilly," is one of the smaller rivers discussed here, however its importance in local river fishing history and lore might be the greatest. The North Fork of the Stilly gained a following during the 20th century that was rivaled by few rivers in Washington.

The hubbub centered upon a run of steelhead that returned to the same tributary, Deer Creek, every year during summer and early fall. These summer-run fish were relatively small (rarely over ten pounds) but extremely enthusiastic about taking dry flies, not a common steelhead trait. Dry fly-fishing on the Stilly caught on in the early part of the 20th century and by the 1940s and '50s had a devoted following. Local outdoor and sports writers gave voice to those who spent months every year on a stretch of the Stilly in the town of Oso, where it is joined by Deer Creek.

Unfortunately, much of the Deer Creek watershed is prime timberland, and logging operations that began in the 1950s had taken a heavy toll by the 1980s. Soil no longer held down by tree roots flowed freely into the creek and millions of tons of silt buried the gravel critical to the spawning fish. A steelhead run that once numbered around 2,000 fish a year dwindled to well below 100 by the late 1980s. Massive mudslides were discovered. A relentless outcry from Stillaguamish devotees eventually brought attention to the problem and an extensive restoration project was initiated to stabilize soil conditions. A pair of heavy floods in the early 1990s also washed away much of the silt. A significant portion of the damage has been undone. Salmon, steelhead, and cutthroat trout numbers have climbed back from the brink of extinction.

The North Fork of the Stillaguamish River is a joy to fish. If you don't have access to a boat or simply would rather hike, bushwhack, and wade, you'll definitely enjoy the Stilly. When rainfall is at normal levels, there are many places to ford, allowing access to much more water than big rivers such as the Skykomish or Skagit. The river supports populations of sea-run cutthroat trout, several species of salmon, and Dolly Varden trout as well, so check with a well-informed local to find out what might be in the river at any given time.

The Stillaguamish River is one of the few in Washington with fly-fishing-only regulations, although these are in effect for only part of the year. If you aren't fishing with a fly, check a Washington State Fish and Wildlife pamphlet to be sure you're in compliance.

Directions: Take I-5 north to Arlington (roughly 45 minutes to an hour). From Arlington, take WA 530 east toward Oso. The river fishes particularly well in the vicinity of Oso (downstream and in the town itself) all the way up to where the road ceases to follow it, about 5 miles from the town of Darrington. The stretch of river between Hazel and the confluence of the Boulder River has much good water and is worth exploring.

YAKIMA RIVER

Location: The Yakima River offers about 90 miles of trout fishing. One hub is the town of Ellensburg, about 110 miles east of Seattle.

Season: Year-round wild rainbow and cutthroat trout

Contact: Worley Bugger Fly Co. (888-950-FISH, www .worleybuggerflyco.com) is located in Ellensburg and has an extensive range of fly gear and guide services. The Evening Hatch (509-962-5959, www.flyfishnorthwest.com), also in Ellensburg, has a small fly shop, guide services, a deluxe riverside tent campground for clients with hot showers and a cook, and other amenities. Emerald Water Anglers (206-545-2197, www.emeraldwateranglers.com) leads full-day, gourmet float trips down the Yakima.

Heads up: The state's best trout river. If you prefer fishing the west side of the Cascades, it's still a great fall-back fishery when other rivers are washed out or closed.

Description: Less than a dozen years ago, this river was designated catch-and-release only between Snoqualmie Pass and Roza Dam, above Yakima. There are about 75 miles of such river in this "Blue Ribbon" stretch, which is perhaps Washington's only good, consistent trout stream. The Yakima flows from the slopes of the Cascades past farmland and into canyon country before spilling into the Columbia River. If you go to Ellensburg, a hub for fly-fishing shops and outfitters, you're about 15 minutes from Yakima Canyon, one of the most popular fishing stretches. The river also offers completely different scenery for a west slope angler. The semidesert canyon changes dramatically from one season to the next. In spring things turn green, and the hillsides are smothered in purple wildflowers. Guides report regular sightings of bighorn sheep on the cliffs, sometimes sparring during mating season. In the fall everything turns bright red and orange, and the harsh summer sun takes on a golden luminescence.

To expand your fishing choices, explore some of the popular lakes in this area, such as Lakes Lenore and Lenice.

Directions: Take I-90 east over Snoqualmie Pass to exit 109. At the stop sign turn right onto Canyon Rd. and enter the city of Ellensburg. Call or stop in at the contacts listed for directions to specific fishing sites. Canyon Rd. itself reaches the head of Yakima Canyon, the most popular reach of the river, about 4 miles past the turnoff above.

OLYMPIC PENINSULA RIVERS

Location: West of Seattle, on the other side of Puget Sound

Heads up: Incomparable

Contact: Good information is available from Three Rivers Resort and guide service in Forks (360-374-5300).

Description: Despite plenty of god-awful clear-cutting on the Olympic Peninsula, the area remains more remote and wild than anything you'll see on the Seattle side of Hood Canal. Several rivers in this region run through large areas of protected, old-growth temperate rain forest, in both national forest and national park land. This is the place to come for lots of trees, solitude, rain, moss, mist, elk, bears, and the opportunity, on rare occasions, to catch very large fish. A 20-pound steelhead or 40-pound Chinook is not unheard of. The Olympic Peninsula fishing experience is probably the one most unique to Washington State. Fishing here offers a chance to see a landscape that, at least in part, looks much as it must have when Captain George Vancouver first explored the area in the late 18th century. Realistically, a fishing trip to the peninsula is at least a two-or three-day affair.

Perhaps the best place to base yourself is the town of Forks. Situated near the northwest corner of the peninsula, Forks is within an hour's drive of exceptional fishing.

In the town's immediate vicinity are the Sol Duc, the Bogachiel, and the Calawah—three rivers that converge to form the Quillayute River. The rivers of the Quillayute system have some outstanding summer salmon fishing, but what they are probably best known for is winter steelhead. The rivers' lower reaches see a good deal of drift boat traffic most winters—somewhat surprising given the remote location. Guided trips are available through a number of local guide services. Fishing the upper stretches of these rivers is most often done by foot and can be very rewarding. The farther you ascend, the more spectacular the scenery becomes.

If a beautiful setting is a high priority on a peninsula fishing trip, the Hoh River should be first on your list. This is not to suggest that it's all looks and no substance, fishingwise. The Hoh has one of the best summer Chinook salmon runs in the state, not only in number of fish but also in size. Fish over 40 pounds are not uncommon. Winter steelhead are also more than respectable, with a healthy run of big, native fish.

What separates the Hoh from any other river in Washington is its surrounding environment. The stretch of the Hoh that is within Olympic National Park has never been logged—the land here is lush, untamed rain forest of incomparable beauty. Some of the largest spruce and fir trees in the world grow in this valley. The Hoh River owes much of its character to the forest's influence. When a tree falls into the water, that's where it stays. Cover is instantly provided for fish and other wildlife and the water's flow is diverted. Moss hangs everywhere. Don't expect to see blue sky while you're fishing the Hoh; instead, keep your eyes open for river otter and Roosevelt elk.

Another approach to fishing the peninsula involves heading to the north coast to fish for winter steelhead. A number of smaller rivers flow into the Strait of Juan de Fuca and generally receive far less fishing pressure than the bigger rivers.

Timing the run correctly is of great importance. Late winter through early spring is usually best, but it pays to check with someone who knows if the fish are in. These rivers favor the angler more interested in hiking than floating. Some of the better known rivers are the Hoko (which has a fly-fishing-only section), the Sekiu, the Pysht, and the Lyre.

Directions: See *Getting to the Olympic Peninsula*, page 182. Once on the peninsula, you'll need to follow directions from outfitters or fishing guides to reach the specific river that interests you.

ALPINE LAKES FISHING

Location: Alpine Lakes Wilderness, 362,000-plus acres of forest land roughly between I-90 and WA 2 east of Seattle

Contact: Mount Baker/Snoqualmie Forest Service (425-775-9702, www.fs.fed.us/r6/mbs); Wenatchee National Forest (509-662-4368, www.fs.fed.us/r6/Wenatchee. Also contact the Washington Department of Fish and Wildlife Web sites for permit and license information (see *Where to Connect*).

Heads up: More than 700 lakes and ponds. The season is generally midsummer to mid-fall only.

Description: If you'd like to hike a lot and fish a little, all while taking in spectacular views, pick your lightest gear and hit one of the trails in this backyard (and visited accordingly) wilderness. Glacial force scoured out pretty potholes in every low spot. The more you're willing to hike, the more likely you are to find a quiet spot of your own, beyond the hordes of picnicking day hikers. Rainbow, cutthroat, brook, and brown trout are what to look for here. Despite the fact that they've been cooped up in an icy puddle for a while, they can offer plenty of challenges. They're sensitive to noise and light, easily spooked by a big body casting a dark shadow over their placid paradise. Sometimes winter weather kills off the fish, so contact the forest service for current conditions. There are so many options for alpine lakes fishing in the area that a list here would barely scratch the surface. Get some hiking guidebooks (see *Where to Connect* in "Hiking") that give good trail descriptions in the wilderness area and talk to the rangers near the destination you're thinking about.

Directions: From Seattle, take I-90 east. Exit 45 will take you to Olallie and Talapus Lake trailhead, which also offers access to the Pratt Lake Trail and more lakes. Farther out on I-90, exit 54 takes you to Margaret Lake and Lake Lillian. Off US 2, FR 6412, FR 6830, and other forest roads offer good options. And there's much more. A few hundred lakes more.

Sportfishing

Longer Hops

WESTPORT

Location: About 130 miles southwest of Seattle
Fish: Coho and Chinook salmon, halibut, bottom fish, and sometimes tuna

Charters: There are many charter companies headquartered here. Coho Charters (800-572-0177, www.westportwa .com/coho/charter) takes boats out for all fisheries. Neptune Charters (800-422-0425, www.westportwa.com/neptune /index.html) offers much the same thing. Their gift shop in downtown Westport is a place you wouldn't want to swing a fishing rod, for fear of knocking the rack of seraphim angels into the shelf of Mount St. Helens glass art.

Heads up: Traditional coho mecca

Description: In the last decade, salmon fishing—for which Westport and the Grays Harbor area are famous— has been so poor that some businesses up and folded. The area's been developing its innate possibilities as a surfing and bird-watching destination in the years since, softening its macho image. Those who loved to fish Westport continued to visit and take charters out for halibut, rockfish, and, farther offshore, tuna, but it wasn't quite the same. Now, after a long hiatus, the wetsuit and binocular sets will have to move over—salmon season has been surging again, with people catching their legal limit of two Chinook or hatchery coho by midday. The coho season is generally open late June to the beginning of September. Halibut opens around May 1. Bottom-fishing season ranges from about March to October.

Many boats also offer whale-watching trips if you're looking for something to do in the non-fishing hours. Besides surfing and bird-watching, of course. (Check those two chapters for the Westport lowdown.) Also, though the razor clam season can be short because of marine toxins, you can dig for these sweet bivalves in the area in season.

Directions: Take I-90 south from Seattle about 65 miles to exit 104, US 101 north toward Aberdeen/Port Angeles. Take WA 8W toward Montesano and Aberdeen. Continue through Aberdeen and follow WA 105 to Westport.

ILWACO

Location: Long Beach Peninsula, about 180 miles southwest of Seattle

Fish: Coho and Chinook salmon, halibut, bottom fish, and sometimes tuna

Charters: Pacific Salmon Charters (800-831-2695, www.pacificsalmoncharters.com)

Heads up: Essentially the same fisheries as Westport, but with different après-fish activities available

Contact: The Long Beach Peninsula Tourist Bureau Web site (www.funbeach.com) will give details on the area, plus links to other peninsula sites. I can personally recommend two great places to stay: The Shelburne Inn in Seaview, which has been getting great write-ups for years and has the most delicious B&B breakfasts on the planet (plus a nice pub), and the wonderful Moby Dick in Nahcotta, which has a sauna with a view and the least fussy (and best) dinners I've had in the area.

Description: Ilwaco is just about on the southwest tip of Washington, and has a fishery very similar to Westport's, with the Columbia River just next door. Choosing between the two towns is somewhat a matter of non-fish amenities. For instance, Westport has wadeable beaches, whereas only a lunatic would go past their ankles in the wicked Long Beach surf. The peninsula, on the other hand, has a couple of very interesting features. Fort Canby State Park, right next to Ilwaco, has the distinction of being Lewis and Clark's old camping grounds, and an interpretive exhibit takes you through the history in detail. Ledbetter Point State Park, at the northern tip of the peninsula, is a fantastic birding destination (and sanctuary) and offers a gorgeous, wild walk on a windswept beach. In between these two is some serious beachfront kitsch (anyone for a photo of the world's largest frying pan?), going head to head with a handful of great inns and restaurants. There are enough festivals to fill the summer, including sandcastle building, kite flying, and chamber music. Lastly, be sure to sally through Oysterville, a historic town on the Willapa Bay side of the peninsula with beautiful old homes and lovely water views. You'll pass immense oystershell mountains on your approach, signs of the oyster-growing industry. A roadside stand in Oysterville sells them whole, smoked, or jarred.

Directions: Take I-5 south about 55 miles to Olympia. Take exit 104 to WA 8 west. In about 40 miles it becomes WA 12. Exit at Montesano, turning left onto US 107. Follow it to a T with US 101 in about 10 miles. Turn left. Continue on 101, winding along Willapa Bay (a beautiful drive, take it slow) to the junction with US 103 on the Long Beach Peninsula. Turn left to go to Ilwaco.

Bill McMillan:
The Interior Sport
of Steelhead Fly-Fishing

" QUIET, ALMOST DIFFIDENT man, country squire and Thoreau in equal measure. . . . In his virtuoso approach, steelhead fly fishing could still be grace and tradition." So says writer Trey Combs of Bill McMillan in his 1991 doorstop of a book, *Steelhead Fly Fishing*. After spending an afternoon with Bill, I can affirm that this is a man whose fiery nature has been tempered by a slow, deep, almost painful thoughtfulness about life. Steelhead devotees admire his legend, a man who used to fish at least 300 days a year, who perfected fly-fishing techniques that withstand trends and changing waters, whose book *Dry Line Steelhead* is described by Combs as "a graduate course in steelhead fly fishing." Others, like myself, are moved by his belief in fishing as a contemplative sport and by a life devoted to conservation and self-awareness in equal measure.

McMillan grew up on the Washougal River in southwest Washington, and currently lives on the Skagit River, north of Seattle. We first met when he was knee-deep in the waters of Piper's Creek here in the city, a bushy-haired, bearded man with deep-set, thoughtful eyes who looked to be in his 50s. He was wearing some sort of official vest to survey coho spawning for Washington Trout, an influential fish conservation organization he helped found. Not surprisingly, he was entirely comfortable talking to me about fish and creek restoration while standing thigh-deep in moving water. Recently I traveled to the cabin on the Skagit to learn more about his ideas on fishing and, as it turned out, life.

McMillan calls his fly-tying and writing shack Inner Sanctum. It's a tiny one-room shed-cabin, and there's a fishing net hanging by the door. From the rafters dangle plastic Ziploc bags, maybe 50 of them, all filled with colorful feathers for his fly-tying. Drawings of fish made by his son, now a fisheries biologist, are stuck around on the walls, and an old fly-tying table is covered with tools, a vise, and a set of pipes.

Here's what I learned about McMillan's life in a couple of hours.

On how he became involved in conservation:

"As a graduation present from high school my father said, 'I'd like to take you some place where you've always wanted to go fishing.' At that time one of the places that was first getting some notoriety for remarkable steelhead fishing was northern B.C., but it was very difficult to access. I'd read a few articles on this and said, you know, this is where I'd really like to go. . . .

My dad at first was taken aback, and then he thought: why not? I haven't taken a trip since before I had you.

McMillan's father rented a boat, and they floated down the

Babine River, catching steelhead. "It was my first experience seeing a river that had the humpback salmon. The bank was literally stacked a foot and a half high with all these rotting carcasses. At first the smell was just unbelievable. It was so overpowering it would just almost knock you out. . . . Little by little we got used to it, and finally got to the point where we didn't pay much attention to it. But it just so impressed me, that incredible abundance of fish. . . . I decided at that point . . . that I wanted to become a fisheries biologist."

Disenchanted with the hatchery-focused program he enrolled in at the University of Washington, McMillan quit, eventually helping to found Washington Trout, a fish conservation group whose main premise was that it was not connected with fishing itself. From the late 1970s to the early '90s much of McMillan's daily life was devoted to conservation, primarily as a volunteer. After a painful divorce, precipitated in part, he says, by his tunnel vision about fish conservation, he decided to rethink his "full frenzy" for this kind of work. "You pack this loaded gun inside yourself," he says. "You're constantly trying to create arguments against something, and you become wound up. We tend to think the world ought to be the way it was when we were born, and it breaks our hearts to see it changing." McMillan offers further explanation in the form of a story about the changing Northwest landscape. "One of the things that split me open was the eruption of Mount St. Helens. I used to go there as a Boy Scout. . . . The pristine rivers, lakes. . . . I didn't even want to consider that it didn't exist anymore. Yet five years later the South Fork of the Toutle River, which had been choked by ash, had more wild steelhead returning than any other river in the Columbia basin. Why? Because we left it alone. Everything I'd been trying to make perfect had been blown apart. . . . So I try to detach myself somewhat from believing my vision of the way things are supposed to be is the one." How does he remain a conservationist? "My life has to do something, and conservation work seems to me to have the least impact. I want to do what has the least impact—not so much my work or my beliefs but the way I live my life. I'm trying to live a life that's as nonconsumptive as possible. I used to be mad at the other guy, you know?"

On how he reconciles fishing and conservation:

"Fishing is the act that connects me with the outdoors. It's the only way to experience fish without a collection permit. It's a way to see beneath the water and study an animal I otherwise wouldn't have access to. But it becomes more and more difficult to rationalize our own impact: even catch-and-release involves mortality. Then again, if humans don't have some sort of connection with nature, there's no reason for them to live a life that recognizes it."

Bill had told me that he questioned the new, more "technical" direction fly-fishing had taken in recent years, a direction away from conservation toward consumption. I asked him to give me an example of this. He picked up a simple reel that he'd owned for years and handed it over. "Reels now cost $150 to $1,200, and all they're meant to do is hold a line," he said.

On his history as a steelhead fisherman:

"I'd done a lot of reading on fly-fishing since I was eight or nine years old. My dad started me fly-fishing when I was five or six. Steelhead fishing is very different from trout fishing. I spent two full years fishing with my father before I hooked my first steelhead. . . . It was that period of time just before adolescence and I really wanted to catch a steelhead. Sometimes I'd go out with my father and I'd come back so heartbroken I'd want to go cry. Everytime we went out he'd catch one, sometimes two or three. I caught lots of other things—salmon, sea-run cutthroat—but steelhead's what I wanted. Finally after two full years I caught my first steelhead."

I asked him what he thought had changed in that time.

"I came to firmly believe that fishing is some sort of spiritual connection inside. You have to be in the right frame of mind. You have to have confidence, for one thing." He hesitated for a moment. "There's an old Indian saying that an animal gives itself to you when you go hunting, and that you always have to honor that animal by treating it properly. For instance, West Coast Indians bury the first fish. They have ceremonies to honor it. They realize the very deep connection. The most successful hunters, the most successful fishermen, had something going for them other folks evidently did not. They had some sort of connection. I think it just takes persistence and time . . . deep desire. Once you get past that threshold, why then it tends to become fairly easy."

McMillan currently works part-time doing spawning surveys for Washington Trout, and is president of the board. The organization now has nearly a million-dollar budget, and a 2,000-person membership. See *Where to Connect* for more information.

Where to Connect

Clubs and Organizations

- Northwest Fly Anglers (www.northwestflyanglers.org) has been around since the 1970s and offers classes, river cleanups, events, guest speakers, and a library of books and videos.

- Northwest Women Flyfishers (www.northwestwomenfly fishers.org/) supports and educates women in the art of fly-fishing, offers fishing outings, and works on conservation issues. It is about 140 members strong.

- Pacific Rivers Council (541-345-0119, www.pacrivers.org) is a West Coast river conservation organization.

- People for Puget Sound (206-382-7007, www.pugetsound .org) is a nonprofit citizens' group working to restore Puget Sound health.

- Puget Soundkeeper Alliance (206-297-7002, www .pugetsoundkeeper.org) is another nonprofit working for the health of Puget Sound.

- Seattle Poggie Club (206-524-8880, www.seattlepoggies .com) is Seattle's oldest salmon fishing club.

- Washington Fly Fishing Club (www.wffc.com) is a conservation-oriented club that was founded in 1939 and is based on Mercer Island.

- Washington Trout (425-788-1167, www.washingtontrout.org) is a nonprofit conservation-ecology organization dedicated to the preservation and recovery of Washington's native fish and the ecosystems they depend on. They are extremely active, studying fish and ecosystems and raising consciousness about the impact of fish hatcheries on native fish runs.

- Wild Steelhead Coalition (www.wildsteelheadcoalition.com) is dedicated to reversing the decline of wild steelhead.

Shops

- Avid Angler Fly Shoppe (17171 Bothell Way N.E. Suite A130, 206-362-4030) is in Lake Forest Park.

- Creekside Angling Company (1180 N.W. Gilman Blvd., 425-392-3800, www.creeksideangling.com) is a well-regarded Issaquah fly-fishing outfitter.

- Kaufmann's Streamborn (1918 4th Ave., 206-448-0601, www.kman.com) is a major downtown fly-fishing shop and a great source of information.

- Ted's Sport Center (15526 WA 99, 425-743-9505) is north of Seattle in Lynnwood, with a complete selection of fishing tackle.

Books

- Combs, Trey. *Steelhead Fly Fishing: Tackle and Techniques, the Great Rivers, the Anglers and Their Fly Patterns.* New York: Lyons and Buford, 1991.

  ———. *Steelhead Fly Fishing and Flies.* Portland, OR: Frank Amato Publications, 1976. Still a classic of northwest fly fishing.

- *Evergreen-Pacific Fishing Guide Washington Waters: Hot Spots for Salmon and Bottom Fish.* Shoreline WA: Evergreen Pacific Publishing, 1998.

- Haig-Brown, Roderick. *Return to the River: The Classic Story of the Chinook Run and of the Men Who Fish It.* New York: Lyons and Buford, 1997.

- Hogan, Dec. *Steelhead River Journal: Skagit-Sauk.* Portland, OR: Frank Amato Publications, 1995. This and other Amato fishing publications can be ordered at www.amatobooks.com

- Love, Glen. *Fishing the Northwest: An Angler's Reader.* Corvallis, OR: Oregon State University Press/Northwest Readers, 2002. A recent anthology of Northwest fishing stories.

- Morris, Holly, ed. *A Different Angle: Fly Fishing Stories by Women.* Seattle, WA: Seal Press, 1995.

- Raymond, Steve. *Steelhead Country.* Seattle, WA: Sasquatch Books, 1994. Northwest author's essay collection on local rivers, tackle, and, of course, the mighty steelhead.

- Rudnick, Terry. *Foghorn Outdoors Washington Fishing.* Emeryville CA: Travel Publishing, 2002.

- Shorett, Dave. *Washington's Central Cascades Fly Fishing Guide.* Seattle, WA: Lake Stream Publications, 2001.

- Thomas, Greg. *Fly Fisher's Guide to Washington.* Belgrade, MT: Wilderness Adventure Press, 1999.

Fly-Fishing & Sportfishing

Links

www.wa.gov/wdfw/fish/regs/fishregs.htm for fishing regulations

www.wa.gov/wdfw/lic/formpage.htm for fishing licenses

www.wa.gov/wdfw/fish/plants/weekly for stocking schedule for lakes and streams

www.waterdata.usgs.gov/wa/nwis/current?type=flow for stream-flow data

www.tidepool.org for information on various subjects including salmon issues, hatchery news, and so forth

THE UNDULATING ATMOSPHERICS of Puget Sound are one of our city's most famous features. But for many people, even locals, Puget Sound is mostly about surface. The dark, cold waters are a sparkling backdrop to our skyline, provide protected passage to commercial vessels, and offer an excuse to take to a sailboat, ferry, or kayak. Few people, even locals, have ventured more than a fishing hook or a chilly set of toes below the Sound's skin, and therefore have no idea what goes on in the depths, though they may gotten a tantalizing taste through the Seattle Aquarium exhibit windows.

It's not surprising more people haven't been

down there, of course, since it's cold and deep. But this lack of attention to the ecosystem below has also meant the Sound has been regularly used as a place for our growing city to dump refuse and waste.

Those who do know the Sound's riches and fragility firsthand include an estimated 20,000 western Washington scuba divers who regularly take a look at our city from the other side of the glass.

"There are more nutrients in our water than in the Caribbean," says Karlista Rickerson, president of the Washington Scuba Alliance and a longtime local diver. Water from local rivers and the slow flushing of nutrients through this inland sea make for an incredibly rich sea habitat. The Sound shelters both the world's largest octopus, the giant Pacific, and one of the planet's smallest, the rubescent. Opalescent squid migrate near-shore seasonally in huge numbers, and divers hit the water off docks at night to watch them change color just before they mate. Some divers are particularly attracted to colorful invertebrates, such as lemon yellow nudibranchs and orange, feathery sea pens, while others seek out rarities, such as the six-gill shark, seen in few other waters. Seattle is fortunate to have many diving destinations, from decent beginner shore dives to epic, advanced boat dives within thirty minutes of the city. Only slightly farther away the gentle (and warmer) waters of Hood Canal and the diving mecca of the San Juan Islands draw divers from across the country. British Columbia diving, 3 to 10 hours away, depending on destination, is rated about the best in North America, if you're looking for a temporary break from the local scene. A smaller pool of divers also explores saltwater alternatives, diving from Lake Washington park shorelines, or into freshwater lakes on the Olympic Peninsula.

While our region is a dive destination for those in the

know, many people are deterred by our cold, glacier-fed northern waters or rumors of bad visibility. Some people can only stand an hour or so in a dry suit in Puget Sound, even in midsummer. The coldest diving season, winter, also tends to be the best for viewing. January, February, and March can offer 30- to 35-foot visibility, and much more in a good year. In summer during a plankton bloom visibility can decrease to four feet or less, but intrepid divers keep exploring, albeit staying close to shore or boat, and dive buddy. Or they wait for the feeding frenzy that clears up the water, jumping in just as soon as things look better.

In recent years it has often been divers who have raised the alert about the status of fish and the health of the water. "Divers start noticing what's missing," says Rickerson. "Particularly older divers take note of what used to be here. This has led to activism." Hazards for divers, especially near shore, include old drift nets and fishing line, which can be deadly if a diver becomes entangled and is unable to cut free. Currents are also a concern, though this to some extent depends on location—there are several destinations near Seattle where currents are rarely a problem.

Diving locally is not the easy, tropical vacation experience you'll have in Hawaii or the Caribbean, but it can be at least as rewarding. If you find yourself hooked on the idea, you'll soon find a passionate group of cohorts among local club members, dive-shop visitors, and outfitters. This chapter will get you started with descriptions of some of the most popular and accessible nearby shore dives and boat dives, and an overview of the local dive meccas. Get to know what lies beneath Puget Sound, and you'll never see it in the same way again.

Sea
Gardens

NOT ONLY IS THE WATER HERE COLDER, the plankton thicker, and the abundance of sea life staggering, but the diving habitat is very different from that most divers will have experienced at tropical destinations.

Except in the San Juan Islands, there are no rocky dropoffs here as there are in, say, Hawaii. Dives near Seattle are frequently to the sites of sunken boats, shipbuilding areas, sunken or crumbling docks and their pilings, or collections of debris piled up to create an artificial reef. Look for such fish as schooling pile perch, skinny tube-snouts, and shiners, and such bottom fish as sole, sanddabs, and flounder—the Sound is home to more than 200 fish species. Seals might swim by these near-shore habitats to see what you're up to.

Fish here are rarely bright, and they tend to blend in with their surroundings. Salmon offer a perfect example of local camouflage strategy. Dark on top and pale on the bottom, it is almost impossible to see salmon from the surface, because they blend in with the dark watery void, and nearly as difficult if you are looking up at them, when their underbellies mimic the lighter water near the surface. Rocky areas are particularly good for finding wolf eels and octopuses, both eagerly sought by divers for their rarity.

Another typical (though ever more endangered) local habitat is eelgrass: swaths of bright green blades that grow up to 4 feet tall or more in shallow shoreline areas. These beds are now thought of almost like underwater old-growth by scientists, who say they are crucial habitat for some salmon species and a nursery for other marine life. Many divers love to hone in on these underwater meadows to make a leisurely inspection, which might turn up Dungeness crabs, juvenile fish, tiny invertebrates such as snails clinging to blades, or nudibranchs feeding off these smaller species. Watch for pipefish here, whose shapes mimic the grass.

Over 500 species of seaweed are drifting about, including immense beds of knobby bull kelp growing up to 100 feet long. Swimming through are a large variety of fish and sometimes marine mammals, which hunt amongst the waving strands.

City Limits

SEACREST, ALKI BEACH, AND THE PIPELINE (SHORE DIVES)

Location: West Seattle

Difficulty: Beginner–advanced

Outfitter: Deep Fathom Supply (2645 Harbor SW near Seacrest Waterfront Park in West Seattle, 206-938-7784)

Description: West Seattle, southwest of downtown, offers a big swath of shoreline that draws urban divers. Protected by wind, with a gentle current and easy shore access, Seacrest is probably the top dive site. Sunken boats and I-beams provide habitat for octopuses, giant lingcod, shrimp, rock crabs, and other species. In recent years the site has drawn particular attention for the presence of six-gill sharks, a rarity currently under study by local scientists (see page 286). Night dives are especially popular.

Alki Beach is located along the busy strip past Seacrest. It's a popular park shared by in-line skaters, runners, baby strollers, and opportunistic gulls, and feels, in spite of the sometimes chilly winds, like a slice of Southern California. Across from the park is a commercial strip with coffee shops, pizza joints, and fish-and-chips restaurants. This site offers perhaps less to see than Seacrest, but it is more affected by north winds and sailboats that sometimes tack close to shore. The habitat is old wharf pilings, with some eelgrass and sand at the bottom. Expect to see a range of sea stars, nudibranchs, plumose anemones, crabs, and such fish as perch, tube-snouts, and English sole. The eelgrass bed farther out is a good place to look for a variety of species as well.

The Alki Pipeline is farther along at the south end of Constellation Park on Alki Point. Once used for sewage overflow during especially rainy winters, the pipe is enclosed by large rocks that draw fish and such invertebrates as plumose, swimming and elegant anemones, tube worms, decorator crabs, and sea slugs in winter. This is also a night dive destination.

Directions: Take I-5 south to exit 163A, West Seattle. Stay right on the exit toward West Seattle. Continue across the West Seattle Bridge and take the Harbor Ave. S.W. exit. Turn right at the light onto Harbor, then continue to Alki. You will pass Salty's Restaurant, a Seattle institution. Just past here is a fishing pier and bait shop. Park here for Seacrest. A buoy indicates the dive spot. For Alki Beach, continue on Alki Ave. to the southwest seawall near the intersection with 64th Ave. S.W. Parking along Alki is available, though it can be very limited on sunny weekends. Also note that most parking is for 2 hours only. The Alki Pipeline is on the west side of Alki, off the end of 63th Ave. S.W. and Beach Dr. S.W. at Constellation Park

Six-Gill Sharks

UNTIL RECENTLY, BIOLOGISTS usually saw a six-gill shark in the Puget Sound area only when it was dead or dying, washed up near shore. Lately, however, sightings have increased to the point where divers head out to a location, particularly at night, in hopes of spotting this ordinarily deep-sea species. According to the Washington Department of Fish and Wildlife (WDFW) biologist Wayne Palsson, commercial fishers are accidentally catching them, and bottom troll surveys in 2002 caught six or seven, while previous surveys turned up only one or two. The juveniles are most often seen and are 6 to 8 feet long or more. Mature specimens, infrequently sighted, grow up to 16 feet. They aren't the largest sharks in the Sound (basking sharks, a plankton-eating species, can stretch to 20 or 30 feet) but they're the largest fish most divers will ever catch sight of around here.

The six-gill fishery has been closed since sightings have increased, primarily because no one can yet say how many there are or what role they play in the local ecosystem. "We're using the precautionary principle," says Palsson. "There's way more that we don't know" about the species than what they do know. Various groups in the state are now launching studies of six-gills to gather more information.

Backyard

RICHMOND BEACH PARK (SHORE DIVE)

Location: In Shoreline, about 5 miles north of Seattle
Difficulty: Beginner
Book: *Northwest Shore Dives*
Description: This park just past North Seattle features a sandy beach and a decent beginner-intermediate dive or a satisfying snorkel for those looking for something nearby and sheltered. Bull kelp thrive here in late summer, giving cover for fish and other sea life. The beginning of the dive is quite shallow, from 10 to 12 feet, over sand and cobble. Farther out there is less to see and a steep drop-off. You might

spot perch, flounder, anemones, sea squirts, sea stars, and nudibranchs. Note that access to the beach is over a pedestrian bridge, so gear must be hauled for some distance.

Directions: Take I-5 north to exit 176 (175th St. and Aurora Ave. N.). Turn west at the bottom of the ramp and then right onto Aurora Ave. Turn left onto N. 185th St., which becomes Richmond Beach Rd. Continue to 20th Ave. W. and turn left to Richmond Beach Park. At the entrance, go down a hill to the parking area, where you will see a footbridge leading to the beach.

EDMONDS UNDERWATER PARK (SHORE DIVE)

Location: In Edmonds, about 14 miles north of Seattle
Difficulty: Intermediate
Outfitter: Edmonds Underwater Sports
Description: Just north of the Edmonds ferry dock, one of the first underwater parks established on the West Coast draws avid divers from all over the region. The park is well set up with outdoor showers and an underwater park map near the entry point. Local volunteers, in particular diver Bruce Higgins, have devoted years to improving on the original feature here, a 300-plus-foot dry dock that was sunk in 1935. Other structures include reef balls, various pipes, and an old tugboat, and several trails established to find them all. Some of the healthiest eelgrass beds anywhere are here. The dry dock itself is a mosaic of colorful tube worms and frilly white sea anemones. You'll find all kinds of invertebrates, including sea cucumbers, scallops, a variety of anemones and nudibranchs, but divers rave in particular about the big fish. This area has been a marine reserve since the 1970s, and fishing is prohibited. As a result, the huge lingcod and cabezon cast serious shadows. Hazards include the nearby

ferry dock—be sure not to stray in that direction. There can also be a long surface swim to get to the sites, and occasional current concerns.

Directions: Take I-5 north to the Edmonds/Kingston Ferry exit, and follow signs to the ferry. As you approach the ferry ticket area, do not get into line but go to the left with non-ferry traffic. Turn left onto Dayton Street. When approaching the ferry dock move to the right lane and cross over the train tracks on Railroad Ave. The park is on the left in about 0.3 mile.

EDMONDS OIL DOCK (SHORE DIVE)

Location: In Edmonds, about 14 miles north of Seattle
Difficulty: Intermediate
Outfitter: Edmonds Underwater Sports
Description: A second marine sanctuary in Edmonds, also easily accessible and protected, it is good for a change of scenery or an escape from the Underwater Park crowd. The pilings of the long, T-shaped dock draw fish like a reef might, and provide a haven for tube worms, huge sun stars, and other creatures. Beginners or snorkelers might hang out in the shallows to look around. Any more wandering requires a tolerance for swimming and more advanced skills: water can get deep, wind can be a problem, and if you wander too far you might rub up against boat traffic. Divers are especially fond of the area just north of the dock, where large rocks shelter schools of ratfish. Divers have also seen wolf eels, octopuses, and shrimp, and occasionally are investigated by curious California sea lions.

Directions: Follow directions to Edmonds for Edmonds Underwater Park (see page 288). When you approach the stoplight and ferry ticket area, turn left onto Dayton St.

Cross railroad tracks and follow this road as it curves left and becomes Admiral Way. Edmonds Marina Beach Park appears shortly on your right.

THREE TREE POINT–NORTH SHORE (SHORE DIVE)

Location: In Burien, about 13 miles south of Seattle
Difficulty: Intermediate
Outfitters: Poseidon Diving and WaterSports; TLSea Dive Center
Description: South of West Seattle, this point of land draws sea life with the currents. Both the south and north shores are accessible and worth visiting. Burien castoffs, including various pipes, bottles, busted beer kegs and other above-water eyesores, are transformed into an artificial reef on the sandy, silty bottom of the north shore and provide habitat for a variety of invertebrates and fish. Night divers are sometimes rewarded with sightings of giant Pacific octopus, stubby squid, rubescent octopus, and even six-gill sharks. An eelgrass bed is good for close-up study, sometimes yielding spiny lumpsuckers, tube-snouts, and other hard-to-spot species. Currents are considered moderate. Be aware that beach access is limited—on either side of the access point is private property. Don't trespass. Also, parking is limited to five or six cars.
Directions: Take I-5 south and exit at 154A, Burien/Sea-Tac, heading west on WA 518 toward Burien. Continue past the airport exit into Burien, across 1st Ave. S. Drive one block past 9th Ave. S.W. and turn left onto Ambaum Blvd. Turn right onto S.W. 152nd St. Continue on this street to where 152nd curves left onto Maplewild Ave. S.W. Follow this about 1.5 miles and turn right onto S.W. 170th St. Park at the end of S.W. 170th.

TITLOW MARINE SANCTUARY (SHORE DIVE)

Location: Tacoma, about 35 miles south of Seattle

Difficulty: Intermediate, depending on the current

Outfitters: Tacoma branches of Lighthouse Diving Center and Underwater Sports

Description: Down in Seattle's southern sister, Tacoma, the popular Titlow dive site is visited regularly by dive classes. Like many other Puget Sound locations, the attraction is a rotted ferry pier whose rows of pilings are draped and spangled with sea life. In particular, the translucent white blanket of plumose anemones, when seen through sunlight in the green water, is "like a cathedral" says diver Karlista Rickerson. There is also a crumbling wooden barge southwest of the pilings that provides its own habitat. The bottom is sandy and shell-speckled. Hermit crabs, sea urchins, sea pens, nudibranchs, and a variety of fish, including flounder, perch, and ratfish, are all seen here. This dive should be planned during slack tide, since the currents are otherwise quite strong. Also, watch for boat traffic at the nearby marina.

Directions: Take I-5 south to exit 132 for WA 16 west (Gig Harbor/Bremerton). Take the Jackson Ave. exit before the Tacoma Narrows Bridge. Turn left onto Jackson. Turn right onto 6th. Take 6th downhill to the water. Parking is adjacent to the railroad tracks near Titlow Beach.

SUNRISE BEACH COUNTY PARK (SHORE DIVE)

Location: Gig Harbor, about 45 miles southwest of Seattle

Difficulty: Intermediate

Book: *Northwest Shore Dives*

Outfitter: None currently in the area; contact Tagert's

Dive Locker in Port Orchard (360-895-7860), which once had a Gig Harbor outlet, for more information.

Description: This is a very popular dive because of the abundant sea life in a concentrated area. "It's pretty much a slam-dunk," according to the folks at Bandito Charters, who say it's one of their most popular boat dives. You'll understand why you'd bother to charter here when you head down to the water—there's a long, steep hill between the parking lot and the dive site. Favorite inhabitants of the rock ledges are the wolf eels, which are abundant. Both these and octopuses are fed by divers, *usually* without incident (watch those fingers). The drawback for a shore dive, besides the walk in and out with heavy gear, is the fact that strong currents are common. Divers say a visit can be glorious or truly awful, depending on how well you time it. This became a protected area in 2001—only salmon fishing is allowed—so it is possible there will be a healthy increase in numbers and size of fish here in coming years.

Directions: Take I-5 south to exit 132, WA 16 west (Gig Harbor/Bremerton). Follow WA 16 across the Tacoma Narrows Bridge. After the bridge drive just over 3 miles to the Gig Harbor/City Center exit. After exiting, turn right at the stoplight onto Pioneer Way. Drive downhill into Gig Harbor. At the bottom of the hill, turn left onto Harborview Dr. The road curves right into Stinson Ave., then right (get into right turn lane) onto Harborview Dr. again. Stay right onto Vernhardson St. This becomes 96th St. for 0.3 mile. Turn left onto Crescent Valley Dr. N.W. Drive 0.6 mile and turn right at the fire station onto Drummond Dr. N.W. At the top of the hill (less than a mile), turn right at the stop sign onto Moller Dr. N.W. then left onto Sunrise Beach Dr. N.W. Follow this for 0.5 mile and turn left into the park.

The Best of Backyard Boat Dives

While there are plenty of shore dives within 30 miles of Seattle, they're mostly concentrated around old pilings or docks accessed from sloping beaches. You can add some variety by getting on board a charter, which can shuttle you to an otherwise inaccessible wall dive or wreck. Some of these dives are suitable for the newly certified, but there are also some extremely advanced dives, including an eerie trip to see the remains of Galloping Gertie, the elegant but doomed suspension bridge that originally spanned the Tacoma Narrows and bucked its way to oblivion during a windstorm in November 1940.

VASHON ISLAND BOAT DIVES

Outfitters: Bandito Charters; Spirit Diver; Sound Wave Scuba

Book: *Northwest Boat Dives*

Description: Much of Vashon Island diving, tantalizingly close to Seattle, is off-limits to shore divers because of poor or restricted access. Four sites are particularly appealing for boat dives, however, and readily available for a reasonable price. The Cove Motel lives up to its name, with shelves and rock outcroppings that offer nooks and crannies for a variety of species. Octopuses have been seen here. Maury Island Barges, a slightly deeper dive at 40 to 70 feet, is the broken up remains of a sunken barge, and fairly well protected from currents. KVI Reef offers a manmade reef and sunken boats.

In a different category is the more difficult Dalco Wall dive, locally known as one of the best wall dives in Puget Sound. Just west of the Vashon/Point Defiance ferry landing, Dalco is a sandstone wall with a sheer drop to 95 feet and a steep slope beyond. Divers enjoy working their way down the wall to investigate the many holes and cracks that shelter octopus, wolf eels, and other species. The dive is potentially dangerous because of strong Tacoma Narrows currents—only advanced divers should attempt it, and they will have to be aware of tides and currents.

Between Vashon and West Seattle, Blake Island is another great destination (also beloved of kayakers and sailors) for area charters, with an artificial reef where wolf eel, lingcod, octopus, and the other regulars hang out.

TACOMA BOAT DIVES

Outfitters: Bandito Charters; Spirit Diver; Sound Wave Scuba

Book: *Northwest Boat Dives*

Description: South of Vashon, the area around the Tacoma Narrows, the sliver of water separating the Olympic Peninsula from the other side of Puget Sound, is a frequent destination for intermediate and advanced diving. Dive boats offer several drift dives here in the fast currents, with a variety of fish and a chance to visit the old stanchions of the first Tacoma Narrows bridge, which collapsed into the water on November 7, 1940. A trip to Galloping Gertie, named for her tendency to sway in the wind, requires more advanced dive skills, and is usually offered only to those with a deep water specialty. "There's an overwhelming sense of something black in front of you," as diver Karlista Rickerson describes the approach, "and then suddenly you realize you're at a road bed." The bridge, now on the National Register of His-

Scuba

toric Places, is considered to be the "largest manmade structure ever lost at sea," about the size of five and a half Titanics placed end to end, according to the Gig Harbor Peninsula Historical Society and Museum. The bridge undulated 3 to 5 feet during a 35-plus-mph windstorm, causing officials to close it. No one was on the structure when it began to twist and then break apart, eventually falling into the deep waters of the narrows.

The museum offers an online exhibit about the bridge, complete with historic photos (www.gigharbormuseum.org).

Short Hop

HOOD CANAL (SHORE AND BOAT DIVES)

Location: About 90 miles west of Seattle
Books: *Northwest Shore Dives; Northwest Boat Dives*
Outfitters: Mike's Diving Center; Hood Sport N'Dive; Pacific Adventures
Description: The long, narrow, deep channel of Hood Canal, actually a fjord, has long been a draw for Northwest divers looking for protected diving and warmer water. The currents here are deep (the canal itself reaches depths of 600 feet) and, unlike other meccas like the San Juan Islands, easy to swim against. In the summer surface water temperatures can reach 70°F. For this reason many dive shops, including those in Oregon, travel here with classes for certification. The west side of the canal is ground zero, with more access and lots of rocky areas near shore. Popular areas include Octopus Hole and Sund Rock. The latter, a marine protected area, was "almost lifeless" in the early 1990s, according to Wayne Palsson of the Washington Department of Fish and Wildlife. Since the protection went

into effect in 1994, rarely seen area species such as vermilion and yellow-eye rockfish can be found here, along with swarms, says Palsson, of copper rockfish. Mid-canal offers boat diving out of Pleasant Harbor. The east side has few access points and is not as rocky.

People are particularly drawn to Hood Canal to see octopuses and wolf eels, which seem to be spotted more frequently here, perhaps because their habitat is concentrated into a smaller space than in other Puget Sound–area dive sites. Summer diving is the warmest, of course, and also the optimal time to go hiking, camping, or, if you've brought your gear, windsurfing. Of course this is also the time of lowest water visibility, and occasionally algae blooms will make conditions difficult. Winter visibility can be 50 to 60 feet or more, though the canal can also get cold, even icing over during particularly chilly winters. The mix of seasonal advantages means Hood Canal has divers all year: "We've got 50 to 300 divers here every year, 50 weekends out of 52," say the folks at the Hood Sport N'Dive Shop.

Directions: To get to Hoodsport drive south on I-5 to Olympia and take exit 104 (US 101) to Shelton exit (US 101N). Continue north 28 miles.

Octopus Week

I N A BACKROOM at the Seattle Aquarium, Roland Anderson, an aquarium curator, pushes back the lid on a dark tank of water and suggests I dabble my fingers in it. It takes a few moments to work up my nerve. Anderson's just been explaining to me that octopuses (they're no longer called octopi, which Anderson says sounds "pedantic") have beaks and can bite. He's the expert, though, and who knows when I'll have another chance to say hello to this generally reclusive species. I take a

Scuba

deep whiff of air that smells like iced seaweed and attempt a flirty finger wave an inch below the water's surface. And watch. Something is emerging from the corner—a long, ruddy arm that gathers speed as it goes, like a row of dominos falling. And when it touches me I . . . jerk back.

"Now try it without jerking back" Anderson encourages, a smile on his flushed face. Summoning confidence, I extend my arm and try the hand flutter once more. This time the octopus takes full possession of my fingers in its slick, muscular grip, suckers attaching themselves to me one by one. It's the strangest handshake I've ever encountered. The grip gets tighter and tighter until Anderson reaches in, unpeeling the arm like a stick-on tattoo. As a gift to my new acquaintance I'm next assigned to feed this burly cephalopod a frozen trout. While I cling to the slimy fish, the octopus first touches, then oozes its way over it, enveloping dinner until all I've got is a tenuous grip on the fish tail. I let go, and the octopus makes it disappear. It's as deliberate and unhurried as a magic trick. I am under the thrall of the magician.

"They've fascinated humans for millennia," says Anderson. "They're related to clams, but they have eyes that look back at you." They also have sophisticated forms of camouflage, including the ability to change color, and in captivity can puzzle out mazes and open jars.

This explains why the aquarium's annual Octopus Week has been so successful. Held in February, the event draws huge crowds, which gather around for such moments as the octopus weigh-in—the Aquarium's resident giant Pacific octopus (Dofleini) is checked for size—and the release of an octopus into the wild. Puget Sound is home to the largest octopuses in the world: they can weigh over 100 pounds and have an arm span of over 20 feet. All this growing takes place within the average life span of three years. One female can produce 70,000 eggs at a go, which she then protects by hibernating in a den, guarding her progeny for several months until they hatch. As part of

Octopus Week, local scuba divers take part in a survey to try to gather more data on the species. The underwater census-takers drop in at likely octopus locations and count up all the creatures they find during several days of Octopus Week, keeping track of both the giant Pacific and the tiny red octopus (rubescens). Rocky sites are the most likely place to find octopuses. For more information on these events, contact the Seattle Aquarium (www.Seattleaquarium.org). Local clubs and shops and *Northwest Dive News* also cover the event.

 Meccas

SAN JUAN ISLANDS (SHORE AND BOAT DIVES)

Location: Anacortes, the ferry gateway to the San Juans, is about 80 miles north of Seattle

Book: *101 Dives*

Outfitter: Island Dive and Watersports

Description: Just as they are meccas for sea kayaking, and sailing, these islands are internationally known for cold-water diving. The rocky islands offer great reefs (rare in western Washington) and wall dives as well as kelp beds that grow lush in late spring. The rock is known for sheltering incredibly colorful sea life, from tube worms to sea anemones, bright sponges, and red and green sea urchins. You'll probably see a wide variety of fish, including lingcod, rockfish, and cabezon, all generally bigger than those sighted farther south, where they are more likely to be fished out. Rare abalone are still found off Lopez Island, and the elusive and highly intelligent giant octopus is also regularly sighted. There are several good shore dives, but more popular are the boat dives, both full-day and multiday outings that may include drift diving or a trip north to British Columbia waters.

Directions: To get to the ferry launch to the San Juan Islands, drive north on I-5 to Mount Vernon and then take WA 20 west to Anacortes, and follow signs for ferries.

PITCHING TENT

san juan county park

SEVERAL INTERMEDIATE SHORE dives are available from San Juan County Park on San Juan Island, and if you stay there you'll have immediate access to all of them. The rocky shores attract a vivid array of invertebrates, from yellow sponges and cup corals to citrus-orange nudibranchs and sunflower sea stars. Consult Stephen Fischnaller's *Northwest Shore Dives* or a local outfitter for details on these dives.

The San Juan Island off-season is considered to be between October and April, and you'll have the best luck getting a spot at these times. Summer can draw mobs, especially on sunny weekends. The campsites are popular with kayakers, who can put in nearby, and whale-watchers, since this locale is known to be prime orca territory. Most sites offer water views.

Reservations are strongly recommended in high season, though it may take you some time to grasp the byzantine regulations. The campground is open year-round. Fees can be steep for camping in high season, but are a little lower in the off-season. The reservation line (360-378-1842) is open for nonresidents between March 19 and August 29, Monday through Friday from 12 to 4 P.M. though they reserve the right to change those particulars at any time. You must reserve at least five days in advance, but not more than 90 days in advance. That said, of course it's worth it. Strolling to the dive site from your tent? Priceless.

BRITISH COLUMBIA (SHORE AND BOAT DIVES)

Location: 3 to 6 hours north of Seattle

Outfitters: Diving Locker; God's Pocket Resort; Porpoise Bay Charters

Description: Mulling over all the stellar diving choices in the Seattle area? Here's another option: the inland and coastal salt water of the Vancouver, B.C., area. For at least three years in a row, *Scuba Diving* readers have rated British Columbia North America's number one diving destination. Marine life is relatively well-protected and there are a variety of interesting dive habitats. It's also an excellent place to travel if you are accompanied by the scuba-allergic, because there are plenty of other things to do, and the area is extremely scenic. Right near Vancouver are wrecks in the Gulf Islands, also a great place for sailing and kayaking. The Campbell River area is known for spectacular drift dives. In Port Hardy you can swim with white-sided dolphins, and in Barkley Sound, on Vancouver Island's wild west coast, visit wrecks in what is known as the graveyard of the Pacific. Huge six-gill sharks and gigantic California mussels also inhabit the area. Outfitters can connect you with shore dives, day charters, and multiday live-aboard options.

Karlista Rickerson

SOMETIMES ACTIVISTS—AND SPORTSPEOPLE—ARE just waiting for the right catalyst. Vashon scuba diver Karlista Rickerson is a case in point. She grew up on Vashon Island, bringing home sea stars, jellyfish, and clams from her regular forays on local beaches, accustomed to Sound waters as an extension of her backyard. But it wasn't until

Mother's Day in 1981 that she tugged on scuba gear and went in deeper. "My youngest son went to welding school and got certified as a diver. He and his brother decided to take me diving for Mother's Day. They took me in a 'uni-suit,' a Pillsbury doughboy thing. I had 35 pounds of lead on me. They took me on a moonlight dive so I could see the phosphorescence, and I was so entranced I went and got certified." Since then she has been diving in Palau, Truk, Fiji, the Great Barrier Reef, the Caymans, and the Bahamas, and when she's home she tries to dive three times a month "if I can find a dive buddy." These days she always brings an underwater camera. "I was always trying to describe what was under there to my husband when I came back from a dive, but I couldn't quite remember everything."

Rickerson helped start the Washington Scuba Alliance in 1992, an advocacy group for underwater parks as safe havens for marine life which works with a variety of government departments and volunteer divers. "She's been an enthusiastic citizen monitor and force for conserving Puget Sound resources," says Washington Department of Fish and Wildlife biologist Wayne Palsson. For more information contact Rickerson at (206) 463-2497. Rickerson sells her photographs of Puget Sound fish on notecards or as enlargements. If you want to see a preview of the giant sculpin, crescent gunnel, giant sea anemone, or other species you'll find at local scuba sites you can give her a call.

Where to Connect

Clubs and Organizations

- Bottom Dwellers (206-329-6901, www.bottomdwellers.org). Gay and lesbian Seattle-area divers.

- Depth Chargers (253-661-1934, www.scubaset.com has a

link to Depth Chargers) is a Federal Way dive club connected to the ScubaSET dive shop.

- Kelp Krawlers (Ed Main at 360-507-5987, www.kelpkrawler .com). Active Olympia-area divers.

- Marker Buoy Dive Club (206-361-9584, www .markerbuoydiveclub.org) is a very active Seattle-based club with meetings in Ballard. Frequent night dives in West Seattle; they also go much farther afield.

- Moss Bay Divers Association (425-827-6584, www .mossbaydivers.com) is a Kirkland-based club.

- Northwest Aquanuts (Scott Dennis at 253-854-1193) is a long-standing South King County club with outings and community service projects.

- The Pacific Northwest Aquatic Alliance (www.onwaa.org) promotes efforts to create responsible artificial reefs in the Pacific Northwest.

- Washington Scuba Alliance (Karlista Rickerson at 206-463-2497, www.oceanwildernessnetwork.org—click "Take Action Now" and then "Washington") is an activist group working to establish marine protected areas and to promote underwater parks for divers and snorkelers.

Shops and Outfitters

Seattle Area
The quality of your experience at the shop has a lot to do with who is working there at the time—local shops generally have a big turnover.

- Bubbles Below (425-424-3483, www.bubblesbelow.com) is a Woodinville-based dive store.

- Deep Fathom Supply (206-938-7784 or 800-442-DIVE) is located near Seacrest Waterfront Park on Alki Beach in West Seattle.

- The Dive Shop (425-482-2800, www.thedive-shop.com) is located in Bothell.

- Fifth Dimension Scuba Diving Center (253-854-6692, www.fifthd.com) has two locations, one in Kent for south Sound diving, and one on the eastside in Issaquah.

- Lighthouse Diving Centers (206-524-1633 for the Seattle store, www.lighthousediving.com) is a big local center with three locations: Lynnwood, Seattle, and Tacoma.

- Poseidon Diving and Watersports (810 SW 151st St. in Burien, 206-835-1314) is located about a mile from Three Tree Point.

- ScubaSET Adventure Center (253-661-9299 or 877-929-4422, www.scubaset.com) is located in Federal Way.

- Silent World Diving Systems (800-841-DIVE, www .silent-world.com) is located in Bellevue.

- TLSea Dive Center (23405 Pacific Highway S., 206-824-4100 or 888-448-5732) is located in Des Moines and offers a wide range of diver training, equipment, and trips.

- Underwater Sports (10545 Aurora Ave. N., 800-252-7177, www.underwatersports.com) is a big, established dive store with several branch locations. The Edmonds branch (264 Railroad Ave., 425-771-6322) serves the Edmonds Underwater Park.

Hood Canal
- Hood Sport N'Dive (360-877-6818; www.hoodsportndive .com) offers sales, repairs, and kayak rentals for diving and can connect you with lodging options.

- Mike's Diving Center (2 miles south of Hoodsport on US 101, 360-877-9568) has been operated by Shirley and Mike Smith for the past 27 years. The center offers classes, rentals, repairs, and one-on-one dive outings. They rent a house to divers that sleeps up to six.

- Pacific Adventures (206-714-1482, www.pacadventure.com) is the only charter service for diving in the area. They have a boat out of Pleasant Harbor, at mid-canal.

British Columbia

- Diving Locker (800-348-3398, www.kochersdiving.com) store has been around since 1972, with several British Columbia locations. They offer free Sunday dives, night dives, and all kinds of trip possibilities, including Barkley Sound and Campbell River. Some trips are coordinated with dive lodges at destinations.

- God's Pocket Resort (250-949-1755, www.godspocket.com) is highly recommended by several Seattle-area divers. A land-based scuba resort on the inside (east side) of Vancouver Island, they are only a few minutes from Browning Passage. They offer two or more boat dives a day, three meals, and lodging.

- Porpoise Bay Charters (800-665-3483, www.porpoisebaycharters.com) is another recommended dive company on Sechelt Inlet on British Columbia's Sunshine Coast. They offer charters, beachside cabins, and dive packages with meals and lodging included. Kayaks also available.

Charters

- Bandito Charters (253-973-0370, www.banditocharters.com) in South Puget Sound offers charters to Vashon, Tacoma, and other sites.

- Island Dive and Watersports (800-303-8386, www.divesanjuan.com) is a premiere San Juan Island dive outfitter with locations on Orcas and San Juan Islands. They have full-day and multiday trips and can arrange travel plans to and around the islands.

- Sound Wave Scuba (206-718-4019, www.soundwavescuba.com) based on Vashon Island has two dive boats for Puget Sound and occasional San Juan Island dives. Many advanced south Sound dives.

- Spirit Diver (call Exotic Aquatics at 206-842-1980, www .web.idirect.com/~diving/home.htm) is run by retired Washington State Ferries captain Alan Gill.

Books and Resources

- Bliss, Dave. *Northwest Boat Dives: 60 Ultimate Dives in Puget Sound and Hood Canal.* Seattle, WA: Sasquatch, 1997. Limited number of boat dives in the area, but offers helpful GPS coordinates.

- Fischnaller, Stephen. *Northwest Shore Dives*, 3d ed. Olympia, WA: BioMarine Images, 2000. Big guidebook to western Washington shore dives with color photos and lots of description.

- *Northwest Dive News* (360-240-1874, www.Nwdivenews .com) is an entertaining and informative monthly newsprint dive magazine.

- Pratt-Johnson, Betty. *101 Dives: From the Mainland of Washington and British Columbia.* Victoria, B.C.: Heritage House Publishing Co., 1997. This highly regarded guidebook covers everything from shore dives, boat dives, and kayak dives to night diving, junk collecting, marine hazards, sea life, and anything else you want to know. Wide range of locations.

Sailing

I **F KAYAKING AND** canoeing bring you closer to the experience of Northwest natives, who once laced the Sound and inland waters with their wooden craft, sailing will put you in contact with the water the way nonnative explorers saw it. You could do worse than read the first 75 or so pages of Jonathan Raban's *Passage to Juneau* before you set foot on deck in our area, to get both a portrait of a modern Seattle sailor and a start on the history of Captain Vancouver and his crew as they tacked and jibed their way through the Inside Passage at the end of the 18th century.

Though there is at least one traditional ("khakis and Top-Siders," as one man put it) sailing club here, sailing in this town, in typical Northwest

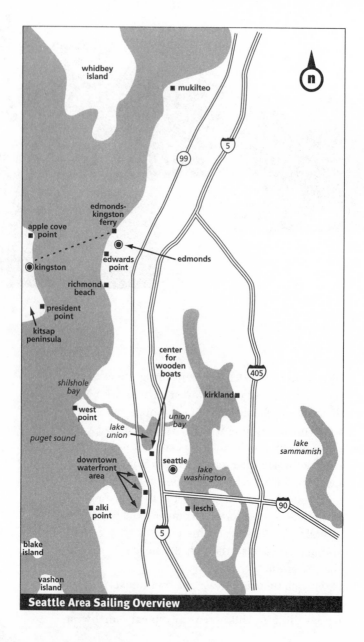

Seattle Area Sailing Overview

fashion, is a fairly democratic sport. Engineers, artists, and fishermen find their way to owning a boat if they want one, or they volunteer at a club and get cheap access without the overhead. Huge yachts are docked all over the city, but so are crumbling follies.

The sailing year is equally loose. Unlike most of the East Coast, our winters are mild enough that you don't ever have to take your boat out of the water. The busiest season is still spring through late fall, though, when you'll find races every night of the week. Summers seem to stretch forever, as sailors take advantage of the long nights in the months before and after the summer solstice—even if you can't knock off work before five you'll still have at least four hours of daylight ahead of you in midsummer. A common occurrence in this season is for wind to die right around 5 P.M. and to pick up again at 6, going light and steady for the rest of the evening. In spring and fall the winds can be stronger, averaging perhaps 10 to 15 knots.

Experienced sailors will find all kinds of camaraderie, with formal clubs and many impromptu racing teams. Those new to the pastime can get involved in a variety of ways. The city of Seattle has two boathouses at Green Lake and Lake Washington offering reasonably priced sailing classes for all levels. Several other good schools are linked to clubs or charter businesses. And even boat rental companies that outfit kayakers and other boaters have gotten into the picture. *Where to Connect* outlines some of the many options.

In-city sailing takes place either in Lake Washington and Lake Union or in Puget Sound, generally off the shores of the enormous Shilshole Bay Marina. If you're heading farther afield, charters are available for exploring nearby islands, South Puget Sound, and the San Juan Islands, or as far north as British Columbia. You'll probably want your own boat to cut loose, à la Raban, all the way to Alaska.

City Limits

SHILSHOLE BAY

Location: Northwest of downtown

Outfitter and Clubs: Windworks Sailing Center; Seattle Sailing Club; Corinthian Yacht Club

Map and Book: Maptech Waterproof Chart Book: Puget Sound and San Juans; *A Cruising Guide to Puget Sound*

Heads up: Just south of the marina are a couple of Seattle's best-known seafood restaurants: Ray's Boathouse and Anthony's Homeport. In the evening people line up to try to get an outside, sunset-view table at Ray's upstairs café, where they'll provide blankets if it gets cold.

Description: There are a few places to dock a sailboat on salt water in Seattle besides Shilshole Marina, but this is the big one, and it's where most of the clubs and rentals are. Managed by the Port of Seattle, the marina is near the city's traditional maritime hub, Ballard. It's the second-largest marina in the state, with about 1,500 boats, most of them sailboats. There's a promenade here that leads to Golden Gardens Park, one of the city's few accessible sand beaches, and thus quite popular on sunny days. Shilshole is a good place to start a sail, keeping a couple of potential problem areas in mind. Just south of the marina is the outlet for the Ballard Locks, and, as the people at Windworks Sailing Center describe it, "people come tearing out of there" in their powerboats. Be cautious. Heading the other direction toward Golden Gardens things quickly get shallow, so it is best to head away from shore as soon as possible. The drop-off ledge is only about 10 to 15 feet from shore, and taking a depth reading a quarter-mile out will often to give you an unexpected result—it is too deep to measure.

There are a few popular day sails from the area, most with guest moorage that is either free for a couple of hours or fairly low-priced. Heading north to Edmonds you'll see islands and more of Puget Sound, and the harbor there has quite a few shops and restaurants within walking distance. (This is also the location of one of the best shore dive sites in Washington, if you've got the gear; see "Scuba," page 288.) Kingston, just across the water (watch for the Edmonds-Kingston ferry plying the route) is on the Kitsap Peninsula, and the towns along the shoreline are a bit less developed than what you'll see on the mainland side.

If you head south from Shilshole you can visit downtown Seattle from the water, docking in Bell Street Harbor and wandering the waterfront or walking up to Pike Place Market. Sure, you could also go in a rental car, but this view is much preferred. To the southwest, Blake Island, also a scuba and kayaking destination, is a good place to sail for an overnight excursion. Bring your own food or go to the touristy salmon bake with traditional Native American performances. There are a couple of gorgeous beaches, too. See "Sea Kayaking," page 44, for more details.

Directions: Take I-5 to exit 172 (N. 85th St.). Head west on N. 85th St. Continue approximately 3 miles (N. 85th St. will change to 85th St. N.W. after you cross 15th Ave.) until you come to a four-way intersection with stop sign and flashing red light. Turn right onto Golden Gardens Dr. Follow the winding road down the hill and under the railroad bridge to another stop sign. The water is in front of you. Turn left onto Seaview Ave. N.W. Continue approximately a quarter-mile to the main marina building, which is light brown, green, and yellow, with a big Port of Seattle sign. Parking is in front of the marina building or on the street.

LAKE UNION

Location: North of downtown

Club and outfitter: Center for Wooden Boats; Sailing-in-Seattle

Map: Maptech Waterproof Chart: Seattle and Lake Washington

Heads up: Sailing within view of downtown

Description: It may be the most cramped sailing destination in Seattle, but it packs a lot into a tiny space. About a half-mile wide and one and a half miles long, Lake Union is as much the city's center as downtown or the Pike Place Market, and is the best place to get to know the heart of Seattle by sailboat.

Known by Native Americans as "Tenas Chuck" (Little Water) to Lake Washington's Big Water, Lake Union was once virtually landlocked. It was also almost a third larger than it is today; sawmills filled in a bay with their refuse in early settler days. It was also around this time, 1854, that Thomas Mercer, an early pioneer, suggested renaming the lake Union, since a canal linking this lake with Lake Washington seemed inevitable. The canal, which connected Lake Union with Lake Washington via the Montlake Cut, and Puget Sound via the Fremont Cut and Hiram Chittenden Locks, was considered complete in 1934.

At the south end of the lake, where you might rent a boat or take a free sail with the Center for Wooden Boats, a 12-acre dry dock repairs ships, and a couple of aviation companies launch float planes for scenic rides or trips north to the San Juan Islands. Every inch of shoreline is in use from here north, whether for a kayak rental shop, yacht sales, a street-end park, a Hooters restaurant, or a floating home. Most of Seattle's famous houseboats are here and east in Portage Bay, a few hundred altogether. Cormorants air out their wings on pilings, Canada geese nibble at the tulips in houseboat planters, and all kinds of ducks paddle around gathering food and dodging the human activity. Their main hazard is yours, too—traffic can get nearly as congested on summer days as on notoriously choked I-5, though in winter you can sometimes almost have the place to yourself. Float planes launch from South Lake Union; keep out of their flight path. Rental shops send kayak novices out to poke around the shoreline; don't expect them to know when you might tack in their direction, or even how to avoid you. Do not expect all boaters to be sober on summer evenings.

Looking north from the south end you'll spot the sculptural rust heap known as the Gas Works, a former gasification plant that was converted to a park in the 1960s. Maintaining the site's industrial character, rather than overlaying it with something more green and pastoral, was (and still is) considered a radical departure from tradition.

Heading west from the Gas Works, a narrow passage connects Lake Union to the locks, where boats are lowered to sea level and a fish ladder allows several species of salmon to travel between salt water and fresh. (Don't be surprised to see a muscular coho leaping from Lake Union's waters.) The locking-through process can be lengthy, particularly in summer, and small sailboats are often more easily trailered to Shilshole Bay. Heading east you'll pass under the I-5 and University Bridges into Portage Bay. On the north side of the water before and after you pass under the bridges are, from west to east, the historic Kalakala ferry, Ivar's Seafood, and one of the studios of Seattle's glassblowing celebrity, Dale Chihuly. More houseboats are squeezed into Portage Bay, as well as offices, the Agua Verde Paddle Club, NOAA, and more maniacial boaters.

Events that swell boating numbers include Opening Day in early May, the informal races known as the Duck Dodge every Tuesday evening in summer, the Fourth of July fireworks display, and the parade of Christmas Boats near the end of the year. Seafair, held on Lake Washington the first weekend in August, also brings out boats—and loaded coolers—in full force.

Directions: Directions depend on which outfitter or club you're headed to. The Center for Wooden Boats is just a few minutes from downtown Seattle at the south end of Lake Union, off Valley St. between Fairview Ave. N. and Westlake Ave. N.

Let the Games Begin

BOATS ARE ON THE WATER in Seattle year-round, and sails are definitely unfurled by early spring, no matter what the weather. But it isn't officially boating season until the captain says so—that is, until the fanfare and tam o'shanter antics of Opening Day. An almost 100-year-old tradition, organized by the Seattle Yacht Club the first Saturday each May, this event is a great, free spectacle. Head down to the Montlake Cut as early as you can that morning and bring something to sit on. A couple hundred decorated boats will parade through the cut at midday, with bright spinnakers and crews dressed in caps (the tam o'shanter part) and sport jackets (the yacht club part). Other excitement includes tugboats twirling in dervishy circles, fireboats spouting like whales, and a clanging, crashing, floating band. The Windemere Cup regatta is also on Opening Day, with a huge variety of crew teams competing.

LAKE WASHINGTON

Location: The east side of Seattle

Map: Maptech Waterproof Chart: Seattle and Lake Washington

Clubs and outfitters: Mount Baker Rowing and Sailing Center; Sail Sand Point; Sailing-in-Seattle

Heads up: There are restaurants and cafés at Leschi Marinas.

Description: If Lake Union is a strong, handsome, serviceable tugboat, Lake Washington is to some extent an oversized yacht. Some of the city's most expensive houses line much of the west side of the lake, interrupted by one of the many small waterfront parks that dot this shoreline. On the east side, well, Bill Gates built his eco-mega-mansion here. Need we say more?

As the second-largest natural lake in our state—200 feet deep in places and over 15 miles long—Washington will give you room to claim your own temporary patch of floating real estate. A couple of obstacles to keep in mind are the Evergreen Point Floating Bridge and the Mercer Island Bridge, both of which offer passage only at their elevated ends. A major annual logjam is Seafair, an enormous hydroplane racing event in early August that attracts a crowd, particularly old-school, pre-dot-com Seattleites and people from out of town. During Seafair the skies roar with Blue Angel formations and TV news stations air footage of yet another thunder boat flipping into the air, igniting an inferno, breaking a neck, or at least concussing a skull to the point that the racer responsible actually wants to come back the next year and climb back into a floating, beer-company-emblazoned death trap for another go. If this sounds like your sort of thing, stock up on brewskis and have a look. If not, leaving town is a good idea.

Some beautiful parks share the lake's shoreline, including Seward Park, on the outstretched thumb of Bailey Peninsula south of Leschi. Watch for bald eagles fishing here. They have established a nest site at Seward, which shelters some of the city's last old-growth trees. The park is also home to a variety of woodland birds and beaver and muskrat. At the north end of Washington is the mouth of the Sammamish River; at the south is the Cedar River, both of which offer salmon fishing.

Directions: Outfitters are in different locations. To get to the Leschi Marinas, home of the Corinthian Yacht Club, take I-5 to downtown exit 165A (James St.). Stay straight onto 6th Ave. Turn left onto Yesler Way. Turn left onto 32nd Ave. Turn right onto Lake Dell Ave. This becomes East Alder. Turn right onto Lake Washington Blvd. Leschi will be on your left.

Stowaway

I F YOU WANT TO GO SAILING, even if you're a complete novice, one of the best ways to do it, for free, is to walk the docks at Leschi or Shilshole late spring through fall at around 5 P.M. Ask if anyone needs a crew member, and chances are someone will be looking for a warm body to fill a slot on his or her boat.

Cruising

SOUTH PUGET SOUND

Location: 15 to 60 miles south of Seattle
Club and Outfitters: Tacoma Women's Sailing Associa-

tion; Puget Sound Sailing Institute; Island Sailing Club at Swantown Marina, Olympia

Map: Maptech Waterproof Chart: Seattle and Lake Washington

Heads up: Faraway, so close

Description: South of Seattle, just a bit farther than your usual city day sail, the islands and ports of South Puget Sound offer an abundance of hidden charms that are still little known to people outside the area. This is a great destination in late July or August if you'd like to get away from crowds in the San Juans or Gulf Islands. In a sense this is a more authentic Northwest adventure, as the marinas and harbors haven't pitched toward tourism, and the little pit-stops along the way are decidedly short on saltwater taffy and T-shirt shops. There are places to stop and hike, state-run marine parks, and tons of scuba diving and kayaking destinations (see those chapters for more information).

Directions: Olympia is a good place to launch. To get to the Swantown Marina, take I-5 south about 58 miles to exit 105, and take ramp toward Port of Olympia. Merge onto E. Bay Dr. Make a slight right onto Plum St. S.E. This becomes E. Bay Dr. N.E. In less than a mile, turn left onto Marine Dr. N.E. The marina is at 700 Marine Dr.

SAN JUAN ISLANDS

Location: Anacortes is 85 miles north of Seattle

Outfitters: Anacortes Yacht Charters; Charters Northwest; San Juan Sailing

Map and Book: Maptech Waterfront Chart Book: Puget Sound and San Juans; *A Cruising Guide to Puget Sound*

Heads up: Island-hopping heaven

Description: The hundreds of islands of the San Juans are an ideal cruising getaway, and you'll want at least a week here if you can swing it. The city of Anacortes has a state ferry dock and is the gateway to the San Juans. Several outfitters are located here.

Despite their role as a tourist hub, the San Juans are comprised mostly of islands that are not accessible by public transportation, and those islands and surrounding waters still shelter all kinds of wildlife. You may spot resident orcas breaching and spy hopping, and you're bound to see seals and perhaps sea lions. Oyster farms on some of the San Juans have piers where you can sail up and buy a sack of fresh bivalves, and most rented sailboats will include traps so you can catch your own Dungeness crabs for dinner. Summer is high season—not only for sailing but for kayaking, camping, and touring around by car. Several harbors provide well-protected anchorages, including Deer Harbor on Orcas Island; Roche, Reid, and Friday Harbors on San Juan Island; and Hunter Bay on Lopez Island. Of course, you'll also want to get away from the main islands and claim a bay of your own. A system of marine parks, many accessible only by boat, provide anchorage, primitive campsites, and sewage disposal. Beyond the San Juans, some boaters continue north to Victoria, for a night or two. The city is known for its British bent, with high tea at the famous Empress Hotel and Union Jacks snapping in the wind. The city also has some great bookshops and restaurants, if you're not a fan of crumpets or crustless sandwiches.

Directions: To get to Anacortes drive north I-5 to Mount Vernon, then take WA 20 west to Anacortes. Take the "R" Ave. exit and go north to 22nd St. Turn right. Anacortes Marina is directly ahead one block.

Natural Selection

OR THE LAZY SAILOR who wants to kick back, snack on the cheese platter, and let someone alert them when the orcas come into view, there are a few sailboat tours that specialize in the natural history and wildlife in and around the San Juans. Amante Sail Tours (360-376-4231), based out of Deer Harbor on Orcas Island, takes guests on a 33-foot sailboat for 3 hours for a reasonable price. Brisa Charters (877-41-BRISA, www.olympus.net/brisa_charters/main.html) sails from Port Townsend on 3-hour tours aboard a 45-foot Lapworth sloop.

In a slightly different category, the historic schooner *Adventuress* (360-379-0438, www.soundexp.org) in Port Townsend belongs to a nonprofit specializing in environmental education, which offers day sails or week-long San Juan trips. This school's for the not-so-lazy-sailor and can involve full days of learning to navigate a tall ship and intensive natural and maritime history study. These are generally prearranged group trips, but you may be able to get aboard through the Sierra Club or another organization. The emphasis is on ecology; the food is vegetarian.

VANCOUVER, B.C., THE GULF ISLANDS, AND BEYOND

Location: Vancouver, B.C., is about 160 miles north of Seattle.

Outfitters: Anacortes Yacht Charters; Charters Northwest; San Juan Sailing

Map: Canadian Chart Book (ask at Armchair Sailor, 2110 Westlake Ave., 206-283-0858, www.armchairsailorseattle .com)

Heads up: O Canada!

Description: The Gulf Islands, the Canadian alternative to the San Juans, are equally scenic and perhaps more equipped with restaurants, marinas, and everything else the freewheeling sailor might demand. Beyond the southern Gulf Islands is Vancouver, an international city with a busy downtown, a huge Chinatown, and a polyglot street life that sets provincial Seattle heads spinning. Anchorages here include the Coal Harbor Marina in Vancouver Harbour and the Union Steamship Marina on Bowen Island. North of Vancouver, between Vancouver Island and the mainland, are the northern Gulf Islands. Desolation Sound has some of the warmest seawater north of the Gulf of Mexico in summer, generally very mild conditions, and a big helping of wilderness. To go beyond you'd need a month or two, so we'll stop with that. To get to most of these destinations you can either set off from the San Juans or drive to British Columbia.

In general, winter north of Puget Sound can bring serious storms—people head up to Vancouver Island these days to stay in hotels and watch the waves tear up the beach. May through September is the safest time for sailing. However, as in Seattle itself, July is perhaps the earliest you can reasonably expect to stay warm and dry.

Directions: Take I-5 north to the U.S./Canada border. In British Columbia, I-5 becomes Hwy. 99N. Continue on this to Vancouver. From here you can follow signs to the appropriate B.C. ferry terminal for your destination. Visit www .Bcferries.com for schedules and itinerary suggestions.

Build It
Yourself
Boating

F IT WEREN'T FOR THE WARM BEER, Roger Coulter might not be building a boat in his backyard right now. "I went up to Desolation Sound with a few friends on a kayak trip, and I kept wishing for a dory. We were struggling because the beer was always warm. A double-ender dory would have had five times the volume of the sea kayak, and we could have carried a big cooler with ice in it. And a sail, so I wouldn't have to paddle. I prefer rowing, anyway." And that's how he came to build his first boat in 10 years, a 20-foot nontraditional Swampscot Dory, in his Capitol Hill backyard.

Disenchanted with college (he says he had perfect grades but felt he wasn't learning anything), Coulter headed off to Maine for a semester to study boat-building. "I'd mastered systems, but had learned nothing. I thought boat-building wouldn't allow for shortcuts. Actually I was wrong about that, but I did learn quite a bit." He built two small rowboats, a medium rowboat, and a 20- foot Caledonia yawl. His grades went down when he got back to school, but he figures that meant he was learning something. After college he moved out to Seattle and got what was for him a dream job at the Center for Wooden Boats. He also made the friends who took him to Desolation Sound in a kayak. This led him to want to build boats again, and to be standing out in his backyard in a rainy Seattle winter, building a dory with two masts, and thinking of cold beers and summer.

Where to Connect

The Basics

This may look like an exhaustive list of resources, but it's not—just a few of the more well-known books, clubs, and shops. There are plenty of gems here, and you'll be able to get out on the water using only these contacts. If you're ready for more, however, check out the magazine *48 Degrees North*, available in local boating shops. *Boatless in Seattle*, listed below, though not yet out in a new edition, is one big "where to connect" for local boating.

Clubs and Nonprofit Sailing Organizations

- Center for Wooden Boats (1010 Valley St., 206-382-2628, www.cwb.org) is a boat-lover's dream museum of classic wooden watercraft. It's also a working museum: sailing and rowing classes are offered, and various watercraft, including rowing shells, sailing dinghies, and rowboats are available to rent. Free classic boat rides every Sunday from 2 to 3 P.M.

- Corinthian Yacht Club (7755 Seaview Ave. N., 206-789-1919, www.cycseattle.org) is one of the country's most active clubs, with two locations: Shilshole Bay and Leschi Marinas.

- The Mountaineers (206-284-8484, www.mountaineers.org), organizers of all things outdoorsy, covers sailing as well. Members can sign on for an inexpensive basic crewing course, and go on sailing outings with the group.

- Mount Baker Rowing and Sailing Center (206-386-1913, www.cityofSeattle.net/parks/Boats/mtbaker.htm) at Seattle's Stan Sayers Park is another Parks and Recreation club with affordable classes in all ability levels for sailing, rowing, and sailboarding, and beginning canoe and kayaking for youth and adults. They have drop-in sailboat rentals for those with current Mount Baker Sailing Certificates (call for more info), a youth sailing team, and sailing camp.

- Puget Sound Racing Yacht Club (www.psryc.org) is dedicated to racers.

- Sail Sand Point (206-525-8782, www.sailsandpoint.org) is a youth-focused community nonprofit sailing center off Sand Point's Magnuson Park in Seattle, "providing water access to all."

- Seattle Canoe and Kayak Club at the Green Lake Small Craft Center (5900 W. Green Lake Way N., 206-684-4074, www.cityofseattle.net/parks/Boats) is one of the city's best boating deals. Sponsored by Seattle Parks and Recreation, the center has classes in canoeing, rowing, sailing, and kayaking, and boat rentals for members.

- Seattle Women's Sailing Association (206-444-4025, www.swsa.com) is "uniting women with a common interest in sailing." They offer membership to men as well, and offer classes, day sails, overnight cruises, and racing.

- Seattle Yacht Club (206-325-1000, www.seattleyachtclub .org) on Portage Bay was established in 1892 and has nearly 3,000 members.

- Shilshole Bay Yacht Club (2442 N.W. Market St., www.shilsholebayyc.org) meets at the Yankee Grill in Shilshole and has a racing series, the Ballard Cup, cohosted by the Sloop Tavern.

- Sloop Tavern Yacht Club (2830 NW Market St. in Ballard, 206-782-9402) "was founded by a group of live-aboard and free spirited sailors and welcomes those new to sailing."

- Tacoma Women's Sailing Association (253-851-8155, www.twsa.org) is a great contact for South Sound sailing. They are a coed group and the oldest women's sailing organization in the United States. Membership is $20 and you don't need a boat to join.

Shops

- Captain's Nautical (2500 15th Ave. W., 206-283-7242) sells charts, books, and navigation and optical instruments.

- Doc Freeman's (1401 N.W. Leary Way in Ballard, 206-633-1500) is a long-time purveyor of marine supplies.

- Hardwick and Sons (4214 Roosevelt Way N.E., 206-632-1203) is not a marine store, but a hardware store in the University District that has to be seen to be believed. "It has all the obscure tools a boatbuilder could ever want," says boatmaker Roger Coulter.

- West Marine (1000 Mercer St., 206-292-8663, or 6317 Seaview Ave. N.W., 206-789-4640) is a national chain selling marine supplies and equipment.

Rentals and Classes

- Anacortes Yacht Charters in the Anacortes Marina (360-293-6683, www.ayc.com) offers a range of San Juan Island charters.

- Charters Northwest in the San Juan Islands (800-258-3119, www.chartersnw.com) is a full-service bareboat charter company

- Elliott Bay Yacht Center (206-285-9499, 800-422-2019, www.ebyc.com) offers skippered and bareboat charters and classes.

- Island Sailing Club, in Kirkland and Olympia (800-303-2470, www.islandsailingclub.com), offers lessons and half- and full-day charters.

- Moss Bay Rowing and Kayaking Center (1001 Fairview Ave. N. #1900, 206-682-2031, www.mossbay.net) is located on South Lake Union and offers sailing, rowing, and paddling classes, and rents rowboats, canoes, rowing shells, and small sailboats.

- Puget Sound Sailing Institute (800-487-2454, www.pugetsoundsailing.com) is a sailing club and school. Owner

Mike Rice has won the American Sailing Association Instructor of the Year Award for several years running, including 2002. The classes take place in Tacoma, Edmonds, or Roche Harbor on San Juan Island.

- Sailing-in-Seattle (206-298-0094, www.sailing-in-seattle .com) is a husband-and-wife team with a 33-foot sailboat. They offer instruction and several skippered cruise options, including a 5-hour sail on Lake Washington and a Lake Union sunset cruise.

- San Juan Sailing at Squalicum Harbor in Bellingham (800-677-7245, www.sanjuansailing.com) operates a sailing school, charters, and brokerage services.

- Seattle Sailing Club (206-782-5100, www.seattlesailing .com), at the Shilshole Bay Marina next to the J dock, has been around since 1968 and is the oldest sailing school in the Northwest. They offer classes as well a club billed as "the reasonable alternative to boat ownership." Members have unlimited day-sailing access to a fleet of 22- to 36-foot sailboats and reduced charter rates for overnights and longer. Membership recommended for the frequent sailor.

- Starpath School of Navigation (206-783-1414, www .starpath.com) offers training in marine navigation and weather online or at their school in Seattle.

- Windworks Sailing Center (206-784-9386, www .windworkssailing.com), at Shilshole Bay Marina, offers sailing lessons and bareboat (25- to 43-foot) and skippered (up to 63-foot) charters. Locals can join their club and rent boats for a discounted rate.

San Juan Island Charters
- Anacortes Yacht Charters (800-233-3004; www.ayc.com) offers skippered and bareboat charters for San Juan Islands and north.

- Charters Northwest (800-258-3119, www.chartersnw.com)

is located in Friday Harbor on San Juan Island. They have a fleet of day-sailers from 23 to 48 feet, as well as bareboat charters.

Events

- The Duck Dodge is every Tuesday night in the summer on Lake Union.

- The Corinthian Yacht Club's Puget Sound Sailing Regatta in spring and Puget Sound Sailing Championships in fall are both big local events.

- Seattle Yacht Club's Opening Day is on the first Saturday in May.

Books

For more ideas or great browsing visit or call the Armchair Sailor (2110 Westlake Ave., 206-283-0858, www.armchairsailorseattle.com).

- Blanchett, M. Wylie. *The Curve of Time: The Classic Memoir of a Woman and her Children who Explored the Coastal Waters of the Pacific Northwest.* Seattle, WA: Seal Press, 2002.

- *Evergreen Pacific Cruising Guide: Washington Waters.* Shoreline, WA: Evergreen Pacific Publishing, 1994. NOAA chart reproductions for area.

- Hacking, Sue Muller. *Boatless in Seattle: Getting On the Water in Western Washington Without Owning a Boat.* Seattle, WA: Sasquatch, 1999.

- Mueller, Marge, and Ted Mueller. *Seattle's Lakes, Bays and Waterways: Afoot and Afloat Including the Eastside.* Seattle, WA: Mountaineers Books, 1998.

    ———. *The San Juan Islands: Afoot and Afloat*, 3d ed. Seattle, WA: Mountaineers Books, 1995.

- Raban, Jonathan. *Passage to Juneau: A Sea and Its Meanings.* New York: Vintage Books, 2002. Voyage from Seattle to Juneau with a literary luminary.

- Scherer, Migael. *A Cruising Guide to Puget Sound: Olympia to Port Angeles Including the San Juan Islands.* Camden, ME: International Marine Publishers, 1995.

Links

www.atmos.washington.edu/data provides almost too much information on water, weather, mountain forecasts, and the like. Data-lovers will go crazy.

www.boatwashington.org is a boating safety site.

www.nwboat.com for Northwest boat travel with an annual guidebook and many sailing links.

www.seattleboating.com

www.48north.com is the site for *48 Degrees North,* a sailing magazine, which is also available at boating stores around town.

outsidepix.com

Surfing

WHILE SOME OUTSIDERS are under the mistaken impression that Seattle is located on ocean shores, the only surfing you'll find within city limits is on the web. The Emerald City is on Puget Sound, which is a body of water to be reckoned with, but too protected to see any serious waves. If you're willing to make the minimum 2½-hour drive—and there are plenty of Seattleites who are—there are miles of killer waves on the Washington and Oregon coasts.

The Seattle surf culture is a different breed from the beach bum brigades of warmer climates. First of all, there is no rolling out of bed and into the surf. The closest reliable surfing is at least 130 miles away, so if you sleep in late you won't have time to catch many waves. Also, Seattle surfers can't look out the window to check weather and swells. Consequently, this is by necessity a more motivated and nerdy bunch, forced as they are to check several coordinates before leaving town. These determined souls awaken at 4:00 A.M. to comb through beloved, bookmarked Web sites for buoy data on coastal weather, wind, tides, and swells.

You can surf year-round off the Washington coast, but don't plan to perfect a Coppertone tan. Even in summer the water never gets above 60°F, and most of the time it fluctuates in the brisk 40–50°F range. You'll want to wear a 3 to 4 mm wetsuit, and unless your feet are made of neoprene, spring for the booties as well. Also, you may have heard that it rains quite a bit in Seattle. The same is true for the coast, but it doesn't bother the devotees much, one of whom comments, "You're going to be wet anyway, plus it keeps the crowds down."

Don't dismiss the signs warning "Beach logs can kill." They're amusing at first, until you witness a piece of buoyant old growth plowing toward you in the surf. Are we having fun yet? (Wait until you hear about the treacherous currents.) What with the bleary-eyed, crack-of-dawn drives, icy water temps, murderous logs, and unreliable weather, surfing here isn't a terribly casual sport. You have to be a little obsessed to do it with any consistency (and "crappy time in the water" is every serious surfer's duty). If your partner doesn't possess the same hankering to hang ten, beware: many a relationship has been shipwrecked on these rocky shores.

Aficionados argue that the many challenges of Seattle-area surfing only make it that much more rewarding. There's an adventurous, rough-and-tumble, pioneering Northwest spirit to the whole endeavor, and certainly a well-deserved sense of pride in accomplishment. Perhaps that's why Seattle surfers are excessively secretive about the locations of the sweetest spots—they've gone through hell and high water to find them, so why shouldn't you? The party line is that a big part of the payoff is in the discovery, which makes it tough for a newbie (or a guidebook writer) to get the goods on where to go. You can try asking around, but a lot of the responses will sound like this: "There's a break off of Whidbey Island. . . . It's a longboarder's break, with over a 10-foot swell in the winter . . . but that's all I'll say." Osmosis may be your best bet. Try being friendly—but not too friendly—to surf shop employees and anyone with the telltale wetsuit burn on the back of their neck.

I've described the locations considered common knowledge, but outside of Westport you'll need to do a lot of your own sleuthing—keep your spider senses alert. Seattle surfers explore as far south as the Oregon coast and north into British Columbia. I've included some information on both places for those of you who harbor as much free time as you have interest in the sport. Take heart in knowing that whether you prefer a right or a left (the direction the wave breaks when you're in the water facing the beach), a shortboard or long, there are plenty of surfing options for both beginners and pros.

Meccas

WESTPORT

Location: 130 miles southeast of Seattle
Difficulty: Beginner–advanced
Outfitters: The Surf Shop is a must-stop for its long history alone. You'll find everything you might want to rent, including surfboards, boogie boards, wetsuits, and other

accoutrements. They'll also point you toward the beach. When you're truly addicted, head to Northwest Surfing Customs to learn how to design, shape, and glass your own stick. Boarding Factory is the surf shop closest to Westhaven State Park, and many surfers hang out to "talk story" at Jetty Java, the coffee shop next door.

Description: As far as Seattle-area surf towns go, Westport is pretty developed. Since it's openly pro-surfer, you'll find plenty of businesses and restaurants ready to serve summertime crowd. The beach is part of Westhaven State Park, and there are three breaks to test your mettle. The Jetty, a right, is best with a 5- or 6-foot swell and an east wind. There are also right and left breaks near the jetty in the beach break. The Cove, also known as Half Moon Bay, is a right, but breaks fast and caters to shortboarders. The Groins, finger jetties, is a left, and offers a longboader's break that's best in fall.

Directions: Take I-5 toward Olympia to exit 104 (US 101 north). Follow signs to WA 8 to Aberdeen. From Aberdeen follow WA 105 to Westport.

SHORT SANDS

Location: In Oregon, about 200 miles southwest of Seattle
Difficulty: Beginner–intermediate
Outfitters: There are several tiny coastal towns along this stretch of the Oregon coast, but your best bet for gear is 10 miles north at Cannon Beach. Check out Cleanline Surf (503-738-2061, www.cleanlinesurf.com) or CB Surf and Mercantile (503-436-0475) for rental and retail needs.

Description: Located in picturesque Oswald West State Park, Short Sands is a small cove with a nice curved beach that makes a great spot for beginners or body boarders. Fans say that in the summer this beach-break is "just like Hawaii" (except for the full-body wetsuits and the conifers stretching down to the beach). Be prepared to carry your gear along the half-mile trail leading from the parking lot to the beach. There are both right and left breaks but the waves tend to be diminutive, so it's best for longboarders. Experienced surfers looking for something a little more hard-core can head 10 miles north to Seaside Point, where the turfy localism is rumored to be as fierce as the point-break.

Directions: It's at least a 4-hour drive from Seattle, so stock the car with snacks. Follow I-5 south to Longview, about 125 miles. Then head toward Astoria on US 30. At Astoria, follow coastal US 101 south, toward Seaside and Cannon Beach. Oswald West is about 10 miles south of Cannon Beach on WA 101.

PITCHING TENT

oswald west state park, oregon

OSWALD WEST STATE PARK is a beautiful campground beneath the evergreens just before the beach, on a gorgeous stretch of the Oregon coast. Campers get wheelbarrows at the entrance at US 101 to cart their gear down the long trail to the camping areas.

Camping at the park is available March to November and is first-come, first-served. Sites are around $10 to $15, depending on the season. With a place this wonderful, you know you'll need to be there very early to get anything, and aim for as far outside summer as you can. There are 30 sites, all walk-in. For more information call 800-551-6949 or check out www.oregonstateparks.org/park_195.php.

NEAH BAY

Location: Northwest coast of the Olympic Peninsula, several hours by car and ferry from Seattle

Difficulty: Intermediate–advanced

Outfitter: North by Northwest (in Port Angeles) is the closest surf shop around, so be sure to stop on the way out. They won't tell you where to go or give you a map, but they will rent you gear and wish you luck. As it says on their Web site, "We believe the search will be the reward."

Description: Just inside the teetering northwest corner of Washington, Neah Bay faces north to the Strait of Juan de Fuca. You'll want to make sure the swells are pretty high if you're planning to surf hereabouts—they need to be in order for the narrows to get any action. The waves are unpredictable but can suit either a long- or shortboard. Keep in mind that this is Olympic rain forest territory—if you are hoping for sun, you'll be better served elsewhere. Please be mindful of preservationist efforts to protect these shores from manmade damage. There are a couple of small fishing resorts, but if you don't take their lodging options, be sure to come with a decked-out VW van or build in time at the end of the day to head back to Port Angeles for a meal and a bed.

Directions: Take I-5 north to Edmonds. Take the Edmonds ferry to Kingston. Follow WA 104 west to US 101 north toward Port Angeles. Continue west on WA 112, along the north coast of the Olympic Peninsula to the bay. This can be a 4-hour journey, so set that alarm clock loud.

LA PUSH

Location: The Olympic Peninsula, about 4 or 5 hours from Seattle

Difficulty: Beginner–advanced

Outfitters: Gear up in Seattle before you head out, or stop at North by Northwest in Port Angeles. La Push is on the map, but don't expect to find an abundance of amenities in this 800-year-old Native American fishing village. Forks, the lumber town 14 miles to the west, isn't glamorous but holds more (but not myriad) options.

Description: With both right and left breaks and a remote setting, La Push is a favorite of surfers of all levels. Located on the Quileute Indian Reservation, this rocky, reefy break makes for nice peaks and bowls. There are several beaches to choose from: First, Second, Third, and Rialto. First Beach is likely the easiest to access, especially if you're lugging your gear. La Push is also known for reliable whale-watching, so prepare to share the sand with Shamu seekers February through April.

Directions: Follow the Neah Bay directions (see above) to Port Angeles, but instead of continuing west on WA 112, take a slight dip south on US 101 toward Forks. Just before Forks you'll turn west on to WA 110, La Push Road. Head toward the water.

TOFINO

Location: The west coast of Vancouver Island, about 8 hours from Seattle by car, depending on car ferry choice.

Difficulty: Beginner–advanced

Outfitter: Live to Surf (250-725-4464, www.livetosurf .com) is Tofino's original surf shop, founded waaaay back in 1984. Located on the Pacific Rim Highway, it offers sales and rentals for surfing, skimboarding, and skateboarding.

Description: Heralded by serious surfers as one of the most beautiful surf spots in the world, Tofino is a long trek from Seattle but promises spectacular scenery and waves you'll never forget. The town is located on lushly forested and largely untouched Vancouver Island, and, being on an island, boasts many beaches. Long Beach, located within Pacific Rim National Park, is said to be the best for surfing, rather famously so. Canadians, not surprisingly, aren't as prone to localism as stateside surfers are, so sleuthing for less obvious spots won't prompt a turf war. The populous bears aren't likely to be itchin' for a fight either, but if you see one on the trail, give it a wide berth, just in case.

Directions: Let's just say it's a hell of a lot longer than the road to Tipperary. First, get yourself to the city of Victoria, on Vancouver Island (you have several options from Seattle, including airplane, seaplane, hydrofoil, car, and ferry). Stock up with tea and crumpets in Victoria—it's a gnarly 5-hour drive from here.

When the Shark Bites

THERE'S AN UPSIDE to surfing in water so chilly wetsuits are required year-round: you're unlikely to be sharing the waves with sharks. There has been only one recorded shark attack off the Washington coast—it was the work of a great white, but it wasn't fatal. Oregon surfers have suffered a few more bites (17 attacks, one fatal), but those have mostly occurred along the southern part of the coast. If you do happen to get nibbled there's good news: you may have a better chance of survival than unlucky surfers in tropical climes, since the frigid water slows blood flow from a gaping wound. According to Kenny Doudt, a surfer who was brutally mauled by a great white at Cannon Beach, Oregon, in 1979, "Hypothermia is what saved me." Cowabunga, dude.

Where to Connect

Club

Seattle Surfrider (www.seattlesurfrider.org) is the local chapter of the national foundation dedicated to conservation, activism, and education surrounding the preservation of beaches and marine ecosystems. Check out the newsletter for upcoming events, programs, and volunteer projects.

Shops

- Cheka-Looka (2948 Eastlake Ave. E., 206-726-7878, www.chekalooka.com) is an in-city surf shop the locals adore for its wide selection of gear and excellent customer service. Definitely should be the first stop for novices and pros alike. The Web site has links to surf reports and surf cams, weather reports, tide charts, and swell reports.

- North By Northwest (902 S. Lincoln St. in Port Angeles, 360-452-5144, www.nxnwsurf.com) is *the* surf shop in the Strait of Juan de Fuca and anywhere off the northern coast of the Olympic Peninsula. Friendly salespeople are committed to preserving the north coast, but don't ask for a map or directions. They also sell skateboard and snowboard ephemera.

- Northwest Surfing Customs (Westport, 360-589-2099, www.surfnwsc.com) is for the surf addict. Surfing and wave-reading lessons, also custom surfboard shaping, and glassing—design your own stick. The Web site has all the forecasting links.

- Perfect Wave (8209 124th Ave. N.E. in Kirkland, 425-827-5323, www.perfectwave.com) has gear and . . . bikinis. The Web site has links to surf reports and surf cams, weather reports, tide charts, swell reports. Board repair, board rentals, and lessons.

- The Surf Shop (207 N. Montesano St. in Westport, 360-268-0992) is a definite must-stop for Westport surfers. Rents and sells gear. Owner Al Perlee opened the store in 1986.

- Urban Surf (2100 N. Northlake Way, 206-545-9463, www.urbansurf.com) sells and rents gear. Also supplies gear for in-line skating, snowboarding, windsurfing, and kite-boarding.

Events
- Check Web sites or a full-bodied surf shop like Cheka-Looka to find out about seasonal surfing contests. Westport holds the Northwest Longboard Clean Water Classic in late winter, and the Summer Surf Jam takes place in Tofino when the weather is balmy (by Northwest standards).

Links
www.wannasurf.com has links to northwest Washington and Oregon. Read surfer commentary and hot-spot ratings (and once you've checked them out, post your own).

www.surfline.com features info about surfing the world over, inuding ratings, descriptions (by season), and recommendations for food and lodging. Webcams, forecasts, articles, and interviews as well. Head to the travel section and click on the map for more.

www.northwestwaves.com is "100 percent dedicated to the Northwest surfer." This site offers forecasts, webcams, and wave predictions.

www.buoyweather.com for weather and swells information.

http://tbone.biol.sc.edu/tide/sites_uswest.html has tide tables for the Northwest.

BECAUSE HIGH WINDS blow primarily in winter, just when the water hits its lowest temperatures, windsurfing has never been one of Seattle's top sports. That said, a jaunt to Golden Gardens or Alki Beach on a decent wind and weather day will likely turn up at least a few intrepid boardsailors in full wetsuits. To windsurf in the city you'll need to be flexible. Many windsurfers cruise on longboards in summer, then switch to shorter, faster boards in winter when the wind kicks up. Either way, no windsurfer could eke out an existence in the Seattle area without periodic trips to the windsurfing hub of the Northwest, the Columbia River Gorge, about 4 hours

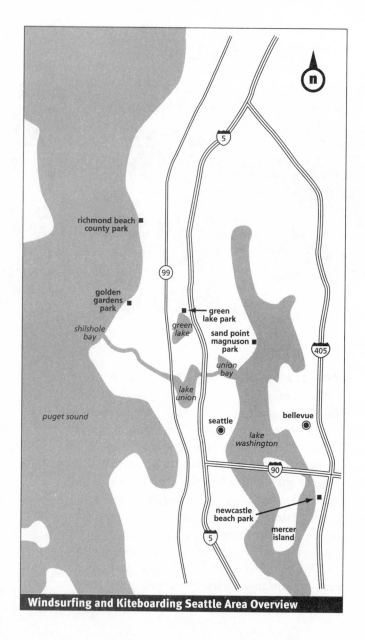

Windsurfing and Kiteboarding Seattle Area Overview

south. The town of Hood River is equipped with shops, outfitters, and camps geared toward the sport.

The other survival strategy of many Seattle windsurfers in the last few years has been to pick up the related but more radical sport of kiteboarding. Using a kite, board, and handlebars, boarders can catch air not available to windsurfers. "For every 10 or more days of good kiting available in this city there's maybe one day of short-board windsurfing," says Robin Ogaard, whose shop, Urban Surf, is pretty much ground zero for the kiteboarding community and employs kiteboarding pros. Though Ogaard hesitates to label it an extreme sport, manufacturers are doing it for him. With names like Popsycho, Frenzy, Hazmat, and Mutant, kiteboarding equipment is clearly meant to be worn by the stoked water outlaw in you. After all, windsurfers generally stay near the water's surface, but kiteboarders regularly go airborne. Spend some time on the Web (or with *Kiteboarding magazine*) to get a sense of the culture. In Seattle the sport just took hold a couple of years ago (though its been around longer in meccas such as Hawaii and France) and is fairly welcoming to newcomers, even if you don't yet know your Melon Grab from your Hoochie Glide. Insurance companies are still ironing out the kinks in a policy for rental equipment, so you can't rent the gear yourself, and new gear is dauntingly expensive—$1,100 to $2000, not counting the mandatory full wetsuit. Fortunately, there are ways to try out the sport before you make a full investment. Urban Surf will rent you kiteboarding trainer gear, designed to be used on land, which helps you learn to fly the kites. They also have several instructional videos. The Seattle Kitesurfing Association (www.seattlekitesurfing.org) offers weekly free lessons and a get-together starting in late spring at Golden Gardens Park.

And, by the way, no one's quite sure yet which name will stick with this sport. You'll see kiteboarding, kitesailing, and kitesurfing used, but they all mean the same thing: Wear a helmet.

City Limits

GREEN LAKE PARK (WINDSURFING)

Location: A few miles north of downtown
Outfitter: Urban Surf
Difficulty: Beginner
Contact: Parks and Recreation Department (206-684-4075, www.cityofseattle.net/parks)
Description: This popular urban lake is a great place to learn windsurfing; it is small, sheltered, and generally not mired in boat traffic (rowing classes are the main competition). Some years the lake, which is working hard to turn into a swamp, has to be closed because of algae blooms. Check the parks department Web site for more information.
Directions: Take I-5 north to exit 170 (Ravenna Blvd.) toward N.E. 65th St. Merge left onto N.E. Ravenna Blvd. This leads into E. Green Lake Dr. N. Turn left into the Green Lake Park parking lot in about 0.3 mile.

SAND POINT MAGNUSON PARK (WINDSURFING AND KITEBOARDING)

Location: Lake Washington
Outfitter: Urban Surf
Difficulty: Intermediate
Contact: Parks and Recreation Department (206-684-4946, www.cityofseattle.net/parks/parkspaces/spmp/windsurfing.htm) has information on rules and launching.

Windsurfing & Kiteboarding

Description: Mellower than Puget Sound, Lake Washington is good for the intermediate sailor. There's enough room for kiteboarders to spread out, so you'll see people doing both sports, though kiteboarders say it's a tough spot for beginners because of a difficult launch and landing. Good southerly winds in winter and spring.

Directions: Head north on I-5 to the N.E. 65th St. exit. Take this and head east approximatly 4 miles (stay on the arterial) until you have crossed Sand Point Way N.E. into the N.E. 65th St. entrance to Sand Point Magnuson Park. Go straight to the lake. The windsurfing launch is just south of the boat ramp. Set up your rig on the grassy area nearby.

GOLDEN GARDENS PARK (WINDSURFING AND KITEBOARDING)

Location: Northwest of downtown
Outfitter: Urban Surf
Difficulty: Intermediate–advanced
Description: This can be a challenging site for windsurfers. Puget Sound's crazy chop takes some finesse, and powerboats and sailboats share the same waters. Local windsurfers say its great on northerlies. Kiteboarders claim this sandy stretch of beach as their home base, it seems—free lessons with the kitesailing association take place here, and last year's barbecue fired up here as well. Golden Gardens offers great views of the Olympics and Puget Sound on a sunny day and is very popular with picnickers and sunbathers. North of Golden Gardens, Carkeek Park is another kiteboarding destination for more advanced boarders.

Directions: Take I-5 to the 85th St. exit and head west. Follow 85th west to the dead end at the bluff. Turn right and go downhill. Go under the railroad tracks and you'll be at the park entrance.

Backyard

RICHMOND BEACH (WINDSURFING AND KITEBOARDING)

Location: About 11 miles north of Seattle in Shoreline
Outfitter: Urban Surf
Difficulty: Intermediate–advanced
Description: Generally less crowded than Golden Gardens, Richmond Beach in Shoreline, a Seattle suburb, is popular with windsurfers and kiteboarders for its fairly consistent southerlies. The beach is large but can be rocky at low tide. Because it's on Puget Sound, with its unpredictable chop, it should be considered intermediate or advanced, depending on conditions.
Directions: Take I-5 north to exit 176 (N. 175th St.) toward Aurora Ave. N. Turn left onto N. 175th St., and then right onto Aurora Ave. N./WA 99. Turn left onto N. 185th St. This becomes N. Richmond Beach Rd., then N.W. 195th St. Turn left onto 20th Ave. N.W., which becomes N.W. 190th. The park is at 2021 N.W. 190th.

NEWCASTLE BEACH PARK (WINDSURFING)

Location: Just south of Bellevue on the east side of Lake Washington
Outfitter: Urban Surf
Difficulty: Intermediate
Contact: Bellevue Parks Department (www.ci.Bellevue.wa.us)

Description: Newcastle Beach Park is the largest Bellevue park on Lake Washington and a windsurfing hub on the Eastside. There's a 200-foot-long swimming beach here as well as all kinds of other amenities. The park gives access to a sheltered cove where you can try out windsurfing in low-key fashion, or move farther out and get some wind and chop. Considered best on southerly winds.

Directions: Take I-5 north to I-90 and head east over Lake Washington. Take the I-405 exit south. From I-405 take the 112 Ave. S.E. exit and head west. Head north on Lake Washington Blvd. S.E. and turn left into the park at the end of the road.

Mecca

THE GORGE, HOOD RIVER

Location: About 230 miles southeast of Seattle in Oregon
Difficulty: Beginner–very advanced
Outfitters: Big Winds; Storm Warning; Second Wind; Windance
Heads up: In July the Gorge Games includes windsurfing, paragliding, and all kinds of other edgy endeavors.
Description: The area around this channel of the Columbia River (referred to in one tourist book as "a chasm of majesty") is known for a huge variety of sports opportunities; windsurfing is one of the most popular. There are many sites to choose from, including some for beginners and big-swell–high-wind areas that will challenge anyone. Kiteboarders are making headway, though they can be in competition with windsurfers, since kiteboards take more room to launch. The Sandbar is a popular kiteboarding site. For more

information on Gorge sites, or on windsurfing in the area in general, check out Windance Sailboards (800-574-4020, www.windance.com), which has a great Gorge guide online for details on local sites. The Columbia Gorge Windsurfing Association (541-386-9225, www.windsurf.gorge.net/cgwa) is a strong advocate for obtaining and maintaining access to the water. When you're done with all the wind play, carbo-load in lively Hood River at one of the many good cafés—there's Mexican, Thai, vegetarian, and every other option.

Directions: Take I-5 south about 162 miles to exit 7, I-205 south, and head toward WA 14/I-84. Merge onto I-84 east (exit 22) in about 15 miles and head toward The Dalles. In about 55 miles take exit 63 toward Hood River/City Center. Turn right on 2nd St. Turn left onto Oak St. Several Hood River windsurfing and kitesailing shops are on Oak St., and can provide outfitting or directions to launch points.

Where to Connect

Clubs

- Mount Baker Rowing and Sailing Center (206-386-1913, www.cityofseattle.net/parks/boats/mtbaker.htm) at Seattle's Stan Sayers Park on Lake Washington offers wind-surfing lessons.

- Northwest Boardsailing Association (http://home .mindspring.com/~nwba/) organizes local windsurfing events.

- Seattle Kitesurfing Association (www.seattlekitesurfing .org) is a hub for the local kitesurfing community and helps newcomers get started in the sport.

- Seattle Women's Windsurfing Association (www.geocities .com/seattlewwc/) is just what it sounds like. They have events and their Web site has club member comments on local windsurfing spots.

Shops
Seattle
- Urban Surf (2100 N. Northlake Way, 206-545-9463, www .urbansurf.com) rents, sells, and offers lessons. They have windsurfing, kiteboarding, surfing, and in-line skate gear. They hold a yearly windsurfing and kiteboarding swap, generally at the end of April.

Hood River
- Big Winds (207 Front St., 541-386-6086, 888-509-4210, www.bigwinds.com) has been around for 16 years. "We're still here, still stoked" and ready to rent or sell windsurfing or kiteboarding equipment. They also give lessons.

- Second Wind (210 Oak St., 541-386-4464) has lots of used gear.

- Storm Warning (112 Oak Street, 541-386-9400, 800-492-6309, www.e-stormwarning.com) has a big selection of new and used windsurfing equipment as well as kiteboarding equipment and telemark and backcountry gear.

- Windance (108 OR 35 in Hood River, 800-574-4020, www .windance.com) sells and rents equipment. Their Web site is an incredible source of information about the Gorge and local windsurfing.

Event
- Starting around April the Seattle Kitesurfing Association, in association with Urban Surf, holds weekly Kite Nites at Golden Gardens Park to introduce people to the sport with free trainer kiteflying. Check out the SKA Web site or call Urban Surf for details.

Link

http://home.earthlink.net/~crzybdhd/wind/index.html is a Northwest windsurf site with great links to videocams of windsurf spots, windspeed information, and descriptions of other windy sites worth visiting.

SEATTLEITES PRIDE THEMSELVES on being year-round cyclists, gearing up in windbreakers, pricey waterproof bike pants, and hip neoprene panniers for the slog through puddles under a downpour. The same cannot be said for in-line skaters, who, like visiting out-of-towners, rust under the relentless precipitation of winter. Prime skate season is summer, no doubt about it, with July, August, and September offering the most reliably dry conditions. In winter a week-long dry spell that dries out the puddles might also bring out the die-hards.

That said, this is actually a fairly glorious place to skate when the weather cooperates. We're nearly as famous as San Francisco for our hills, but that just means we've got miles of flat, cruisable waterfront at the bottom of each slope. Some of the most scenic stretches of paved trail anywhere in the country are in and around our city, skirting rivers, lakes, and Puget Sound. You can go to Alki Beach for a sunset roll with a view of the city and mountains, or drive 15 miles to Snohomish County for a 14-mile out and back riverside getaway on a path flanked by a horse trail. Right in town we are lucky to have the Burke-Gilman and Sammamish River Trails, 27 miles of railroad right-of-way that provides a commuter path for cyclists all week, and an urban-to-rural escape route for bikers, skaters, joggers, skateboarders, and the rest of the city on weekends. Finally, of course, you can always blaze your own trail through the city. When the manic summer season hits, you'll see wild skating fanatics switchbacking up neighborhood hills, navigating through summer festival crowds, maybe even mixing it up with the skateboarders at the local skate park. Once you've exhausted the options below (and maybe consulted the "Road Biking" chapter for more ideas), you can always dream up a route of your own.

Where to Connect lists a couple of skating schools, for those just getting their, er, bearings. These offer a chance to hone skills, or the opportunity to get out of the rain and into a rink during the outdoor skating downtime.

Note: This may seem obvious, but these are just about all great places to go running as well.

City Limits

BURKE-GILMAN AND SAMMAMISH RIVER TRAILS

Location: Northeast of downtown
Length: 27 miles one way
Difficulty: Beginner
Outfitter: Urban Surf
Description: These two linked trails comprise one of the longest paved bike-skate-jog-walk routes in the country, and on any nice day half the city seems to come out in the afternoon to make use of them. The Burke-Gilman Trail, or BGT as it is fondly known, begins in Ballard and stretches next to the ship canal in Fremont for great views of the water and boats, past Gas Works Park and through the University District, skirting the campus under tall trees. These miles of trail are probably the most congested on the entire stretch, since they're used by bike commuters to and from campus and the rest of the north end of town. Farther on the trail loops up and over the top of Lake Washington to Bothell, passing several waterfront parks along the way. In Bothell it becomes the Sammamish River Trail for 10 pastoral, peaceful miles to its termination at Marymoor Park. For a short- or midlength city excursion you might want to start on the first half of the BGT. Directions to Gas Works Park, a popular meeting place for skaters with an outfitter, Urban Surf, located across the street, are below. For a marathon blade start near the university or farther north and roll out to Marymoor, stopping at beaches and small parks along the way.

Directions: Take I-5 northbound to the 45th St. exit. Turn right onto 45th. Turn right onto University Ave. Turn right onto Pacific. Make a left at the stop sign half a mile later. The road will curve to the right. Gas Works Park will be on the left side just after Anthony's Restaurant.

ALKI BEACH

Location: West Seattle
Length: 2.5 miles or more one way
Difficulty: Beginner
Outfitters: Urban Surf; Gregg's Greenlake Cycle
Description: The first place pioneers showed up to claim Seattle in 1851, Alki may also be the first place most beginners try out their skates. It's sort of a modified Venice Beach, with fewer T-shirt shops and more rainy days. The wide, paved path is shared with cyclists, walkers, and wandering pedestrians, so it can be tough to negotiate. Best to come in the morning or midday during the week. Weekends in summer are good for honing supernatural agility or getting your money's worth out of your wrist guards and kneepads. The highlights here are stunning views of the city, a few blocks of snack emporiums at the ready, and a wide sandy beach to sprawl on when you're done. Sunset can be pretty swell.

Directions: From I-5 or WA 99 (Aurora Ave.) take the West Seattle Bridge to West Seattle. Take the Harbor Ave./Avalon Way exit on the right. Turn right onto Harbor Ave. S.W. Bear left onto Alki Ave. S.W. Alki Beach Park is on your right—look for street parking.

GREEN LAKE PARK

Location: North of downtown
Length: 2.8-mile loop

Difficulty: Beginner–intermediate

Outfitter: Gregg's Greenlake Cycle

Description: Like Alki, this park is short on distance but long on popularity. If your goal is to people-watch, you won't run out of characters. If you want a clear path, you're in the wrong place. Right across the street, Gregg's Green-lake Cycles rents skates to newbies, who can be seen clutching telephone poles at corners, waiting for the traffic to let them through so they can career into the lane in front of you. Or maybe you're one of them! The Green Lake path, which circles the lake, has separate sides for "wheels" and "feet," but the dogs on extendable leashes don't seem to know that. On the upside, the path is newly repaved, and the park itself is an urban retreat for all kinds of birds—you may spot a great blue heron, hear the trilling of red-winged blackbirds, watch a pied-billed grebe build a nest, or spy a bald eagle fishing in the lake.

Directions: Take I-5 north to exit 170 (Ravenna Blvd.) toward N.E. 65th St. Merge left onto N.E. Ravenna Blvd. This turns into E. Green Lake Dr. N. Turn left into the Green Lake Park parking lot in about 0.3 mile.

MYRTLE EDWARDS PARK AND ALASKAN WAY

Location: West of downtown on the waterfront

Length: 2.5 miles or more out and back

Difficulty: Beginner–advanced

Outfitters: Urban Surf; Gregg's Greenlake

Description: Myrtle Edwards Park on Seattle's waterfront offers great views of Puget Sound, nearby islands, and the Olympics, and a 1.25-mile-long flat, paved trail for joggers, cyclists, and skaters. There's an interesting grain terminal here where peregrine falcons and other raptors sometimes come to hunt pigeons. More advanced skaters can take the option recommended by Washington In-Line Skating Adventures, exiting the park heading south on Alaskan Way past Pier 70 to Pier 66, then crossing the street to an asphalt trail, which, if taken to the end, can tack another 2 miles or so onto your skate. There's some rough concrete along the way, and wandering tourists to be aware of, but for the intrepid this is a great place to take in the piers, docks, and ferry boats that are quintessential Seattle.

Directions: Take I-5 to exit 167 (Mercer St./Seattle Center). Keep right at the fork in the ramp. Turn right onto Fairview Ave. N. Turn left onto Valley St. Valley becomes Broad St. Turn right on Alaskan Way. The park will be on your left after Pier 70. There's a parking lot here that is metered and can be full. Across the street to the east are more pay parking lots and street parking uphill. Alternately, there is a streetcar that runs along much of Alaskan Way, so you can also park south of here and take that, or (with some skill) roll your way to the park along Alaskan.

Backyard

CENTENNIAL TRAIL

Location: In Snohomish, about 15 miles northeast of Seattle

Length: 7.25 miles one way

Difficulty: Beginner

Outfitter: Bring your own skates

Description: Like the Burke-Gilman Trail, this is a paved path built over a railroad right-of-way. It's definitely worth the drive out of the city to try out this long, 6-foot-wide path used by walkers, bikers, and hikers. A parallel grass path serves as an equestrian trail. From the smell of horse

In-line Skating

manure and cut grass to stretches along the Pilchuck River, the vibe is country-pastoral. Snohomish County Parks and Recreation (www.co.snohomish.wa.us/parks/centennial .htm) manages the path, and intends to extend it from Lake Stevens to Arlington in the near future, a total of about 20 miles of trail.

Directions: Take I-5 north about 13 miles to Everett, and the Snohomish-Wenatchee exit to US 2. Take the third exit off US 2 to Snohomish. The southern end of the trail begins in Snohomish at the intersection of Maple St. and Pine Ave. An additional access point in Snohomish is the Pilchuck Trailhead: From Snohomish follow Maple St. out of town (it becomes Machias Rd. at the city limits) for approximately 1.5 miles. The trailhead is on the right.

CEDAR RIVER TRAIL

Location: Renton, south of Seattle
Length: 6 miles one way
Difficulty: Beginner–intermediate
Outfitter: Bring your own skates
Description: Visit the source of your drinking water. The Cedar River keeps the taps running for most of the city of Seattle, and this path, yet another railroad right-of-way, sticks close to this beneficent amenity much of the way. The trail starts near the freeway in a suburb—not the most atmospheric beginning. The farther you go, however, the more rural it becomes, leaving the sprawl behind. After 6 miles the trail, heading to Landsburg Park, becomes gravel, so you'll have to head back to suburbia or take off your skates and walk.

Directions: Take I-5 to I-90 or across the WA 520 bridge and head east. Turn south at I-405, then east on WA 169 (Maple Valley Hwy.). Take the first right off WA 169 into

Cedar River Park. The trail begins below I-405 at a bridge crossing the Cedar River.

Where to Connect

Club

- Washington In-Line Skating Adventures (www.wilsa.org) has details on social rolls, events, and indoor and outdoor places to skate around town.

Shops and Instruction

- Get Your Bearings Inline Skate School (www.getyourbearings .biz) has classes on indoor and outdoor skating. This school provides instruction for REI.

- Gregg's Greenlake Cycle (7007 Woodlawn Ave. NE, 206-523-1822) sells and rents in-line skate equipment and is located right across the street from Green Lake Park.

- REI (222 Yale Ave. N., 206-223-1944, www.rei.com) sells a limited amount of skating gear.

- Trish Alexander's Skate Journeys (206-276-9328, www .laterskater.com) is the Northwest's largest in-line skate school, with a devoted following. Classes, clinics, and lots of social events.

- Urban Surf (2100 N. Northlake Way, 206-545-9463, www.urbansurf.com) rents and sells in-line equipment and is located right on the Burke-Gilman Trail across from Gas Works Park.

Event

- Seattle Skate for MS (www.msa-sea.org/MSA /FundraisingEvents/Skate.htm) is said to be the largest skating event in the Northwest, with hundreds of participants.

outsidepix.com

SEATTLEITES WITH A hankering for horseback riding have to work a little harder than other local sports enthusiasts. The geography of the region and the difficulty and expense of getting hay west of the Cascades means you'll have to leave town to quench your equestrian thirst. But don't let that put a hitch in your gitalong. Most of the areas listed below are also ripe for hiking, fishing, and other outdoor pursuits that could be combined with a horseback journey for a trip packed with adventure and spectacular scenery. Who could say neigh to that? Prices for renting your own steed range from $30 to $50 for an hour or two to $100 to $200 for a day or two of riding, which can sometimes include overnight accommodations on a pack trip.

Seattle's Equine History

THE PACIFIC NORTHWEST may not have the lasso-looping, yeehaw-yelling reputation of other Western states, but Seattle's history is actually quite noisy with the clip-clop and neighing of horses. Pioneers settling the area relied heavily on horses, and with our city-by-the-sound's notoriously muddy beginnings it's likely that these beasts had many burdens. Local newspapers from the early days report horses hauling lumber and supplies through chest-high muck. This was no John Wayne movie—not everyone owned their own saddle—but the fledgling population was over 20 percent equine: the 1859 census listed 255 white persons and 55 horses (cozily accompanied by 93 hogs and 13 mules). Thankfully, things weren't completely lawless in this pioneer town. In 1879, officers issued Seattle's first speeding ticket: a fine to two men caught racing horses through the city.

By 1884 things were more civilized: this year saw the establishment of the region's first mass transit system. Seattle entrepreneur Frank Osgood established the Seattle Street Railway, which was not a railway at all, but a streetcar line with trolleys pulled by teams of horses. For a nickel, you could ride in style all the way down 2nd Ave. (though 1st Ave. was the more popular thoroughfare, Osgood's streetcar was disallowed for fear that the cars would frighten normal horse traffic). But Seattle, already establishing itself as a high-tech kind of town, soon put these obliging horses out to pasture in favor of something manmade: within three years the "hay-burners" were replaced by an electric traction trolley system.

There was no fear of out-of-work horses loitering in the streets, however. The bustling, burgeoning city had plenty for them to do. Some horses were sent to firehouses, where they heroically pulled Seattle's fire engines to burning buildings (at least until most hook-and-ladders were motorized in the 1920s). In fact, city stats from 1904 reveal that all 2,745 vehicles in Seattle were pulled by horses (be they for garbage, lumber, commodities, building materials, delivery services, or pleasure). By the end of the same year that number had risen to 3,945, but the future was already encroaching—14 automobiles were also added to the tally.

You can still see horses in downtown Seattle, but rather than hauling lumber or industrious pioneers, they are likely to be supporting the city's mounted police, out in full force during the infamous WTO protests. The mounted patrol of the Seattle Police Department (started in 1973) includes 11 horses, a sergeant, and three full-time officers, and is considered especially effective in large-crowd situations (pop veterinary psych has it that horses have a calming effect on humans). The popular peacekeepers got upgraded accommodations in 2001, when the unit moved from an old building in Volunteer Park to new facilities in Westcrest Park, West Seattle. But in case you're starting to think Seattle's urban horses are restricted to work, not play, never fear. During the holiday season horses from outlying farms are trailered into the city to cart tourists around the Pike Place Market in old-fashioned carriages.

Backyard

VASHON ISLAND

Location: Vashon Island, a ferry ride west of the city

Outfitter: West Side Stables (206-463-9828, www.joffray .com/ride) is open seven days a week, year-round, but reservations are required. They prefer riders with some experience for the trail rides.

Description: It's not in-city riding, but it's as close as you'll get short of a carriage ride. A 10-minute trip on the Fauntleroy Ferry, which departs from West Seattle, brings you to verdant and lovely Vashon Island. West Side Stables owner Cici Carson grew up on Vashon and has been riding horses since she was five. She offers 1- and 2-hour guided trail rides for individuals or small groups, English or Western style, through woods, country lanes, and meadows. If you feel like you can't get enough, you can also shop for horses, and once you're an owner you can come back for lessons. Since you'll have forked over the ferry fee, you may want to stay on the island and make a day of it. The bird-watching, cycling, and scuba diving chapters all have Vashon Island entries. Another nearby option is a trip to WolfTown, a nonprofit for rescued wolves and rehabilitated horses. WolfTown operator Teresa Martino also breeds mustang for the Blackfeet Buffalo Horse Coalition, a nonprofit working to bring back the horses of Native American tribes. Tours and seminars are available if you call in advance (206-463-9113, www.wolftown.org).

Directions: Call first for reservations. Take the Fauntleroy-Vashon ferry from West Seattle to Vashon Island. Drive straight into town on Vashon Highway. At the second light (about 8 miles) turn right onto Cemetery Rd. When the road elbows left, continue on it for about 1 mile. The stables are signed on the left.

Mountie Etymology

THE WORD "CONSTABLE" is a contraction of the eastern Roman Empire phrase *comes stabuli* or "count of the stables," and originally referred to the person(s) in charge of the king's horses and militia. The word "cop" is actually an acronym for "constable on patrol" or, if the original meaning is taken into consideration, "count of the stable on patrol."

Short Hop

MOUNT VERNON

Location: About 60 miles north of Seattle

Outfitter: Cultus Mountain Ranch (16011 Beaver Lake Rd., 360-422-5620, www.valleyint.com/cultusmountainranch /Ranch.htm) is open daily, year-round.

Heads up: Mount Vernon is for famous for its spring tulip festival in April (www.tulipfestival.org), when the entire Skagit Valley appears to be awash in vibrant color. Crowds pack the country roads on festival weekends, so consider bringing your bike along—it's much easier to park and tiptoe through the tulips from two wheels. The bird-watching chapter offers an outing a short hop from here, if you want to explore farther.

Description: Just an hour north of Seattle, Mount Vernon is the quaint county seat of scenic Skagit Valley. Located on 38 wooded acres at the foot of Cultus Mountain and adjacent to the Nookachamps River, Cultus Mountain Ranch has hundreds of miles of trails. Local wildlife is abundant (deer, elk, and cougar), as well as plenty of puppies—the ranch owners are also registered dog breeders.

Cultus Mountain offers a range of trail rides through beautiful terrain. The Greenhorn Trail takes beginners on a 1-hour ride through flat, woodsy terrain. The Scenic Trail brings riders through old-growth forest and along the Nookachamps River for 2 hours. The Wrangler's Trail takes more advanced riders on a 4-hour ride up Cultus Mountain for views of the Skagit Valley, the Cascade Range, and Puget Sound sparkling in the distance (highly recommended for a sunset ride). And for those who love to live life in the saddle, the Mountain Trail offers advanced riders 8 hours of steep riding with magnificent views. The facility also offers moonlight rides. Advance reservations recommended.

Directions: Take I-5 north to Mount Vernon and exit 227, College Way. Go east on College about 4.5 miles. Continue as it veers left at a fork (Big Rock Grocery is on the right as you go left). In 0.25 mile turn right onto Gunderson Rd. In 4.5 miles turn right onto Starview Ln. Follow signs to the ranch.

Longer Hop

CLE ELUM

Location: About 80 miles east of Seattle

Outfitters: High Country Outfitters (315 W. 2nd St., 509-674-4903 or 888-235-0111, www.highcountry-outfitters.com) and Hidden Valley Ranch (3942 Hidden Valley Rd., 509-857-2344 or 800-5COWBOY, www.ranchweb.com/hiddenvalley)

Heads up: Sunny-side horse riding. If you're someone who's cuckoo for all things cowboy, you may want to time your trip to coincide with the annual rodeo in nearby Ellensburg. Held each Labor Day weekend for the last 75 years (except during World War II), the Ellensburg Rodeo offers all the excitement of a world-class sporting event held in a historic western town (www.ellensburgrodeo.com). Ellensburg is also the Yakima River fishing hub (see *Mecca* in "Fly-Fishing & Sportfishing," page 265).

Description: Tough to pronounce but easy to get to, Cle Elum ("clay ellum") is a desirable destination for aspiring cowboys and -girls. It features the Cascade Mountains, the Yakima River, and the Wenatchee National Forest in close proximity—all of which make for picturesque riding. And

Horseback Riding

if you find yourself with a little extra time at the end of the day, you can always head over to the quaint neighboring town of Roslyn, where the television show *Northern Exposure* was filmed, and wait for a moose to mosey down Main Street.

High Country Outfitters offers trail rides and pack trips June through September. Both day rides and overnights offer scenic vistas, including Cascade Mountain panoramas and glistening alpine lakes. In the fall, High Country offers day-long trail rides, which last for 6 hours, and overnight pack trips, which include 2 days of riding. In the summer, day rides are offered only on the weekends. A full-day ride is 5 hours, including lunch. A "mini-overnight" includes an overnight stay the night before a day trip in a rustic tent cabin. Extended 3- to 5-day pack trips are available July through September; everything is provided except sleeping bag and sleeping pad.

In addition to horseback riding, visitors to Hidden Valley Ranch will find quite a few other activities, including hiking, fly-fishing, and white-water rafting. Cabins are also available to rent. Open mid-April to the end of October, the ranch offers ride packages with cabin stays (not available for one-night stays). Even if you aren't staying at the ranch, take advantage of the extensive trail ride schedule, with 1½- to 3-hour rides. Hungry pardners may want to partake in a chuckwagon breakfast ride, offered on Wednesday and Sunday mornings, or an evening ride with dinner back at the ranch.

Directions: To get to High Country Outfitters, take I-90 east to Cle Elum and exit 85. Cross the freeway and follow WA 970 toward Wenatchee for 6 miles. Turn left onto Teanaway Rd. Continue for 12 miles and take the right fork onto a dirt road. Follow signs to Beverly Campground, 4 miles. Continue another 4 miles to High Country Outfitters on the left.

To get to Hidden Valley, follow directions for High Country Outfitters to WA 970. Stay on 970 to milepost 8 and turn right onto Hidden Valley Rd. Follow signs to the ranch.

Meccas

LEAVENWORTH

Location: About 135 miles east of Seattle

Outfitters: Eagle Creek Ranch (509-548-7798 or 800-221-RIDE, www.eaglecreek.ws) offers a variety of rides for individuals and small groups, from the short and sweet (4 miles) to the long and luscious (an all-day, lunch-inclusive guided tour through the Wenatchee River Valley, up an elevation gain of 2,000 feet, with views of Mt. Stuart and Glacier Peak). Icicle Outfitters (800-497-3912, www.icicleoutfitters.com) offers day rides from one of the two stables (Lake Wenatchee State Park, 509-763-3647, or Leavenworth/Icicle Valley, 509-669-1518). Trail rides are available from mid-May to late September, with 2-, 4-, and 13-mile (lunch included) options. Pack trips originate from Entiat Valley Ranch (509-784-1145) and range from day-long trips into the Cascade Mountains to 2- to 7-day custom-designed trips. Call for reservations.

Heads up: Leavenworth never met a summer festival it didn't like; consider timing your trip with one. May brings the Leavenworth Spring Birdfest (www.leavenworthspringbirdfest.com) for those with a birding bent, as well as Maifest, a German celebration featuring traditional foods and oompah music (509-548-5807). June holds the Bavarian Bike Brew, an IMBA-sanctioned 8.6-mile cross-country bike race (www.dasradhaus.com), followed by a beer fest of Ger-

Horseback Riding

manic proportions. If you arrive toward the end of June, there'll be no avoiding the 4-day International Accordion Celebration (www.accordioncelebration.com), featuring concerts, competitions, workshops, and plenty of spirited dancing. And if that isn't enough to get you on the road to Leavenworth, surely the Sausage Fest, held each Fourth of July weekend, will tempt your tastebuds (509-548-5807). Plan a multisport trip, and you can do rock climbing, white-water kayaking or rafting, or snow sports, depending on season (see relevant chapters).

Description: The beautifully situated town, with its Bavarian stylings and schnitzel aplenty, is a serious tourist destination, even for people who have little interest in outdoor activity. They're missing a lot, including a rushing river and first-class rock climbing. Even if you aren't a fan of lederhosen, Leavenworth is worth the trip for horseback riders, who can spend the day trotting through evergreen forests and alpine meadows.

Directions: To get to Leavenworth, take I-5 north toward Everett and turn off at US 2, heading east. Continue about 85 miles over Stevens Pass to Leavenworth. Consult individual outfitters for directions to meeting points.

WASHINGTON COAST: OCEAN SHORES

Location: About 130 miles southwest of Seattle

Outfitter: Nan-Sea Stables (255 WA 115, 360-289-0194, www.horseplanet.com) has rides available daily, without appointment, weather permitting.

Heads up: Riders in the sand

Description: What's more romantic than riding a horse on the beach? If you're willing to make the 2¾-hour drive to the Washington coast (and there are plenty of reasons to do so; see "Bird-Watching" and "Fly-Fishing & Sportfishing"), you'll have the chance to star in your own Harlequin paperback. Located 75 miles west of Olympia, Ocean Shores is a 6,000-acre peninsula with 6 miles of majestic beach open for walking, kite-flying, and trotting. Nan-Sea Stables offers ½- and 1-hour rides along the spectacular Pacific coastline, with the option of a sunset ride on a more secluded stretch of beach. Wooded inland trail rides are also an option, with routes determined by your skill (beginner to advanced riders are welcome).

Directions: Take I-5 South to Olympia and exit 104. Follow signs to WA 8, which becomes US 12, continuing through Aberdeen and into Hoquiam. Take exit 109N to Ocean Shores. Take WA 109 about 18 miles and turn left on Hogan's Corner. Continue on the road to Ocean Shores.

METHOW VALLEY

Location: Just over 190 miles from Seattle

Outfitters: Rocking Horse Ranch (18381 WA 20 in Winthrop, 509-996-2768, www.rockinghorseranchwinthrop .com) offers 2-hour to full-day rides on a variety of trails through the Methow Valley. There's a campground at the ranch for those who want to rest saddle-sore backsides. Rocking Horse also offers 2- to 6-day pack trips into the upper end of the Lake Chelan Sawtooth Wilderness. For the basic trip they supply guide and horses, but you bring your own food and camping gear. The deluxe trip includes a guide, horses, a cook, food, and camping gear. Bring your own sleeping bag, pad, and personal gear. Early Winters Outfitting in Mazama, (509-996-2659 or 800-737-8750, www.earlywintersoutfitting.com) offers day rides and pack trips for beginners and experts through the Pasayten Wilderness, with views of waterfalls, streams, and the snowcapped peaks of the north Cascades. Day rides range from 1 hour to all day. On pack trips you can either cook for yourself or have a cook at your service. Each day covers 6 to 15 miles, with optional fishing stops.

Directions: To get to Winthrop in summer take I-5 north about 65 miles to Burlington and head east over WA 20, North Cascades Scenic Highway, to Winthrop. After the pass closes for the winter take I-5 north to Everett. Take US 2 east to Wenatchee. Go north on US 97 to Pateros, then take WA 153 to Twisp and WA 20 west to Winthrop. Consult outfitters listed for a specific meeting place.

Heads up: No need to bring your own cowboy hat; this place has them to spare. In addition to being rich in activities, the Methow Valley offers a wealth of special events throughout the season. Horse fans may want to time their trip to coincide with Winthrop Rodeo Days, held at the Winthrop Rodeo Grounds during the last days of May and August (509-996-2125 or 1-888-463-8469). Thanks to the Methow Valley Sport Trails Association (509-996-3287, www.mvsta.com), sports enthusiasts have an array of options year-round, including a winter triathlon (bike, ski, run) in March, a half-marathon in April, a 21.5-mile relay run in May, and the Boneshaker Mountain Bike Bash race in June. (See "Mountain Biking," page 144, and "Cross-Country Skiing," page 390.)

Description: The Methow Valley and Pasayten Wilderness are known for beautifully dry summers and snowy winters, and, consequently, all the accompanying outdoor sports, including horseback riding. Be sure to check conditions if you're heading over the pass during the snowy months—one main route, WA 20, closes every winter after the first big snowfall. The atmosphere here suits the Western rider almost too well—the entire town of Winthrop has been styled as a Western town, with false storefronts and hand-lettered signs, wrought-iron lamps in antique stores, and a steak on just about every plate. The area is long on amenities, though, with several good hotels, camping in the Pasayten, and great restaurants scattered about. Be sure to drop in to the tiny town of Mazama for a bowl of home-made soup at the Mazama Store.

STEHEKIN

Location: East of Seattle, about 180 miles in the car plus a 1- or 2-hour boat ride on Lake Chelan

Outfitter: Cascade Corrals (509-682-7742, www .courtneycountry.com/cascadecorrals.html) is open from June through Labor Day. They specialize in 4- to 7-day pack trips on Norwegian Fjord horses into the North Cascades National Park and the Sawtooth and Glacier Peak Wilder-nesses. They also offer daily 2½- to 3-hour trail rides from the ranch to Coon Lake, with so many breathtaking views you may want to bring an oxygen tank. Hiking and rafting gear is also available for rent. Log cabins are also available but reservations are highly recommended.

Description: If you really want to get away from it all, plan a trip to Stehekin. Once you get there, you'll find zero roads and only one phone (bring a sack of quarters). But the journey is well worth it. Known as the gateway to North Cascades National Park, remote Stehekin sits on crystal-clear Lake Chelan in a valley surrounded by 8,000-foot peaks. It's the deepest gorge in North America—yes, deeper than the Grand Canyon. The word "Chelan" comes from the native American word *Tsill-ane,* deep notch, and deep it is—the fjordlike lake is the third deepest in the nation, reaching more than 400 feet below sea level. Spectacular scenery is a given, so don't forget your camera.

Unless you've secured a float plane or a private boat, once you reach Lake Chelan you'll need to climb aboard either the *Lady of the Lake* or the newer, speedier *Lady Cat* to cross to this alternative-lifestyle hotbed. Be sure to check the ferry schedule before you leave home, or prepare yourself for lengthy layovers. The Courtney family has lived in Stehekin for over 100 years and operates most of the facilities in the area.

Directions: Take I-90 east over Snoqualmie Pass to exit 85, toward WA 903N/Wenatchee. Turn left onto WA 970 E., which becomes US 97. Take US 97 Alt. ramp toward Entiat/Chelan. Continue about 34 miles through Entiat to just outside of Chelan, where you will see a sign for Lady of the Lake on your right. Turn left and follow signs. There are multiple ferry options from Chelan to Stehekin. Trips range from 1 to 4 hours, depending on boat speed, and just $26–90 round-trip. Contact 800-4-CHELAN or visit www .ladyofthelake.com for options.

Where to Connect

If you're interested in a leisurely day ride or even an overnight pack trip, you need not worry about gearing up for your giddyup—the ranches provide everything you need to ride in high style (follow-up posterior message not included). But enthusiasts who either already own a trusty steed or are considering it may want to check out one or more of the area's tack shops and saddleries. You won't find any in Seattle proper, but there are a couple just across the lake in Bellevue.

- Mills Equestrian Equipment (13620 N.E. 20th St. in Bellevue, 425-746-9330, www.millsequestrian.com)

- Olson's Tack Shop (11408 N.E. 2nd Place in Bellevue, 425-454-9453)

Link
www.polocenter.com/tack/tackuswa.html for countless tack shops (at greater distances from Seattle)

outsidepix.com

YOU MAY HAVE HEARD the term "Cascade Concrete" bandied about. You may, in fact, have encountered this heavy stuff on your boots, boards, and ski bottoms. This is the kind of snow that Pacific Northwesterners often deal with on the slopes, particularly in the early part of the season. At the opposite end of the spectrum is the corn snow of spring, spoken of in reverent terms as the light, dry deliverance every skier has been waiting for. Somewhere in between is what to anticipate most days. (Some years, particularly recent ones, you hope for any snow days at all within a close drive of Seattle.) Sometimes, if you are a child or an adult bent on truancy, you even hope for snow in Seattle itself. This does happen,

371

but most years it's just once, and it doesn't stick around long enough for you to strap on snowshoes. Perhaps every six or seven years there's a chance to break out a sled and slide down a quiet street, but that's not the norm in this maritime climate.

For skiers who can't wait for it to dump right in their backyard, we are fortunate to have a string of tall volcanoes with elevations that guarantee heaps of white stuff. These places, beyond the resort areas, are there for the backcountry skier to investigate. For drier conditions, it's a safer bet to head to the east side of the mountains.

One thing to consider: the potential for high avalanche danger can at times make driving on the roads treacherous. One of the worst avalanche disasters in U.S. history happened in our state, when 96 people in two trains on the west side of Stevens Pass were killed. Sure, this was in 1910. Still, use caution when driving in winter, and be aware that one or more roads over the passes are often closed at some point because of avalanche danger.

The three snow sports chapters—"Cross-Country Skiing," "Snowshoeing," and "Backcountry Skiing & Snowboarding"—will give a taste of the goods on offer. With snow conditions as unpredictable as they are, it's tough to know which areas will be best for an outing on the day you strap your gear to the car rack. The outings described are good starter material, close to home, with plenty for beginners. There is at least one thorough guidebook out for our area on each of these snow sports, all listed in *Where to Connect*. Sidebars illuminate matters of safety, etiquette, winter road travel, and the curious philosophy of the Pacific Northwest snow lover.

General Winter Safety Essentials

THE FOLLOWING LIST combines the Mountaineers' Ten Essentials (page 170) and three winter extras. Check your equipment before every outing, though the avalanche extras can be omitted on safe routes.

1. Map
2. Compass
3. Flashlight
4. Extra food and water
5. Extra clothing
6. Sunglasses
7. First-aid kit
8. Pocketknife
9. Waterproof matches
10. Candle and fire starter
11. Snow shovel and probe
12. Avalanche transceiver and a partner with one
13. Tools to fix boards or skis

There are a few other safety measures you should take. Be sure to let someone know where you're going and when you're likely to be back. This is paramount when venturing into the backcountry. Always check avalanche and weather reports before leaving home (see Avalanche Awareness). If you are going to an area where there will be snowmobilers (e.g. forest service land on the east side of Snoqualmie Pass) be extra cautious and step aside if you hear them coming. Most people who have visited or lived in the Pacific Northwest have mastered the art of layering—only a couple of months out of the year are warm enough to safely leave a jacket behind, even in the city. Out on the snow layering is essential. Start with a non-cotton base layer, such as a stomach-covering sports bra for women, and a long-sleeved synthetic, wool, or silk undershirt for men and women. Ones with zippers ventilate well on those uphill climbs. Follow this with tightly knit wool or fleece, and, crucial in most mountain areas around here, a full suit of rain gear—gaiters, a jacket, and waterproof pants. Bring along plenty of high-energy snacks. You will burn these off, and more, over the course of a few hours in the cold. In an emergency they may be essential to your survival. Don't get too tired. If you feel yourself wearing out, best go find a cup of hot chocolate somewhere, and see if your energy revives—you'll need your wits about you.

Avalanche Awareness

WASHINGTON STATE IS one of the top five in the United States for avalanche deaths, and anyone venturing into the backcountry, even for a cross-country ski or snowshoe, must take this into consideration before deciding where and when to go. Recent years have seen the deaths of many experienced backcountry skiers both here and in British Columbia. If you haven't taken an avalanche safety class, it's time to sign up for one. If you have already learned the ropes, remember that many avalanche victims have had training, but either don't use it or use it improperly. Make sure you know what you're doing and that you employ the techniques you learn. Even then, of course, there is no guarantee that you will always be safe—spending time in the winter backcountry will never be completely risk-free, and the more skilled you become the more likely you are to push limits. Study and use the techniques and heed avalanche center safety warnings, however, and you will limit your risk substantially.

Avalanche Danger Reports

Current avalanche information is available for Oregon and Washington at the Northwest Weather and Avalanche Center (206-526-6677 in Washington; 503-808-2400 in Oregon; online at www.nwac.noaa.gov)

Avalanche Safety Classes

The Mountaineers (206-284-6310, www.mountaineers.org /skiing/avalanche-seminars.htm) is one of Seattle's oldest and largest outdoor activities clubs, with hundreds of classes and outings involving nearly every outdoor sport. They are also involved on local conservation and run Mountaineers Books.

Marmot Mountain Works (425-453-1515, www .marmotmountain.com) offers avalanche safety courses at their Bellevue and Tacoma stores with longtime instructor and guide Gary Brill of Mountain Madness.

Northwest Avalanche Institute (360-825-9261, www .avalanche.org./~nai) is affiliated with the American Avalanche Association. Classes are taught by Paul Baugher, head of the Crystal Mountain Ski Patrol. Their Web site also offers a summary of the previous season's avalanche-related accidents and deaths for the United States and Canada.

Washington Alpine Club (206-467-3042; www.wacweb.org) offers backcountry travel classes similar to those at the Mountaineers.

Books and Additional Resources

Daffern, Tony. *Avalanche Safety for Skiers, Climbers and Snowboarders,* 2nd ed. Seattle, WA: Mountaineers Books, 1999.

Fredston, Jill, and Doug Fesler. *Snow Sense: A Guide to Evaluating Snow Avalanche Hazard,* 5th ed. Anchorage, AK: Alaska Mountain Safety Center, 2001. This book is available at www .alaskaavalanche.com

"Snow Avalanches" is an avalanche safety pamphlet avail-

able at local outfitters and through the forest service. It describes
the basic principles for how to avoid and survive an avalanche.

Before
You Go . . .

A couple other pieces of business:

1. Weather conditions and forecasts can be found at
the NOAA Website: www.wrh.noaa.gov/Seattle.

2. Road conditions, emergency highway closures,
and road construction information are all available from the
Washington State Department of Transportation: www.wsdot
.wa.gov/traffic/road/mnts/mntbas.htm. This site will also list
traction requirements for mountain passes:

Traction Advisory Oversize Vehicles Prohibited: Drive with
care if you are in a passenger vehicle.

Vehicles over 10,000 GVW—Chains Required Passenger
vehicles must have all-season tires.

All Vehicles—Chains Required—Except All-Wheel-Drive
AWD vehicles are not required to show up with chains on the
vehicle, however, the state patrol can ask you to put them on
if conditions change, so stash them even if you never have to
use them.

Ski
Etiquette

- Don't walk on the trail. Move to the side of the trail when
  stopping.
- Skiers coming downhill have the right of way.
- Ski within your ability.
- Ski on the right side of the trail.
- If you fall, fill in the hole.
- Pack out what you packed in.

Where to Connect

Clubs and Schools

- American Alpine Institute (360-671-1505, www.mtnguide
  .com/default.asp) offers backcountry skiing and mountaineering classes.

- The Mountaineers (206-284-8484 or 800-573-8484, www
  .mountaineers.org) offers winter sports courses, seminars,
  and outings around Puget Sound.

- Washington Alpine Club (206-467-3042, www.wacweb.org)
  offers classes, outings, and a cabin on Snoqualmie Pass for
  members.

Shops

- Backpacker's Supply (253-472-4402) is a Tacoma store with
  knowledgeable staff.

- Feathered Friends (206-292-2210, www.featheredfriends
  .com) is just across the street from the flagship REI, but
  smaller and with attitude. They built a reputation for down
  gear (in the damp Northwest, no less) but sell and rent a
  variety of equipment.

- Marmot Mountain Works (425-453-1515, www
  .marmotmountain.com), just east of Seattle in Bellevue,
  this store has cross-country and ski mountaineering equipment as well as backpacking and climbing gear. The staff is
  very knowledgeable with a great reputation. Avalanche
  training courses available.

- OR Factory Outlet Store (2203 1st Ave. S., 206-971-1496,
  www.orgear.com). If you'd like to do some bargain hunting
  check out the factory outlet for this gear manufacturer,
  with clothes, gloves, gaiters, and other brands' merchandise
  as well.

- Play it Again Sports (206-264-9255, across from the flagship REI and next to Feathered Friends, plus four other locations in the area) sells new and used ski and snowboard equipment and offers tune-ups and rentals. You can also trade in used equipment here.

- Pro Mountain Sports (206-522-1627) in the University District is owned by Jim Nelson, a winter-climbing expert.

- Pro Ski Service (206-525-4425, 425-888-6397 in North Bend, www.proguiding.com) is a ski shop connected with Pro Guiding Service, a very reputable group of backcountry mountaineering guides who teach groups and individuals and lead trips into the backcountry. The owner, Martin Volken, was originally trained as a Swiss Mountain Guide in his native country.

- Recreation Equipment Outfitters (REI) (206-223-1944, www.rei.com). The famous REI's flagship store is at 222 Yale Ave. N., with all kinds of equipment, a bookstore, classes, lectures, and everything else. Additional stores in Federal Way, Lynnwood, Redmond, Tukwila, and Tacoma.

- Second Ascent (206-545-8810) in Seattle's Ballard neighborhood is an independent store with new and used outdoors equipment. (See sidebar in "Rock Climbing.")

Links

www.nwsnow.org is a Northwest snowboarding and skiing Web site with news, articles, weather information and discussion forums.

www.turns-all-year.com is described in *Endless Winter*, page 416.

www.gorp.com is a travel and adventure Web site for North America.

outsidepix.com

CROSS-COUNTRY SKIING HAS an avid if not completely coordinated following here in western Washington. The I-90 corridor, that summer magnet for day hikers, becomes the first destination on your ski trip list in winter. Winter days are so short, the light is so dim, that by the time you've hauled yourself out of bed you don't usually have time to look farther. I'm convinced this is the reason why many cross-country skiers (myself included) can be seen on these trails doing a serviceable but not graceful job of skiing from one place to another. The snow is sometimes beautiful, but it's rarely the pretty powder found on the other side of the mountains, and it doesn't inspire the gazelle-like Nordic form a true cross-country expert can achieve. I know—this winter I went to the Methow.

I'd been to this crisp, dry, Nordic trail mecca several times before, in different seasons, but this time I was there for the skiing. I stuck out like a Methow Valley farmer in a Capitol Hill nightclub. I was slogging, while people were schussing effortlessly over the slick, groomed trails. And I vowed to return for a long weekend of lessons from one of the many expert Methow instructors, who have all winter in the dry snow to study nothing but grace.

This is not to suggest that the Sno-Park trails of Snoqualmie Pass aren't worthy of a visit—they're accessible and enormous fun in the right conditions. But do yourself a favor and get out of town once in awhile, south to the higher elevations of Rainier, up to Mount Baker, farther east on I-90 over the pass, or, best of all, up to the Methow for a few days in a cabin hideaway with just you, your main squeeze, and a pair of skinny skis for inspiration.

A few notes: As with all other winter sports, remember when choosing your own trail that avalanche risk varies greatly from place to place, and be sure to learn as much about the warning signs of avalanches as possible (see *Avalanche Awareness*, page 374). Next, if you exhaust the resources here, look to the snowshoe routes, which begin on page 397, or even hiking trails for more cross-country skiing ideas. Forest service roads capped with a fresh blanket of snow are often great for cross-country skiing or snowshoeing, so seek them out. After some warm weather, however, a refreeze will make this icy terrain. Then it's time to retreat to groomed trails—take advantage of what's out there.

Short Hops

THE SUMMIT AT SNOQUALMIE NORDIC CENTER

Location: About 45 miles east of Seattle

Contact: Snoqualmie Summit at 425-434-6646, ski conditions at 206-236-1600, www.summit-at-snoqualmie.com

Facilities: 50 kilometers of groomed trails, 4 kilometers of lighted trails. Rentals, lessons, racing, and snowshoeing. The fee for trail use is around $12.

Description: Seattle-area kids cut their ski edges at Snoqualmie Pass, and most people think of it as a place for a basic, nearby downhill outing, as long as there's decent snow. Not everyone realizes that, high above the chilly chair lifts, a more refined world of groomed cross-country trails, food, rentals, lessons, and cozy warming huts exists. A ticket for trail use gets you a ride up to this well-run Nordic center, where there are beginner routes and many intermediate and even advanced options for trying out your cross-country skills on hilly terrain.

Directions: Take I-90 to exit 54 and follow signs for the Summit at Snoqualmie Nordic Center.

Sno-Parks

WHEN YOU HEAD OUT to cross-country ski or snowshoe this season, chances are you'll be pulling up at a Sno-Park. This program, nearly 30 years old, provides snow plowing at parking lots with access to local trails for nonmotorized winter recreation. Your job is to buy an annual Sno-Park pass so you don't get ticketed at the

Sno-Park site. The current price is around $20, with daily passes for $8. The pass is available at state park headquarters and at over 100 vendors around Washington, including REI, Marmot Mountain Works, other outdoors stores, as well as gas stations and minimarts near ski areas. Many of the Sno-Parks have groomed trails—a guide is available from the Washington State Parks and Recreation Commission. Dogs are not allowed in groomed trail areas.

More information is available from the Washington State Parks and Recreation Commission at 360-902-8500 or www.parks.wa.gov.

KEECHELUS LAKE: IRON HORSE TRAIL

Location: About 55 miles east of Seattle

Contact: Lake Easton State Park (509-656-2230), Washington State Parks and Recreation Commission (360-902-8500, www.parks.wa.gov)

Length: 12 miles out and back

Difficulty: Easy, groomed

Elevation Gain: 70 feet

Maximum elevation: 2,540 feet

Map and Book: Green Trails 207: Snoqualmie Pass; *100 Best Cross-Country Ski Trails*

Permit: A Sno-Park pass is required

Heads up: Flat route, great for gliding and skate skiing. In recent years a tiny kiosk in the parking lot has sold pizza. It might still be there. Cash only. Here, as at other groomed Sno-Parks, dogs are not allowed on trails.

Description: This ski route is atop an old railroad grade that parallels—and offers occasional views of—Keechelus Lake. It's a great beginner stretch with plenty of room to get exercise. The trail, a wide expanse with trees on either

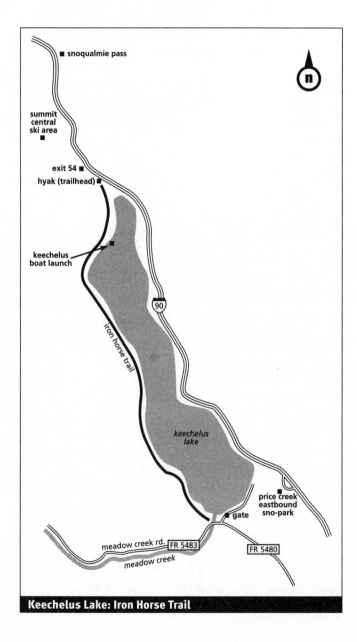

Keechelus Lake: Iron Horse Trail

side, curves around the west side of the lake. At 2.5 miles, a 0.25-mile stretch, marked by signs, runs beneath a cliff and can avalanche under the right conditions. No loitering. Keep on south for as far as you want—at nearly 6 miles the Keechelus Lake dam is a good place to turn back north.

Directions: Take I-90 east from Seattle to exit 54. Turn south. At the stop sign turn left (east again) and follow a road that parallels I-90. Turn right on the road to the Keechelus boat launch, following Sno-Park signs.

CABIN CREEK NORTH—CABIN CREEK SOUTH

Location: About 65 miles east of Seattle

Contact: Washington State Parks and Recreation Commission (360-902-8500, www.parks.wa.gov)

Length: Up to 10 miles of trails

Difficulty: Easy to difficult

Elevation Gain: 200 feet

Maximum elevation: 2,600 feet

Map: Green Trails 207: Snoqualmie Pass

Permit: A Sno-Park pass is required

Heads up: Arrive early at this popular set of trails.

Description: Somehow, wherever you intend to head on I-90, your ski tips always seem to turn in this same direction. The trails here are generally marked, complete with difficulty signs. Races are held regularly (and those trails will be off-limits at the time), so this is a good place to practice technique. Cabin Creek North offers trails from easiest to most difficult, the latter involving some fun hills and zips around tall evergreens. The shorter 2-kilometer loop at Cabin Creek South follows a gentle grade in a semi-circle from one Sno-Park lot to the other—ski back the way you came or move up to the Cabin Creek North trails by

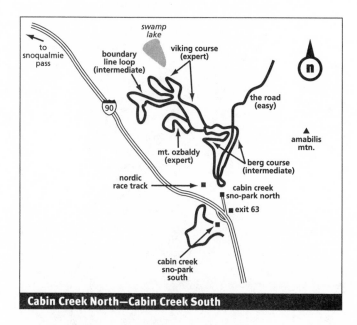

Cabin Creek North—Cabin Creek South

crossing the freeway overpass (skis off). If you want additional challenges, move up to the Amabilis Mountain junket, accessible from the same Sno-Park.

Directions: For Cabin Creek trails, take I-90 east to exit 63. Turn south into the Sno-Park. The north trails are on the north side of the freeway interchange. The southern loop starts from the southeast corner of the lower lot and returns near the entrance to the Sno-Park.

SUN TOP MOUNTAIN SNO-PARK

Location: About 50 miles southeast of Seattle

Contact: Washington State Parks and Recreation Commission (360-902-8500, www.parks.wa.gov); White River Ranger District (360-825-6585)

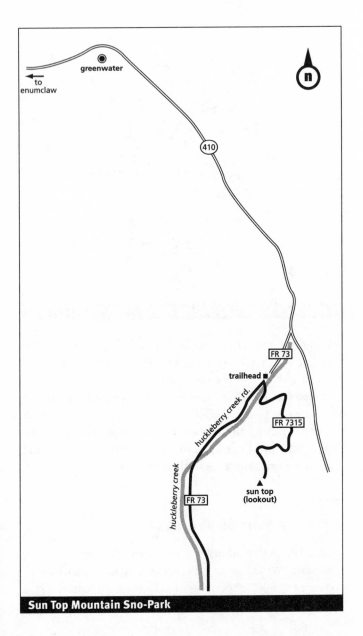

greenwater

to
enumclaw

410

FR 73

trailhead ■

huckleberry creek rd.

FR 7315

huckleberry creek

FR 73

sun top
(lookout)

Sun Top Mountain Sno-Park

Length: Variable—many wandering miles are available.

Difficulty: Huckleberry Creek is easy, the Sun Top Lookout, difficult.

Elevation gain: Huckleberry Creek, 700 feet; Sun Top Lookout, 3,030 feet

Maximum elevation: Huckleberry Creek, 2,900 feet; Sun Top Lookout, 5,230 feet

Map and book: Green Trails 238: Greenwater; *100 Best Cross-Country Ski Trails in Washington*

Permit: A Sno-Park pass is required

Heads up: Wildest Sno-Park in the state

Description: The lower elevation ski here, Huckleberry Creek, starts at 2,200 feet and gains only 700 feet in about 4.75 miles. To do it, follow Huckleberry Creek Road (FR 73) for 0.25 mile and stay left, wandering on side roads willy-nilly. If you manage to get back to the main road again keep going on FR 73, staying left to get deeper into the forest. This is a real wilderness outing with old growth and a chance to see such wildlife as elk and deer. If you go in 4 miles, you may encounter a narrow chute that occasionally avalanches. Take precautions. A second ski trip at Sun Top heads uphill on FR 7315, with a potential for a 3,030-foot elevation gain to the summit. Avalanche risk can be high here. For a description of this trail see *100 Best Cross-Country Ski Trails in Washington.*

Directions: Take I-5 south about 22 miles to exit 142A toward WA 18 east (Auburn/North Bend). In about 4 miles take the WA 164 east exit toward Enumclaw. In Enumclaw, follow signs to WA 410 east. From here drive about 24.8 miles to Huckleberry Creek Road (FR 73) and turn right (south) for about 1.4 miles. This road should be plowed to the Sno-Park (if not, park here and ski in).

Longer Hops

STEVENS PASS NORDIC CENTER

Location: On US 2 about 80 miles northeast of Seattle

Contact: 360-973-3441, snow conditions 206-634-1645, www.stevenspass.com

Facilities: 25 kilometers of groomed trails including ones for skate-skiing, and 6.5 kilometers of snowshoe trails

Description: With a base elevation of about 4,000 feet Stevens can guarantee more snow and colder conditions than the Snoqualmie Pass area. Their Nordic Center is a favorite area destination for many cross-country lovers, with 25 kilometers of groomed trails, room for skate skiing and snowshoeing, and a lodge. Unless you're practicing skate skiing it's fun to wander off the main trail through the woods, where hills provide opportunities to manuever. The resort offers instruction, rentals, and food.

Directions: Take the WA 520 bridge from Seattle to I-405 and head north. Take exit 23 (WA 22 east) toward Monroe. Take a right in Monroe on US 2 and continue about 50 miles to Stevens Pass. The Nordic Center is 5 miles east of the summit.

MOUNT TAHOMA TRAILS ASSOCIATION: RAINIER HUTS

Location: Near Ashford, about 85 miles southeast of Seattle

Contact: 360-569-2451 for snow conditions. For ski hut

Cross-Country Skiing

reservations send SASE to Mount Tahoma Trails, Attn.: Hut Reservation Program, P.O. Box 206, Ashford, WA 98304. Reservation forms and other information are available at www.skimtta.com

Facilities: Hut-to-hut skiing with three huts and one yurt, 50 miles of trail, 20 of them groomed.

Description: And now for a little something different. This destination bills itself as "North America's largest no-fee cross country hut-to-hut ski and snowshoeing trail system" and is run by a nonprofit association. For a minimal processing fee (about $5) and a refundable damage deposit, you can stay in a hut reserved in advance. Huts have kitchens, propane lighting, woodburning stoves and firewood, furniture, and sleeping pads—all you need is a sleeping bag and food. Huts sleep six to eight people and are located at elevations of 4,000 feet and up, right on the outskirts of Mount Rainier National Park. High Hut boasts a 360-degree view, including Mounts Rainier, Adams, and St Helens, and frequent wildlife sightings.

Directions: Call for directions to particular trails. The MTTA office is behind the fire station at the west end of Ashford, and is open Saturday and Sunday during daytime hours December through April.

Meccas

LEAVENWORTH

Location: About 120 miles northeast of Seattle

Contact: 509-548-5477 or 509-548-5115, Leavenworth Mountain Sports at 509-548-7864, www.skileavenworth.com

Facilities: All trails have double-set tracks and skating lanes. Two of the trails pass near the downtown area with access to shops, restaurants, and cafés. The ski hill north of town has 5 kilometers of groomed, lighted trails, while the golf course and waterfront park area has 10 kilometers. South of town, Icicle River (a climbing and rafting mecca) has 7 kilometers of trails. Daily or season passes available.

Heads up: Gustav's is a brew-pub popular with rock climbers and others looking to get away from the standard Bavarian tourist fare. Dogs are allowed on the 3 kilometer waterfront park trail, but not on other trails.

Description: The Bavarian town of Leavenworth is a destination for all kinds of summer sports (see "Rock Climbing," page 208, and "White Water," page 87, for starters) and in winter is dressed in white and on display for tourists. If you're heading east to (or returning from) the Methow or beyond, you will likely pass through here. In keeping with its theme, the town has established three cross-country ski trails. This might be a good place to come with children for a short ski getaway.

Directions: Take I-5 north toward Everett, turning off at US 2. Head east about 85 miles over Stevens Pass to Leavenworth. The golf course and Icicle River Trails are located on Icicle Rd., 2 miles before entering the town of Leavenworth on the right. Ski Hill trails are on Ski Hill Rd., on the left as you enter town. Waterfront Park Trails are a block from downtown (turn right in town) and connect with Golf Course Trail.

METHOW VALLEY

Location: About 200 miles northeast of Seattle

Terrain: Extensive groomed trail system and backcountry huts

Outfitters: Winthrop Mountain Sports (509-996-2886, www.winthropmountainsports.com) in downtown Winthrop is a tiny store that manages to pack a rental shop and well-rounded outdoors store into one small space. Ski and snowshoe rentals and trail passes are all here. Central Reservations (800-422-3048, www.extrabeds.com) will help you find local lodging in inns, hotels, or private cabins. To hear a grooming report (including snow conditions and temperature) for the cross-country ski trails call 800-682-5787.

Heads up: Watch in stores and at trailheads for posters advertising free naturalist-led snowshoe outings. They generally take place on Saturdays and holidays and meet outside the yurt (you'll know it when you see it) in Mazama. Use of snowshoes included. Dogs are only allowed on one trail, the Big Valley Ranch trail, which does not require a pass but is not groomed on a regular basis.

Description: When the damp heart of a western Washington winter is upon you, when the fresh powder (if there ever was any) has turned to slush, when that ceaseless drip-dripping outside . . . well, you get the point. It's time to head east. Five hours or so from Seattle the Methow Valley spends the winter cold and dry, usually with the kind of fluffy white stuff people from Idaho, Wyoming, or Colorado might actually recognize as snow. Downhill skiers are mostly restricted to backcountry and heli-skiing here, but Nordic aficionados (and snowshoers) are in luck: The valley has a well-organized maze of nearly 200 kilometers of cross-country ski trails rivaling the best nordic centers in the United States. The trail system, divided into three distinct areas linked by a cross-valley community trail, is maintained by the Methow Valley Sport Trails Association (www.mvsta.com), which pays for upkeep by selling trail passes. The three areas are vaguely divided into beginner, intermediate, and advanced, though there is some overlap. The Rendezvous Huts, rustic but very cozy backcountry cabins, offer a chance to experience hut-to-hut skiing, a European tradition that is becoming more popular in the United States. I'm not sure if it's the fresh air, the sunlight, or the tasteful but ridiculous faux-Western storefronts in Winthrop, but a trip to the valley has never failed to lift me out of any Seattle winter doldrums.

Directions: Take I-5 north to Everett then US 2 east to Wenatchee. Take US 2/US 97 to Okanogan/Pateros. Continue on US 97 and bear left at the junction with Orondo. About 60 miles past Wenatchee, turn left at Pateros onto WA 153 to Twisp, then take WA 20 west to Winthrop.

Where to Connect

Clubs

- The Outing Club (206-363-0859, www.outingclub.org) offers inexpensive or free clinics, a ski lesson, ski purchase advice, maps, and camaraderie. They have buses that take club members to area ski destinations three times a week, midwinter.

- Washington Ski Touring Club (206-525-4451, www.wstc .org) offers trips, clinics, and other opportunities for cross-country and backcountry skiers. Meetings are held at REI. Yearly membership dues.

Shops

See *Where to Connect* in "Snow Sports Overview."

Events

For up-to-date information on cross-country ski events and races check the Pacific Northwest Ski Association Web site, www.pnsa.org.

Book

- Spring, Vicki, and Tom Kirkendall. *The 100 Best Cross-Country Ski Trails in Washington.* Seattle WA: Mountaineers Books, 2002.

Link

www.parks.wa.gov for Sno-Park information

outsidepix.com

HIKERS FRUSTRATED WITH waiting out the winter season to get back to the mountains, take heart. Snowshoeing, that simplest of winter sports, opens the backcountry year-round. That means not only more time in the mountains, but the chance to acquaint yourself with winter versions of summer favorites. Every trail looks, feels, and sounds different under a blanket of white—Douglas firs sparkle, rivers gush, and the smell of Northwest mud is replaced by the cold, crisp scent of ozone. Keep an eye out for wildlife tracks—the animals you'll spot or see signs of in winter may be different than the summer regulars. Depending on where you are, watch for elk, deer, mountain goat, and mountain sheep, and smaller mammals, including hares, red foxes, Douglas squirrels, lynx, and bobcats. The quieter you are, the more you might see. Always keep your distance, since winter wildlife needs to conserve its energy to sustain body temperature and make it to the more abundant seasons.

A few recommended outings are described below. Any hiking trail—and, for that matter, any unplowed forest service road—can make a great snowshoe trail, given the right conditions. Many of the Internet resources listed, especially forest service and national and state parks Web sites, offer trip ideas.

Be aware when choosing your own trail that avalanche risk may vary greatly from place to place, and be sure to learn as much about the warning signs of avalanches as possible (See *Avalanche Awareness*, page 374). Lots of places in and around Seattle have begun to rent snowshoes, but if you get out much you'll quickly want to buy a pair; a serviceable model can be had for as little as $100, often less than the cost of a handful of rentals. The size of your 'shoe depends on your weight and the kind of snow you'll be facing—on this side of the Cascades, frequently heavy, wet stuff. Pay attention to what you rent, and you'll get a good idea of what to buy. Be sure to wear the right footwear for your adventure. For once, this is a sport that doesn't require a specific boot. Manufacturers are surely out there creating such a monster, but for now you won't feel under-dressed (or at least, I don't) wearing a sturdy pair of hiking boots, ones with ankle support, accompanied by thick socks and, in most conditions, a pair of gaiters that cover the whole shebang. Trekking poles—those telescoping poles used by lots of hikers and backcountry skiers—can be useful here. You could also use a pair of ski poles—anything that helps you keep your balance. They will come in handy when backing up in snowshoes—a specialized procedure that should really be accompanied by the sound of loud beeping. For the most part, of course, snowshoeing is exactly as easy as it looks. One tip: Watch out for the wells around the base of trees, where it's easy to sink in deep.

Finally, snowshoeing is often the preferred means for backcountry snowboarders to scale the mountainsides they're hoping to ride down. In case you want to take the obsession further.

Short Hops

KEECHELUS RIDGE

Location: Off I-90, about 65 miles east of Seattle

Contact: Wenatchee National Forest, Cle Elum Ranger District (509-674-4411, www.fs.fed.us/r6/wenatchee/district /cleelum/skiinfo.html)

Length: 6 miles or more out and back

Difficulty: Moderate to difficult

Elevation gain: 2,100 feet

Maximum elevation: 4,900 feet

Map and book: Green Trails 207: Snoqualmie Pass; *Snowshoe Routes of Washington*

Permit: A Sno-Park pass is required

Heads up: Excellent workout for winter conditioning

Description: Many of the nearby Sno-Park options along I-90 are good for cross-country skiers who want to stay in the tracks, circling lakes or wandering among second-growth forest. Since you've got your snowshoes on, you might as well put them to use on something a bit steeper. On clear days you'll get great views of Mount Rainier and other southern peaks when you stop to catch your breath. Make it to the top and you can look east to more mountains before galumphing your way back down.

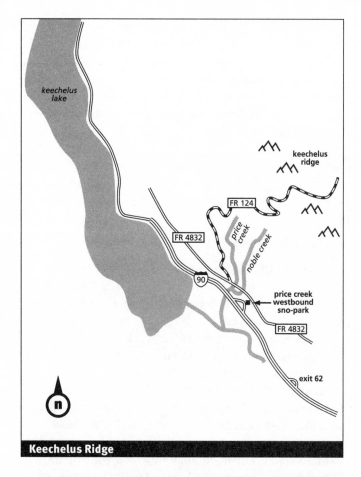

Keechelus Ridge

Route: Leave the Sno-Park and head northwest 0.25 mile to FR 4832. Turn left and go west, then take narrow FR 124. Stick with this road as it winds upward, or cut across the slope on your own trail. Your goal is the peak with radio towers.

Directions: Drive I-90 east from Seattle over Snoqualmie Pass. Take exit 62 (Kachess Lake), located about 10 miles east of the summit. Turn left off the exit back over the freeway, and get back on I-90 going westbound 1.5 miles to the Price Creek Westbound Sno-Park.

HEATHER LAKE

Location: About 57 miles northeast of Seattle

Contact: Darrington Ranger Station (360-436-1155, www.fs.fed.us/r6/mbs/recreation/activities/trails/drd/drd_0701.htm)

Length: 4 miles out and back

Difficulty: Moderate to difficult

Elevation gain: 1,100 feet

Maximum elevation: 2,440 feet

Map: Green Trails 109: Granite Falls

Permit: Northwest Forest Pass (see "Hiking," page 171)

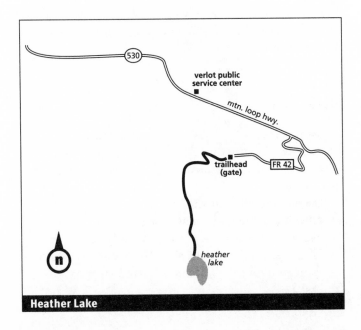

Heather Lake

Heads up: Note the low peak elevation—make sure there's enough snow.

Description: This popular and fairly easy summer hike becomes more challenging, and perhaps more interesting, in winter. A climb on Mount Pilchuck through forest to sparkling, glacier-carved Heather Lake is a strenuous workout but short enough to be manageable for most.

Route: Head up from the left side of the parking area. The trail goes through forest and then climbs beside a creek, traversing west. You'll gain about 1,000 feet before reaching the lake 2 miles in.

Directions: Take I-5 north about 43 miles to exit 208 east to Arlington. Go to Arlington. Turn right on WA9. Turn left onto 84th N.E., following signs for Granite Falls. Turn left onto 92nd E. and left (east) onto WA 530 (Mountain Loop Highway) 1 mile past Verlot Public Service Center. Turn right (south) onto Mount Pilchuck Road (FR 42). Continue 1.6 miles to the gate. Park without blocking the main road or private access roads. FR 42 can be rough and would be best attempted with four-wheel-drive.

KELCEMA LAKE

Location: About 67 miles northeast of Seattle

Contact: Darrington Ranger Station (360-436-1155, www.fs.fed.us/r6/mbs/recreation/activities/trails/drd/drd_0701.htm)

Length: 10 miles out and back

Difficulty: Moderate, though long

Heads up: You may be sharing the early part of the road with sledders, so stay to the side. There may be cross-country skiers all the way along, so avoid stepping in their tracks.

Elevation gain: 1,600 feet

Maximum elevation: 3,182 feet

Map and Book: Green Trails 110: Silverton; *Snowshoe Routes of Washington*

Description: This long but moderate summit hike begins in fairly thick forest with limited views. But climb for a while and you'll be rewarded: The sights up higher can be splendid on a clear day, north to Bald Mountain, and to several peaks down the valley you've left behind. At the top you'll snowshoe through at least a few patches of old growth to a picnic-worthy lake. During the summer this access road makes the lake a popular family destination, but in winter you can often enjoy it in relative solitude.

Route: Follow Deer Creek Rd. (FR 4052) from the eastern edge of the parking area for about a mile through forest, then stay left, following Deer Creek, finally crossing it at about 3.5 miles. The road gets steeper here and recrosses

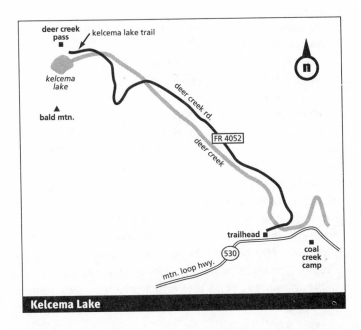

Kelcema Lake

the creek to the Kelcema Lake trailhead at 4.5 miles. Turn left and climb the Kelcema Lake Trail to the lake.

Directions: Take I-5 north about 43 miles to exit 208 east to Arlington. Go to Arlington. Turn right onto WA 9. Turn left onto 84th N.E. following signs for Granite Falls. Turn left onto 92nd east and left (east) onto WA 530 (Mountain Loop Highway) 12 miles past the Verlot Public Service Center. Turn left onto Deer Creek Road (FR 4052), drive to the end of the plowed road, and park.

Meccas

MAZAMA RIDGE

Location: Mount Rainier, about 100 miles southeast of Seattle

Contact: Mount Rainier National Park (360-569-2211, www.nps.mora/recreation)

Length: 4 to 6 miles out and back

Difficulty: Moderate to difficult

Elevation gain: 900–1,200 feet

Maximum elevation: 5,700 feet

Maps and Book: Mount Rainier National Park map; Green Trails 270: Mount Rainier East, and 270S: Paradise; *Snowshoe Routes of Washington*

Heads up: A chance to see Mount Rainier in winter. Get an early start if coming from Seattle, since the days are short and this drive can get long. Check with park headquarters for road conditions into Paradise, and check Mountain Weather and Avalanche Forecast hotline (206-526-6677, www.nwac.noaa.gov) for snow conditions.

Snow camping is an interesting option for any Mount Rainier winter outing, considering the trek it takes to get

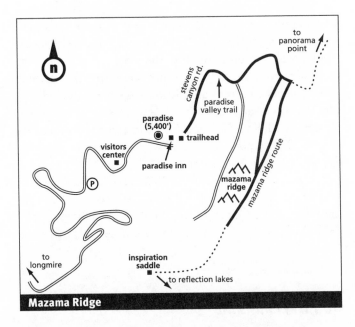

Mazama Ridge

here. If you've got experience, see the Mount Rainier National Park Web site for information on getting a wilderness permit to camp, and for further details.

Free snowshoe treks are frequently offered to the public at the Jackson Memorial Visitor Center at Paradise, usually midday. Sign-up is an hour before, and snowshoes can be borrowed for a $1 donation.

Description: When you tire of hiking to high-country scenery, drive to Paradise and you'll see it from the parking lot. This high-elevation destination is a great place to go when lower routes are still below snow level. Some local clubs bring snowshoers and skiers here for outings, as it's a good midlevel trip. Views of frozen lakes and Mount Rainier are gorgeous, and there are lots of options for striking out on your own if you get the urge.

Route: The Mazama Ridge Trail starts at the east end of the Paradise parking lot and follows Stevens Canyon Rd.

across Edith Creek on a footbridge. From here it goes east around the top of Paradise Valley to Mazama Ridge. A steep climb takes you south (right) to the ridge top at 5,700 feet. From here cross the ridge and turn south (right) to a view toward Mount Rainier and Stevens Canyon. Return the way you came or wander in the meadows if you're good with route-finding. Do not attempt to continue to Inspiration Saddle without talking to a ranger first—avalanche danger lies in that direction.

Directions: Take I-5 south to Tacoma, then head east on WA 7 to Elbe. Bear right on WA 706 and continue east to the Nisqually entrance to Mount Rainier National Park. Take the road all the way to the Paradise Lodge parking area.

WONDERLAND TRAIL

Location: Mount Rainier National Park, about 100 miles Southeast of Seattle

Contact: Mount Rainier National Park (360-569-2211, www.nps.mora/recreation/)

Length: 7 miles or less out and back

Difficulty: Easy

Elevation gain: 1,300 feet

Maximum Elevation: 4,100 feet

Map and book: Green Trails 269: Mount Rainier West; *Snowshoe Routes of Washington*

Heads up: The Longmire Museum (360-569-2211, ext. 3314), open year-round with varying hours, has exhibits on the park. As with most Mount Rainier outings, be sure to check avalanche danger—parts of this route may be risky even during moderate avalanche conditions.

Description: If you've always wanted to hike the Wonderland Trail in summer (see "Hiking," page 192) but never

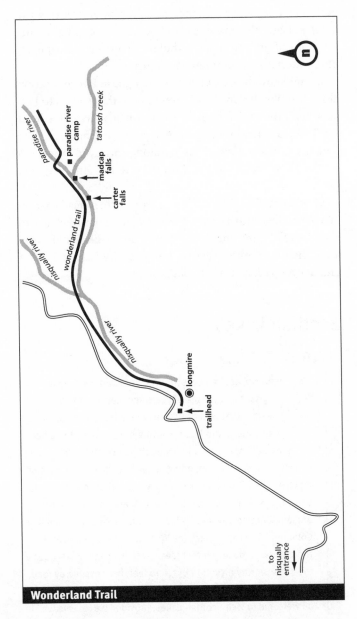

Wonderland Trail

quite made it, here's a chance to visit part of it during the quiet season. Not many snowshoe outings can boast this kind of old growth, or a turbulent river for atmosphere, plus waterfalls to complete the journey.

Route: Snowshoe east from the Longmire Ranger Station along the Wonderland Trail, first next to the road up to Paradise, and then briefly beside the Nisqually River. It's level for 2 miles, then crosses the Nisqually and heads up the Paradise River Valley, climbing along the river to reach a pair of falls, the second at 3.6 miles. Return the way you came.

Directions: Take I-5 south to Tacoma, then head east on WA 7 to Elbe. Bear right on WA 706 and continue east to the Nisqually entrance to Mount Rainier National Park. Take the road 6 miles east to the Longmire Ranger Station and Lodge; park behind the lodge.

Scottish Lakes High Camp

A FRIEND RETURNED SURPRISINGLY AGLOW from a three-day ski trip a couple of years ago. Considering our weather that winter, I suspected she and her boyfriend had snuck off to Kauai, leaving the rest of us to go belly-up in the dark of a western Washington December. She tried to convince me it wasn't so, going so far as to invent the myth of a place called Scottish Lakes, an icy Bali Hai of sorts where the snow is always crisp, the beds are soft, and the hot-tub fires are kept burning day and night, all for a price about equal to a Colorado lift ticket. "Check the Web site" she insisted, and there it was, a backcountry hideaway in the central Cascades at the snow-worthy elevation of 5,000 feet, inaccessible by road, protected and perfect as a Hollywood diva. Apparently we are all welcome to visit Scottish Lakes, provided we reserve well in advance (weekdays might be somewhat more open). There are nine private cabins, a day lodge, sauna, and that mythic hot tub to soak in after a day on an exceptionally well-marked 20 miles of ski trails. They claim great conditions mid-November through late April. The cabins are rustic, with woodburning stoves, and you'll need to bring your own sleeping bag and towel. To check out this wonderland for yourself, visit www .scottishlakes.com or call 888-9-HICAMP.

Where to Connect

Events and Organized Outings

- Mount Rainier National Park (360-569-2211) offers snow-shoe walks with a park ranger/naturalist on weekends. Sign up at the Jackson Memorial Visitor Center one hour before the walk. A $1 donation is requested for snowshoe loans.

- Olympic National Park (360-565-3136) offers snowshoe walks to the public from Hurricane Ridge. Easy to moder-ate. Around $2 donation requested. Sign up at the informa-tion desk an hour before the walk.

- The forest service (425-434-6111) offers guided snowshoe walks from the Forest Service Visitor Information Center off I-90 at exit 52, Snoqualmie Pass. Snowshoes provided. $10 donation, reservations required.

- Renton Recreation Division (425-430-6700, www.ci.renton .wa.us) offers guided snowshoe trips to various wilderness areas for around $15.

Book

- Nelson, Dan. *Snowshoe Routes of Washington.* Seattle, WA: Mountaineers Books, 1998.

MOVING UP A NOTCH in intensity from cross-country and snowshoe treks, back-country skiing (and by that I mean snow-boarding, too) generally involves climbing up high enough, either with skins on your skis or snow-shoes on your feet and a snowboard on your back, to some mountainous terrain where you can swoop down through bowls, catch views over ridgetops, and, for many, carve a series of glorious turns. "The greatest thing about Seattle backcoun-try is that you can go out, take some turns, and be back in the city at a brewpub by nightfall," says backcountry boy Matt Dressler. "You can do a long trek in and major turns on the way out, or go a short distance and do yo-yo up-and-down turns." There's a bit of both described below, and a lot more out there to be explored. Backcountry skiing poses a big enough risk that I don't think this book should be your primary source of information, and really this short list merely suggests what's out there. One of the best places for guidance is Rainer Burgdorfer's *100 Classic Backcountry Ski and Snowboard Routes*.

Longer Hops

BULLION BASIN

Location: About 76 miles southeast of Seattle

Distance: 4 miles

Skill Level: Intermediate with avalanche training

Elevation gain: 2,000 feet

Maximum elevation: 6,200 feet

Season: January through April

Avalanche hazard: Yes, during appropriate conditions

Map and book: Green Trails 271: Bumping Lake; *Backcountry Ski Washington*

Heads up: Some flat spots on the way back may be problematic for boarders. The Snorting Elk pub at Crystal Mountain is great for a post-run beer.

Description: Just as there are local resort skiers who will only ski at Crystal Mountain, there are Bullion Basin addicts who can't seem to resist the potential for great snow and incredible views of Mount Rainier from the top of the ridge. If it's a high avalanche potential day you can stay in the trees by taking the north face down—there are some flat spots here that can be tough for a boarder but fine

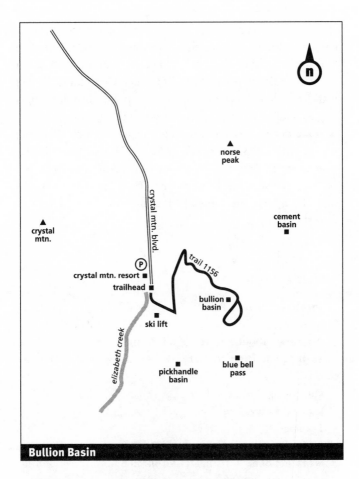

Bullion Basin

for telemarking. The southern slope is open and gentler, but dangerous on high avalanche days.

Route: Go to the upper Crystal Mountain Resort parking area. Climb to the far left of the children's ski area east of the chapel to the road, and climb up through the trees to the Bullion Basin trailhead (a sign may or may not be visible). Climb on a traverse to the north for half a mile to a creek crossing. Here you'll enter steep, open hillside then switchback into the trees. Keep the creek gully on your right. The bottom of Bullion Basin is reached by making a climbing traverse to the south at about 5,600 feet. Go as far up as you want, and descend from any spot along the ridge. If there is any avalanche danger, avoid the south-facing slope.

Directions: Drive south on I-5 to the I-405 exit (Renton). Merge onto I-405 north. Take exit 2 (WA 167) toward Renton/Auburn. Take WA 18 east toward Auburn. Take WA 164 southeast toward Enumclaw. Turn left onto WA 410 east. Turn left onto Crystal Mountain Blvd. and follow it into the resort.

SKYLINE RIDGE

Location: Stevens Pass, US 2 about 80 miles northeast of Seattle

Distance: About 2 miles of climbing

Skill Level: Intermediate skiing, advanced avalanche skills

Elevation gain: 1,400 feet

Maximum elevation: 5,400 feet

Season: November to March

Avalanche hazard: Considerable

Maps and Book: Green Trails 144: Benchmark Mountain, and 176: Stevens Pass; USGS Stevens Pass and Labyrinth Mountain; *100 Classic Backcountry Ski and Snowboard Routes in Washington*

Heads up: A couple of descent options, and the chance of dry snow. You can also ride the lifts to more backcountry skiing at the Stevens Pass Ski Area across the road.

Description: Short but sweet turns here at a very accessible backcountry site. There are spectacular views from the

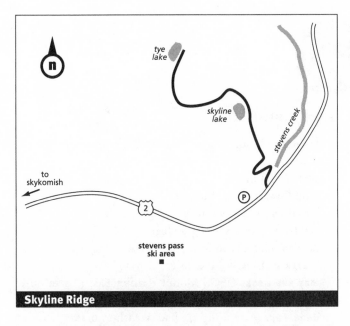

Skyline Ridge

top, and the bowls beyond Skyline Lake are often brimming with good powder.

Route: Climb the slope from the parking lot past the electric substation. Continue up the trail through the trees to open slopes. Begin turning northwest before heavy forest, then uphill to Skyline Lake and the saddle. Intermediate skiers can practice their turns on the short runs available here. More advanced riders can continue northwest into the trees, over the edge into bigger bowls with sheltered powder. To get back to the car, climb back the way you came. You can also descend to the bottom and contour around Skyline Ridge, but this area can have very dangerous avalanche conditions. Practice all safety measures.

Directions: Take I-5 north to US 2, exit 194. Drive east on US 2 past Monroe to Stevens Pass. Park across from the Stevens Pass Ski Area, on the north side of the road.

Mecca

MUIR SNOWFIELD

Location: Mount Rainier, about 85 miles southeast of Seattle

Distance: 9 miles

Skill Level: Intermediate

Elevation gain: 4,500 feet

Maximum elevation: 10,000 feet

Season: October to June

Avalanche hazard: Moderate

Map and Book: USGS Mount Rainier East (7.5 minute); *100 Classic Backcountry Ski and Snowboard Routes*

Heads up: Any hint of bad weather makes this an advanced run, as low visibility can be very dangerous.

Description: This classic trip is no secret, but backcountry skiers want to do it at least once. It's not the place for solitude, since there'll be a line of people making the 4- or 5-hour slog uphill, but when you get to 10,000 feet you'll have a pretty unusual experience waiting for you. First of all, you're above the cloud layer on Mount Rainier, with incredible views all around. Then there's what lies in wait. "Five miles of uninterrupted turns" says snowboarder Julie Walker, with a faraway look in her eyes. The biggest hazard is high elevation, and any bad weather can quickly turn into a dangerous whiteout. Check the reports before going, and be ready to bail out if there is any hint of wind and weather moving in. It's good to have route-finding skills and equipment just in case you've forgotten your crystal ball. Also, late spring is good but be careful later in the summer, when the sun can open crevasses.

Route: You'll probably have no problem figuring out the

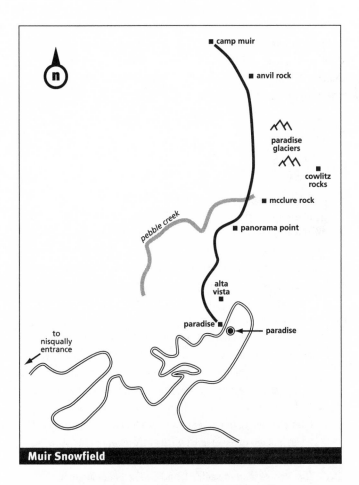

Muir Snowfield

route, since you'll be following a line of people. It starts on the open slopes above the Paradise parking lot to the left of Alta Vista. Continue to the face of Panorama Point at around 7,000 feet, either on the trail, if it's visible, or climbing the windswept side slope. From Panorama head north, continuing up the ridge. Cross Pebble Creek at 6,700 feet, and pass Anvil Rock at 9,850 feet on your right. The Camp Muir notch is visible from here.

Directions: Take I-5 south to Tacoma. Go east on WA 7 to Elbe. Bear right on WA 706 and continue east through Ashford to the Nisqually entrance of Mount Rainier National Park. Continue to the Paradise parking lot next to the ranger station.

Endless Winter

IN HAWAII, LAND OF THE ETERNAL WARM BREEZE, you can find yourself singing "Mele Kalikimaka" under a flocked Christmas tree in a pair of surf shorts. In the Pacific Northwest, with its immense peaks and glaciers, you might be throwing snowballs on Mount Rainier at the end of August. The curious possibility of year-round skiing in our area has not been lost on diehard snowgoers, who cling to the image of endless winter turns the way kids in Malibu once imagined themselves riding their surfboards until the end of time. The year-round skiing phenomenon has become so big that it even has its own Web site, the brainchild, if you will, of a neurobiology Ph.D. with some extra time on his hands, and a hobby to justify.

"At first I just sort of noticed that I was doing it," says Charles Eldridge of his year-round ski habit. He began to challenge himself to ski at least once every month of the year. "It wasn't until four years in that I decided I should make a Web site. People started seeing it and saying 'I'm doing that, too.' I hadn't really realized I wasn't the only one."

To be fair, Eldridge did not create his Web site, www .turns-all-year.com, in order to talk about his obsession with skiing in all seasons. He started it because he was an avid backcountry skier who couldn't find good, up-to-date backcountry trip reports on other sites. Like most backcountry skiers this powderhound was reliant on the thorough but confusingly archived Northwest Weather and Avalanche Center data to plan his trips. Eldridge's Web site offers a place where addicts can quickly sate their desire for this kind of information.

Eldridge started meeting people through the Web site who had been skiing (and snowboarding) more consecutive months than he had. Log on and you'll find the bios of 18 skiers who have been on streaks of 50, 100, and even 281 consecutive months during which they have made turns on at least one day. The criteria for a countable ski trip are as varied as the skiers themselves, but one thing seems to be consistent—the lean months of September and October can test the mettle of the most determined. Their tales of snowy low-points read a bit like something Edgar Allan Poe would have written, had he been out seeking turns instead of being cooped up with a fountain pen. Bill Frans, with 112 months under his belt, describes trying to ski somewhere in October and getting his car stuck. "After excavating it, I turned to the Baker ski area. By the time I reached the parking lot, it was windy, with the rain blowing sideways. The 2–3 feet of new snow on top of the previous year's snowpack was now nothing but sloppy mush. With a 'what else am I going to do on a rainy day' attitude, I emerged from my car to face the inevitable awfulness."

Eldridge's biggest challenge took place in October 2002, a strangely warm and dry fall in the Pacific Northwest, and the month during which Eldridge traditionally held out to its last days to catch new snow on Muir Snowfield. "On October 31st there had been only 6 inches of new snow," he says. By the time he and a friend arrived to do the formalities, the microscopic fresh pow had all been blown away. "The snow was very irregular, huge lumps, big suncups, like icy, hard moguls dirty from dust blowing off ridges." They found a 20-foot-wide strip where the new snow was protected, skied it for about 500 feet, and gave up. "I just felt lucky to have it over with," he says.

So why, with all the frustration, do people keep doing this year after year, racking up decades of year-round skiing credentials? Skier Jonathan Wong (53 months) offers this credo: "It's tempting . . . to mentally impress a four-distinct-season notion of the year on the wacky mountain environment. Alas, in a battle between re-shaping the Pacific Northwest environment before it re-shapes you, there can only be one possible outcome. Soon, everyone will understand that, on the West Coast, there are only two seasons, wet and wetter. The dry bits are purely illusory and are just brief respites designed to allow you to sharpen your edges and wax your bases. Those who still don't understand this are probably still having troubles with their stem Christies."

Where to Connect

There are lots of great backcountry resources in the area. First and foremost, check out the avalanche information in "Snow Sports Overview" (page 374). Here more than anywhere else you're going to need to know your stuff. Then check out local clubs, visit Web sites, and consult the books.

Clubs and Organizations
See *Where to Connect* in "Snow Sports Overview."

Event
- Every May, powder lovin' snowboarders hike up Mt. St. Helens in honor of Mother's Day. Boys don dresses—the more outrageous, the better. Ask around for this year's logistics.

Guide Service
- Pro Guiding Service (206-525-4425, www.proguiding.com) is a well-established group of backcountry mountaineering guides who teach group and private lessons and lead trips into the backcountry. The owner, Martin Volken, was origi-

nally trained as a Swiss Mountain Guide in his native country.

Books

- Beckey, Fred. *Cascade Alpine Guide: Climbing and High Routes,* 3 d ed. 3 vols. Seattle, WA: Mountaineers Books, 2003.

- Blair Jr., Seabury. *Backcountry Ski Washington: The Best Trails and Descents for Free-Heelers and Snowboarders.* Seattle, WA: Sasquatch Books, 1998.

- Burgdorfer, Rainer. *100 Classic Backcountry Ski and Snowboard Routes in Washington.* Seattle, WA: Mountaineers Books, 1999. Probably the most highly regarded local guidebook on the subject.

- Renner, Jeff. *Northwest Mountain Weather: Understanding and Forecasting for Backcountry Use.* Seattle, WA: Mountaineers Books, 1992.

Links

www.turn-all-year.com (see *Endless Winter,* page 416)

www.nwac.noaa.gov for weather and snowpack data from the Northwest Weather and Avalanche Center

Page numbers in *italics* refer to maps.